C-1173   CAREER EXAMINATION SERIES

This is your
PASSBOOK for...

Chief Deputy Sheriff

Test Preparation Study Guide
Questions & Answers

NATIONAL LEARNING CORPORATION®

COPYRIGHT NOTICE

This book is SOLELY intended for, is sold ONLY to, and its use is RESTRICTED to individual, bona fide applicants or candidates who qualify by virtue of having seriously filed applications for appropriate license, certificate, professional and/or promotional advancement, higher school matriculation, scholarship, or other legitimate requirements of education and/or governmental authorities.

This book is NOT intended for use, class instruction, tutoring, training, duplication, copying, reprinting, excerption, or adaptation, etc., by:

1) Other publishers
2) Proprietors and/or Instructors of "Coaching" and/or Preparatory Courses
3) Personnel and/or Training Divisions of commercial, industrial, and governmental organizations
4) Schools, colleges, or universities and/or their departments and staffs, including teachers and other personnel
5) Testing Agencies or Bureaus
6) Study groups which seek by the purchase of a single volume to copy and/or duplicate and/or adapt this material for use by the group as a whole without having purchased individual volumes for each of the members of the group
7) Et al.

Such persons would be in violation of appropriate Federal and State statutes.

PROVISION OF LICENSING AGREEMENTS – Recognized educational, commercial, industrial, and governmental institutions and organizations, and others legitimately engaged in educational pursuits, including training, testing, and measurement activities, may address request for a licensing agreement to the copyright owners, who will determine whether, and under what conditions, including fees and charges, the materials in this book may be used them. In other words, a licensing facility exists for the legitimate use of the material in this book on other than an individual basis. However, it is asseverated and affirmed here that the material in this book CANNOT be used without the receipt of the express permission of such a licensing agreement from the Publishers. Inquiries re licensing should be addressed to the company, attention rights and permissions department.

All rights reserved, including the right of reproduction in whole or in part, in any form or by any means, electronic or mechanical, including photocopying, recording, or by any information storage and retrieval system, without permission in writing from the Publisher.

Copyright © 2025 by
National Learning Corporation

212 Michael Drive, Syosset, NY 11791
(516) 921-8888 • www.passbooks.com
E-mail: info@passbooks.com

PASSBOOK® SERIES

THE *PASSBOOK® SERIES* has been created to prepare applicants and candidates for the ultimate academic battlefield – the examination room.

At some time in our lives, each and every one of us may be required to take an examination – for validation, matriculation, admission, qualification, registration, certification, or licensure.

Based on the assumption that every applicant or candidate has met the basic formal educational standards, has taken the required number of courses, and read the necessary texts, the *PASSBOOK® SERIES* furnishes the one special preparation which may assure passing with confidence, instead of failing with insecurity. Examination questions – together with answers – are furnished as the basic vehicle for study so that the mysteries of the examination and its compounding difficulties may be eliminated or diminished by a sure method.

This book is meant to help you pass your examination provided that you qualify and are serious in your objective.

The entire field is reviewed through the huge store of content information which is succinctly presented through a provocative and challenging approach – the question-and-answer method.

A climate of success is established by furnishing the correct answers at the end of each test.

You soon learn to recognize types of questions, forms of questions, and patterns of questioning. You may even begin to anticipate expected outcomes.

You perceive that many questions are repeated or adapted so that you can gain acute insights, which may enable you to score many sure points.

You learn how to confront new questions, or types of questions, and to attack them confidently and work out the correct answers.

You note objectives and emphases, and recognize pitfalls and dangers, so that you may make positive educational adjustments.

Moreover, you are kept fully informed in relation to new concepts, methods, practices, and directions in the field.

You discover that you are actually taking the examination all the time: you are preparing for the examination by "taking" an examination, not by reading extraneous and/or supererogatory textbooks.

In short, this PASSBOOK®, used directedly, should be an important factor in helping you to pass your test.

CHIEF DEPUTY SHERIFF

DUTIES AND RESPONSIBILITIES
Under general direction, with much latitude for independent or unreviewed action or decision, performs work of a difficult and responsible nature in administering the activities of the county divisions of the Office of the Sheriff performs related work.

EXAMPLES OF TYPICAL TASKS
As Sheriff's Officer, directs the seizure, delivery, transfer, sale or release of real or personal property. Directs the arrest, custody and release of civil prisoners. Supervises the work and assists in training subordinate deputies, and reviews their records and actions in the execution of process. Supervises the legal and clerical employees of the division and is responsible for all correspondence. Supervises the transfer of civil prisoners to the civil jail. Supervises the receipt, deposit and expenditures of fees, poundage and other monies and the accounting therefore, examining and approving financial reports, checks, vouchers, bank reconciliations, etc. Supervises the acquisition of supplies and equipment for the division, and checks inventory control. Participates in conferences with other administrative personnel of the Sheriff's Office, attorneys, judges, etc., on matters relating to policy, procedures, controls and legislation affecting the administration or relating to the functions of the Sheriff's Office. Works closely with staff attorney in analyzing potential or actual legal problems.

TESTS
The test will be designed to measure ability to apply pertinent legal statutes to execution of process; ability to direct subordinates, and to clarify legal and procedural matters; and other related areas.

HOW TO TAKE A TEST

I. YOU MUST PASS AN EXAMINATION

A. *WHAT EVERY CANDIDATE SHOULD KNOW*

Examination applicants often ask us for help in preparing for the written test. What can I study in advance? What kinds of questions will be asked? How will the test be given? How will the papers be graded?

As an applicant for a civil service examination, you may be wondering about some of these things. Our purpose here is to suggest effective methods of advance study and to describe civil service examinations.

Your chances for success on this examination can be increased if you know how to prepare. Those "pre-examination jitters" can be reduced if you know what to expect. You can even experience an adventure in good citizenship if you know why civil service exams are given.

B. *WHY ARE CIVIL SERVICE EXAMINATIONS GIVEN?*

Civil service examinations are important to you in two ways. As a citizen, you want public jobs filled by employees who know how to do their work. As a job seeker, you want a fair chance to compete for that job on an equal footing with other candidates. The best-known means of accomplishing this two-fold goal is the competitive examination.

Exams are widely publicized throughout the nation. They may be administered for jobs in federal, state, city, municipal, town or village governments or agencies.

Any citizen may apply, with some limitations, such as the age or residence of applicants. Your experience and education may be reviewed to see whether you meet the requirements for the particular examination. When these requirements exist, they are reasonable and applied consistently to all applicants. Thus, a competitive examination may cause you some uneasiness now, but it is your privilege and safeguard.

C. *HOW ARE CIVIL SERVICE EXAMS DEVELOPED?*

Examinations are carefully written by trained technicians who are specialists in the field known as "psychological measurement," in consultation with recognized authorities in the field of work that the test will cover. These experts recommend the subject matter areas or skills to be tested; only those knowledges or skills important to your success on the job are included. The most reliable books and source materials available are used as references. Together, the experts and technicians judge the difficulty level of the questions.

Test technicians know how to phrase questions so that the problem is clearly stated. Their ethics do not permit "trick" or "catch" questions. Questions may have been tried out on sample groups, or subjected to statistical analysis, to determine their usefulness.

Written tests are often used in combination with performance tests, ratings of training and experience, and oral interviews. All of these measures combine to form the best-known means of finding the right person for the right job.

II. HOW TO PASS THE WRITTEN TEST

A. NATURE OF THE EXAMINATION

To prepare intelligently for civil service examinations, you should know how they differ from school examinations you have taken. In school you were assigned certain definite pages to read or subjects to cover. The examination questions were quite detailed and usually emphasized memory. Civil service exams, on the other hand, try to discover your present ability to perform the duties of a position, plus your potentiality to learn these duties. In other words, a civil service exam attempts to predict how successful you will be. Questions cover such a broad area that they cannot be as minute and detailed as school exam questions.

In the public service similar kinds of work, or positions, are grouped together in one "class." This process is known as *position-classification*. All the positions in a class are paid according to the salary range for that class. One class title covers all of these positions, and they are all tested by the same examination.

B. FOUR BASIC STEPS

1) Study the announcement

How, then, can you know what subjects to study? Our best answer is: "Learn as much as possible about the class of positions for which you've applied." The exam will test the knowledge, skills and abilities needed to do the work.

Your most valuable source of information about the position you want is the official exam announcement. This announcement lists the training and experience qualifications. Check these standards and apply only if you come reasonably close to meeting them.

The brief description of the position in the examination announcement offers some clues to the subjects which will be tested. Think about the job itself. Review the duties in your mind. Can you perform them, or are there some in which you are rusty? Fill in the blank spots in your preparation.

Many jurisdictions preview the written test in the exam announcement by including a section called "Knowledge and Abilities Required," "Scope of the Examination," or some similar heading. Here you will find out specifically what fields will be tested.

2) Review your own background

Once you learn in general what the position is all about, and what you need to know to do the work, ask yourself which subjects you already know fairly well and which need improvement. You may wonder whether to concentrate on improving your strong areas or on building some background in your fields of weakness. When the announcement has specified "some knowledge" or "considerable knowledge," or has used adjectives like "beginning principles of…" or "advanced … methods," you can get a clue as to the number and difficulty of questions to be asked in any given field. More questions, and hence broader coverage, would be included for those subjects which are more important in the work. Now weigh your strengths and weaknesses against the job requirements and prepare accordingly.

3) Determine the level of the position

Another way to tell how intensively you should prepare is to understand the level of the job for which you are applying. Is it the entering level? In other words, is this the position in which beginners in a field of work are hired? Or is it an intermediate or advanced level? Sometimes this is indicated by such words as "Junior" or "Senior" in the class title. Other jurisdictions use Roman numerals to designate the level – Clerk I, Clerk II, for example. The word "Supervisor" sometimes appears in the title. If the level is not indicated by the title, check the description of duties. Will you be working under very close supervision, or will you have responsibility for independent decisions in this work?

4) Choose appropriate study materials

Now that you know the subjects to be examined and the relative amount of each subject to be covered, you can choose suitable study materials. For beginning level jobs, or even advanced ones, if you have a pronounced weakness in some aspect of your training, read a modern, standard textbook in that field. Be sure it is up to date and has general coverage. Such books are normally available at your library, and the librarian will be glad to help you locate one. For entry-level positions, questions of appropriate difficulty are chosen – neither highly advanced questions, nor those too simple. Such questions require careful thought but not advanced training.

If the position for which you are applying is technical or advanced, you will read more advanced, specialized material. If you are already familiar with the basic principles of your field, elementary textbooks would waste your time. Concentrate on advanced textbooks and technical periodicals. Think through the concepts and review difficult problems in your field.

These are all general sources. You can get more ideas on your own initiative, following these leads. For example, training manuals and publications of the government agency which employs workers in your field can be useful, particularly for technical and professional positions. A letter or visit to the government department involved may result in more specific study suggestions, and certainly will provide you with a more definite idea of the exact nature of the position you are seeking.

III. KINDS OF TESTS

Tests are used for purposes other than measuring knowledge and ability to perform specified duties. For some positions, it is equally important to test ability to make adjustments to new situations or to profit from training. In others, basic mental abilities not dependent on information are essential. Questions which test these things may not appear as pertinent to the duties of the position as those which test for knowledge and information. Yet they are often highly important parts of a fair examination. For very general questions, it is almost impossible to help you direct your study efforts. What we can do is to point out some of the more common of these general abilities needed in public service positions and describe some typical questions.

1) General information

Broad, general information has been found useful for predicting job success in some kinds of work. This is tested in a variety of ways, from vocabulary lists to questions about current events. Basic background in some field of work, such as sociology or economics, may be sampled in a group of questions. Often these are principles which have become familiar to most persons through exposure rather than through formal training. It is difficult to advise you how to study for these questions; being alert to the world around you is our best suggestion.

2) Verbal ability

An example of an ability needed in many positions is verbal or language ability. Verbal ability is, in brief, the ability to use and understand words. Vocabulary and grammar tests are typical measures of this ability. Reading comprehension or paragraph interpretation questions are common in many kinds of civil service tests. You are given a paragraph of written material and asked to find its central meaning.

3) Numerical ability

Number skills can be tested by the familiar arithmetic problem, by checking paired lists of numbers to see which are alike and which are different, or by interpreting charts and graphs. In the latter test, a graph may be printed in the test booklet which you are asked to use as the basis for answering questions.

4) Observation

A popular test for law-enforcement positions is the observation test. A picture is shown to you for several minutes, then taken away. Questions about the picture test your ability to observe both details and larger elements.

5) Following directions

In many positions in the public service, the employee must be able to carry out written instructions dependably and accurately. You may be given a chart with several columns, each column listing a variety of information. The questions require you to carry out directions involving the information given in the chart.

6) Skills and aptitudes

Performance tests effectively measure some manual skills and aptitudes. When the skill is one in which you are trained, such as typing or shorthand, you can practice. These tests are often very much like those given in business school or high school courses. For many of the other skills and aptitudes, however, no short-time preparation can be made. Skills and abilities natural to you or that you have developed throughout your lifetime are being tested.

Many of the general questions just described provide all the data needed to answer the questions and ask you to use your reasoning ability to find the answers. Your best preparation for these tests, as well as for tests of facts and ideas, is to be at your physical and mental best. You, no doubt, have your own methods of getting into an exam-taking mood and keeping "in shape." The next section lists some ideas on this subject.

IV. KINDS OF QUESTIONS

Only rarely is the "essay" question, which you answer in narrative form, used in civil service tests. Civil service tests are usually of the short-answer type. Full instructions for answering these questions will be given to you at the examination. But in case this is your first experience with short-answer questions and separate answer sheets, here is what you need to know:

1) Multiple-choice Questions

Most popular of the short-answer questions is the "multiple choice" or "best answer" question. It can be used, for example, to test for factual knowledge, ability to solve problems or judgment in meeting situations found at work.

A multiple-choice question is normally one of three types—
- It can begin with an incomplete statement followed by several possible endings. You are to find the one ending which *best* completes the statement, although some of the others may not be entirely wrong.
- It can also be a complete statement in the form of a question which is answered by choosing one of the statements listed.

- It can be in the form of a problem – again you select the best answer.

Here is an example of a multiple-choice question with a discussion which should give you some clues as to the method for choosing the right answer:

When an employee has a complaint about his assignment, the action which will *best* help him overcome his difficulty is to
    A. discuss his difficulty with his coworkers
    B. take the problem to the head of the organization
    C. take the problem to the person who gave him the assignment
    D. say nothing to anyone about his complaint

In answering this question, you should study each of the choices to find which is best. Consider choice "A" – Certainly an employee may discuss his complaint with fellow employees, but no change or improvement can result, and the complaint remains unresolved. Choice "B" is a poor choice since the head of the organization probably does not know what assignment you have been given, and taking your problem to him is known as "going over the head" of the supervisor. The supervisor, or person who made the assignment, is the person who can clarify it or correct any injustice. Choice "C" is, therefore, correct. To say nothing, as in choice "D," is unwise. Supervisors have and interest in knowing the problems employees are facing, and the employee is seeking a solution to his problem.

2) True/False Questions

The "true/false" or "right/wrong" form of question is sometimes used. Here a complete statement is given. Your job is to decide whether the statement is right or wrong.

SAMPLE: A roaming cell-phone call to a nearby city costs less than a non-roaming call to a distant city.

This statement is wrong, or false, since roaming calls are more expensive.
This is not a complete list of all possible question forms, although most of the others are variations of these common types. You will always get complete directions for answering questions. Be sure you understand *how* to mark your answers – ask questions until you do.

V. RECORDING YOUR ANSWERS

Computer terminals are used more and more today for many different kinds of exams.
For an examination with very few applicants, you may be told to record your answers in the test booklet itself. Separate answer sheets are much more common. If this separate answer sheet is to be scored by machine – and this is often the case – it is highly important that you mark your answers correctly in order to get credit.
An electronic scoring machine is often used in civil service offices because of the speed with which papers can be scored. Machine-scored answer sheets must be marked with a pencil, which will be given to you. This pencil has a high graphite content which responds to the electronic scoring machine. As a matter of fact, stray dots may register as answers, so do not let your pencil rest on the answer sheet while you are pondering the correct answer. Also, if your pencil lead breaks or is otherwise defective, ask for another.

Since the answer sheet will be dropped in a slot in the scoring machine, be careful not to bend the corners or get the paper crumpled.

The answer sheet normally has five vertical columns of numbers, with 30 numbers to a column. These numbers correspond to the question numbers in your test booklet. After each number, going across the page are four or five pairs of dotted lines. These short dotted lines have small letters or numbers above them. The first two pairs may also have a "T" or "F" above the letters. This indicates that the first two pairs only are to be used if the questions are of the true-false type. If the questions are multiple choice, disregard the "T" and "F" and pay attention only to the small letters or numbers.

Answer your questions in the manner of the sample that follows:

32. The largest city in the United States is
    A. Washington, D.C.
    B. New York City
    C. Chicago
    D. Detroit
    E. San Francisco

1) Choose the answer you think is best. (New York City is the largest, so "B" is correct.)
2) Find the row of dotted lines numbered the same as the question you are answering. (Find row number 32)
3) Find the pair of dotted lines corresponding to the answer. (Find the pair of lines under the mark "B.")
4) Make a solid black mark between the dotted lines.

VI. BEFORE THE TEST

Common sense will help you find procedures to follow to get ready for an examination. Too many of us, however, overlook these sensible measures. Indeed, nervousness and fatigue have been found to be the most serious reasons why applicants fail to do their best on civil service tests. Here is a list of reminders:

- Begin your preparation early – Don't wait until the last minute to go scurrying around for books and materials or to find out what the position is all about.
- Prepare continuously – An hour a night for a week is better than an all-night cram session. This has been definitely established. What is more, a night a week for a month will return better dividends than crowding your study into a shorter period of time.
- Locate the place of the exam – You have been sent a notice telling you when and where to report for the examination. If the location is in a different town or otherwise unfamiliar to you, it would be well to inquire the best route and learn something about the building.
- Relax the night before the test – Allow your mind to rest. Do not study at all that night. Plan some mild recreation or diversion; then go to bed early and get a good night's sleep.
- Get up early enough to make a leisurely trip to the place for the test – This way unforeseen events, traffic snarls, unfamiliar buildings, etc. will not upset you.
- Dress comfortably – A written test is not a fashion show. You will be known by number and not by name, so wear something comfortable.

- Leave excess paraphernalia at home – Shopping bags and odd bundles will get in your way. You need bring only the items mentioned in the official notice you received; usually everything you need is provided. Do not bring reference books to the exam. They will only confuse those last minutes and be taken away from you when in the test room.
- Arrive somewhat ahead of time – If because of transportation schedules you must get there very early, bring a newspaper or magazine to take your mind off yourself while waiting.
- Locate the examination room – When you have found the proper room, you will be directed to the seat or part of the room where you will sit. Sometimes you are given a sheet of instructions to read while you are waiting. Do not fill out any forms until you are told to do so; just read them and be prepared.
- Relax and prepare to listen to the instructions
- If you have any physical problem that may keep you from doing your best, be sure to tell the test administrator. If you are sick or in poor health, you really cannot do your best on the exam. You can come back and take the test some other time.

VII. AT THE TEST

The day of the test is here and you have the test booklet in your hand. The temptation to get going is very strong. Caution! There is more to success than knowing the right answers. You must know how to identify your papers and understand variations in the type of short-answer question used in this particular examination. Follow these suggestions for maximum results from your efforts:

1) Cooperate with the monitor

The test administrator has a duty to create a situation in which you can be as much at ease as possible. He will give instructions, tell you when to begin, check to see that you are marking your answer sheet correctly, and so on. He is not there to guard you, although he will see that your competitors do not take unfair advantage. He wants to help you do your best.

2) Listen to all instructions

Don't jump the gun! Wait until you understand all directions. In most civil service tests you get more time than you need to answer the questions. So don't be in a hurry. Read each word of instructions until you clearly understand the meaning. Study the examples, listen to all announcements and follow directions. Ask questions if you do not understand what to do.

3) Identify your papers

Civil service exams are usually identified by number only. You will be assigned a number; you must not put your name on your test papers. Be sure to copy your number correctly. Since more than one exam may be given, copy your exact examination title.

4) Plan your time

Unless you are told that a test is a "speed" or "rate of work" test, speed itself is usually not important. Time enough to answer all the questions will be provided, but this does not mean that you have all day. An overall time limit has been set. Divide the total time (in minutes) by the number of questions to determine the approximate time you have for each question.

5) Do not linger over difficult questions

If you come across a difficult question, mark it with a paper clip (useful to have along) and come back to it when you have been through the booklet. One caution if you do this – be sure to skip a number on your answer sheet as well. Check often to be sure that you have not lost your place and that you are marking in the row numbered the same as the question you are answering.

6) Read the questions

Be sure you know what the question asks! Many capable people are unsuccessful because they failed to *read* the questions correctly.

7) Answer all questions

Unless you have been instructed that a penalty will be deducted for incorrect answers, it is better to guess than to omit a question.

8) Speed tests

It is often better NOT to guess on speed tests. It has been found that on timed tests people are tempted to spend the last few seconds before time is called in marking answers at random – without even reading them – in the hope of picking up a few extra points. To discourage this practice, the instructions may warn you that your score will be "corrected" for guessing. That is, a penalty will be applied. The incorrect answers will be deducted from the correct ones, or some other penalty formula will be used.

9) Review your answers

If you finish before time is called, go back to the questions you guessed or omitted to give them further thought. Review other answers if you have time.

10) Return your test materials

If you are ready to leave before others have finished or time is called, take ALL your materials to the monitor and leave quietly. Never take any test material with you. The monitor can discover whose papers are not complete, and taking a test booklet may be grounds for disqualification.

VIII. EXAMINATION TECHNIQUES

1) Read the general instructions carefully. These are usually printed on the first page of the exam booklet. As a rule, these instructions refer to the timing of the examination; the fact that you should not start work until the signal and must stop work at a signal, etc. If there are any *special* instructions, such as a choice of questions to be answered, make sure that you note this instruction carefully.

2) When you are ready to start work on the examination, that is as soon as the signal has been given, read the instructions to each question booklet, underline any key words or phrases, such as *least, best, outline, describe* and the like. In this way you will tend to answer as requested rather than discover on reviewing your paper that you *listed without describing*, that you selected the *worst* choice rather than the *best* choice, etc.

3) If the examination is of the objective or multiple-choice type – that is, each question will also give a series of possible answers: A, B, C or D, and you are called upon to select the best answer and write the letter next to that answer on your answer paper – it is advisable to start answering each question in turn. There may be anywhere from 50 to 100 such questions in the three or four hours allotted and you can see how much time would be taken if you read through all the questions before beginning to answer any. Furthermore, if you come across a question or group of questions which you know would be difficult to answer, it would undoubtedly affect your handling of all the other questions.

4) If the examination is of the essay type and contains but a few questions, it is a moot point as to whether you should read all the questions before starting to answer any one. Of course, if you are given a choice – say five out of seven and the like – then it is essential to read all the questions so you can eliminate the two that are most difficult. If, however, you are asked to answer all the questions, there may be danger in trying to answer the easiest one first because you may find that you will spend too much time on it. The best technique is to answer the first question, then proceed to the second, etc.

5) Time your answers. Before the exam begins, write down the time it started, then add the time allowed for the examination and write down the time it must be completed, then divide the time available somewhat as follows:
    - If 3-1/2 hours are allowed, that would be 210 minutes. If you have 80 objective-type questions, that would be an average of 2-1/2 minutes per question. Allow yourself no more than 2 minutes per question, or a total of 160 minutes, which will permit about 50 minutes to review.
    - If for the time allotment of 210 minutes there are 7 essay questions to answer, that would average about 30 minutes a question. Give yourself only 25 minutes per question so that you have about 35 minutes to review.

6) The most important instruction is to *read each question* and make sure you know what is wanted. The second most important instruction is to *time yourself properly* so that you answer every question. The third most important instruction is to *answer every question*. Guess if you have to but include something for each question. Remember that you will receive no credit for a blank and will probably receive some credit if you write something in answer to an essay question. If you guess a letter – say "B" for a multiple-choice question – you may have guessed right. If you leave a blank as an answer to a multiple-choice question, the examiners may respect your feelings but it will not add a point to your score. Some exams may penalize you for wrong answers, so in such cases *only*, you may not want to guess unless you have some basis for your answer.

7) Suggestions
    a. Objective-type questions
        1. Examine the question booklet for proper sequence of pages and questions
        2. Read all instructions carefully
        3. Skip any question which seems too difficult; return to it after all other questions have been answered
        4. Apportion your time properly; do not spend too much time on any single question or group of questions

5. Note and underline key words – *all, most, fewest, least, best, worst, same, opposite,* etc.
6. Pay particular attention to negatives
7. Note unusual option, e.g., unduly long, short, complex, different or similar in content to the body of the question
8. Observe the use of "hedging" words – *probably, may, most likely,* etc.
9. Make sure that your answer is put next to the same number as the question
10. Do not second-guess unless you have good reason to believe the second answer is definitely more correct
11. Cross out original answer if you decide another answer is more accurate; do not erase until you are ready to hand your paper in
12. Answer all questions; guess unless instructed otherwise
13. Leave time for review

   b. Essay questions
   1. Read each question carefully
   2. Determine exactly what is wanted. Underline key words or phrases.
   3. Decide on outline or paragraph answer
   4. Include many different points and elements unless asked to develop any one or two points or elements
   5. Show impartiality by giving pros and cons unless directed to select one side only
   6. Make and write down any assumptions you find necessary to answer the questions
   7. Watch your English, grammar, punctuation and choice of words
   8. Time your answers; don't crowd material

8) Answering the essay question

Most essay questions can be answered by framing the specific response around several key words or ideas. Here are a few such key words or ideas:

M's: manpower, materials, methods, money, management
P's: purpose, program, policy, plan, procedure, practice, problems, pitfalls, personnel, public relations
   a. Six basic steps in handling problems:
   1. Preliminary plan and background development
   2. Collect information, data and facts
   3. Analyze and interpret information, data and facts
   4. Analyze and develop solutions as well as make recommendations
   5. Prepare report and sell recommendations
   6. Install recommendations and follow up effectiveness

   b. Pitfalls to avoid
   1. *Taking things for granted* – A statement of the situation does not necessarily imply that each of the elements is necessarily true; for example, a complaint may be invalid and biased so that all that can be taken for granted is that a complaint has been registered

2. *Considering only one side of a situation* – Wherever possible, indicate several alternatives and then point out the reasons you selected the best one
3. *Failing to indicate follow up* – Whenever your answer indicates action on your part, make certain that you will take proper follow-up action to see how successful your recommendations, procedures or actions turn out to be
4. *Taking too long in answering any single question* – Remember to time your answers properly

IX. AFTER THE TEST

Scoring procedures differ in detail among civil service jurisdictions although the general principles are the same. Whether the papers are hand-scored or graded by machine we have described, they are nearly always graded by number. That is, the person who marks the paper knows only the number – never the name – of the applicant. Not until all the papers have been graded will they be matched with names. If other tests, such as training and experience or oral interview ratings have been given, scores will be combined. Different parts of the examination usually have different weights. For example, the written test might count 60 percent of the final grade, and a rating of training and experience 40 percent. In many jurisdictions, veterans will have a certain number of points added to their grades.

After the final grade has been determined, the names are placed in grade order and an eligible list is established. There are various methods for resolving ties between those who get the same final grade – probably the most common is to place first the name of the person whose application was received first. Job offers are made from the eligible list in the order the names appear on it. You will be notified of your grade and your rank as soon as all these computations have been made. This will be done as rapidly as possible.

People who are found to meet the requirements in the announcement are called "eligibles." Their names are put on a list of eligible candidates. An eligible's chances of getting a job depend on how high he stands on this list and how fast agencies are filling jobs from the list.

When a job is to be filled from a list of eligibles, the agency asks for the names of people on the list of eligibles for that job. When the civil service commission receives this request, it sends to the agency the names of the three people highest on this list. Or, if the job to be filled has specialized requirements, the office sends the agency the names of the top three persons who meet these requirements from the general list.

The appointing officer makes a choice from among the three people whose names were sent to him. If the selected person accepts the appointment, the names of the others are put back on the list to be considered for future openings.

That is the rule in hiring from all kinds of eligible lists, whether they are for typist, carpenter, chemist, or something else. For every vacancy, the appointing officer has his choice of any one of the top three eligibles on the list. This explains why the person whose name is on top of the list sometimes does not get an appointment when some of the persons lower on the list do. If the appointing officer chooses the second or third eligible, the No. 1 eligible does not get a job at once, but stays on the list until he is appointed or the list is terminated.

X. HOW TO PASS THE INTERVIEW TEST

The examination for which you applied requires an oral interview test. You have already taken the written test and you are now being called for the interview test – the final part of the formal examination.

You may think that it is not possible to prepare for an interview test and that there are no procedures to follow during an interview. Our purpose is to point out some things you can do in advance that will help you and some good rules to follow and pitfalls to avoid while you are being interviewed.

What is an interview supposed to test?

The written examination is designed to test the technical knowledge and competence of the candidate; the oral is designed to evaluate intangible qualities, not readily measured otherwise, and to establish a list showing the relative fitness of each candidate – as measured against his competitors – for the position sought. Scoring is not on the basis of "right" and "wrong," but on a sliding scale of values ranging from "not passable" to "outstanding." As a matter of fact, it is possible to achieve a relatively low score without a single "incorrect" answer because of evident weakness in the qualities being measured.

Occasionally, an examination may consist entirely of an oral test – either an individual or a group oral. In such cases, information is sought concerning the technical knowledges and abilities of the candidate, since there has been no written examination for this purpose. More commonly, however, an oral test is used to supplement a written examination.

Who conducts interviews?

The composition of oral boards varies among different jurisdictions. In nearly all, a representative of the personnel department serves as chairman. One of the members of the board may be a representative of the department in which the candidate would work. In some cases, "outside experts" are used, and, frequently, a businessman or some other representative of the general public is asked to serve. Labor and management or other special groups may be represented. The aim is to secure the services of experts in the appropriate field.

However the board is composed, it is a good idea (and not at all improper or unethical) to ascertain in advance of the interview who the members are and what groups they represent. When you are introduced to them, you will have some idea of their backgrounds and interests, and at least you will not stutter and stammer over their names.

What should be done before the interview?

While knowledge about the board members is useful and takes some of the surprise element out of the interview, there is other preparation which is more substantive. It *is* possible to prepare for an oral interview – in several ways:

1) Keep a copy of your application and review it carefully before the interview

This may be the only document before the oral board, and the starting point of the interview. Know what education and experience you have listed there, and the sequence and dates of all of it. Sometimes the board will ask you to review the highlights of your experience for them; you should not have to hem and haw doing it.

2) Study the class specification and the examination announcement

Usually, the oral board has one or both of these to guide them. The qualities, characteristics or knowledges required by the position sought are stated in these documents. They offer valuable clues as to the nature of the oral interview. For example, if the job involves supervisory responsibilities, the announcement will usually indicate that knowledge of modern supervisory methods and the qualifications of the candidate as a supervisor will be tested. If so, you can expect such questions, frequently in the form of a hypothetical situation which you are expected to solve. NEVER go into an oral without knowledge of the duties and responsibilities of the job you seek.

3) Think through each qualification required

Try to visualize the kind of questions you would ask if you were a board member. How well could you answer them? Try especially to appraise your own knowledge and background in each area, *measured against the job sought*, and identify any areas in which you are weak. Be critical and realistic – do not flatter yourself.

4) Do some general reading in areas in which you feel you may be weak

For example, if the job involves supervision and your past experience has NOT, some general reading in supervisory methods and practices, particularly in the field of human relations, might be useful. Do NOT study agency procedures or detailed manuals. The oral board will be testing your understanding and capacity, not your memory.

5) Get a good night's sleep and watch your general health and mental attitude

You will want a clear head at the interview. Take care of a cold or any other minor ailment, and of course, no hangovers.

What should be done on the day of the interview?

Now comes the day of the interview itself. Give yourself plenty of time to get there. Plan to arrive somewhat ahead of the scheduled time, particularly if your appointment is in the fore part of the day. If a previous candidate fails to appear, the board might be ready for you a bit early. By early afternoon an oral board is almost invariably behind schedule if there are many candidates, and you may have to wait. Take along a book or magazine to read, or your application to review, but leave any extraneous material in the waiting room when you go in for your interview. In any event, relax and compose yourself.

The matter of dress is important. The board is forming impressions about you – from your experience, your manners, your attitude, and your appearance. Give your personal appearance careful attention. Dress your best, but not your flashiest. Choose conservative, appropriate clothing, and be sure it is immaculate. This is a business interview, and your appearance should indicate that you regard it as such. Besides, being well groomed and properly dressed will help boost your confidence.

Sooner or later, someone will call your name and escort you into the interview room. *This is it.* From here on you are on your own. It is too late for any more preparation. But remember, you asked for this opportunity to prove your fitness, and you are here because your request was granted.

What happens when you go in?

The usual sequence of events will be as follows: The clerk (who is often the board stenographer) will introduce you to the chairman of the oral board, who will introduce you to the other members of the board. Acknowledge the introductions before you sit down. Do not be surprised if you find a microphone facing you or a stenotypist sitting by. Oral interviews are usually recorded in the event of an appeal or other review.

Usually the chairman of the board will open the interview by reviewing the highlights of your education and work experience from your application – primarily for the benefit of the other members of the board, as well as to get the material into the record. Do not interrupt or comment unless there is an error or significant misinterpretation; if that is the case, do not hesitate. But do not quibble about insignificant matters. Also, he will usually ask you some question about your education, experience or your present job – partly to get you to start talking and to establish the interviewing "rapport." He may start the actual questioning, or turn it over to one of the other members. Frequently, each member undertakes the questioning on a particular area, one in which he is perhaps most competent, so you can expect each member to participate in the examination. Because time is limited, you may also expect some rather abrupt switches in the direction the questioning takes, so do not be upset by it. Normally, a board member will not pursue a single line of questioning unless he discovers a particular strength or weakness.

After each member has participated, the chairman will usually ask whether any member has any further questions, then will ask you if you have anything you wish to add. Unless you are expecting this question, it may floor you. Worse, it may start you off on an extended, extemporaneous speech. The board is not usually seeking more information. The question is principally to offer you a last opportunity to present further qualifications or to indicate that you have nothing to add. So, if you feel that a significant qualification or characteristic has been overlooked, it is proper to point it out in a sentence or so. Do not compliment the board on the thoroughness of their examination – they have been sketchy, and you know it. If you wish, merely say, "No thank you, I have nothing further to add." This is a point where you can "talk yourself out" of a good impression or fail to present an important bit of information. Remember, *you close the interview yourself.*

The chairman will then say, "That is all, Mr. _____, thank you." Do not be startled; the interview is over, and quicker than you think. Thank him, gather your belongings and take your leave. Save your sigh of relief for the other side of the door.

How to put your best foot forward
Throughout this entire process, you may feel that the board individually and collectively is trying to pierce your defenses, seek out your hidden weaknesses and embarrass and confuse you. Actually, this is not true. They are obliged to make an appraisal of your qualifications for the job you are seeking, and they want to see you in your best light. Remember, they must interview all candidates and a non-cooperative candidate may become a failure in spite of their best efforts to bring out his qualifications. Here are 15 suggestions that will help you:

1) Be natural – Keep your attitude confident, not cocky
If you are not confident that you can do the job, do not expect the board to be. Do not apologize for your weaknesses, try to bring out your strong points. The board is interested in a positive, not negative, presentation. Cockiness will antagonize any board member and make him wonder if you are covering up a weakness by a false show of strength.

2) Get comfortable, but don't lounge or sprawl
Sit erectly but not stiffly. A careless posture may lead the board to conclude that you are careless in other things, or at least that you are not impressed by the importance of the occasion. Either conclusion is natural, even if incorrect. Do not fuss with your clothing, a pencil or an ashtray. Your hands may occasionally be useful to emphasize a point; do not let them become a point of distraction.

3) Do not wisecrack or make small talk
This is a serious situation, and your attitude should show that you consider it as such. Further, the time of the board is limited – they do not want to waste it, and neither should you.

4) Do not exaggerate your experience or abilities

In the first place, from information in the application or other interviews and sources, the board may know more about you than you think. Secondly, you probably will not get away with it. An experienced board is rather adept at spotting such a situation, so do not take the chance.

5) If you know a board member, do not make a point of it, yet do not hide it

Certainly you are not fooling him, and probably not the other members of the board. Do not try to take advantage of your acquaintanceship – it will probably do you little good.

6) Do not dominate the interview

Let the board do that. They will give you the clues – do not assume that you have to do all the talking. Realize that the board has a number of questions to ask you, and do not try to take up all the interview time by showing off your extensive knowledge of the answer to the first one.

7) Be attentive

You only have 20 minutes or so, and you should keep your attention at its sharpest throughout. When a member is addressing a problem or question to you, give him your undivided attention. Address your reply principally to him, but do not exclude the other board members.

8) Do not interrupt

A board member may be stating a problem for you to analyze. He will ask you a question when the time comes. Let him state the problem, and wait for the question.

9) Make sure you understand the question

Do not try to answer until you are sure what the question is. If it is not clear, restate it in your own words or ask the board member to clarify it for you. However, do not haggle about minor elements.

10) Reply promptly but not hastily

A common entry on oral board rating sheets is "candidate responded readily," or "candidate hesitated in replies." Respond as promptly and quickly as you can, but do not jump to a hasty, ill-considered answer.

11) Do not be peremptory in your answers

A brief answer is proper – but do not fire your answer back. That is a losing game from your point of view. The board member can probably ask questions much faster than you can answer them.

12) Do not try to create the answer you think the board member wants

He is interested in what kind of mind you have and how it works – not in playing games. Furthermore, he can usually spot this practice and will actually grade you down on it.

13) Do not switch sides in your reply merely to agree with a board member

Frequently, a member will take a contrary position merely to draw you out and to see if you are willing and able to defend your point of view. Do not start a debate, yet do not surrender a good position. If a position is worth taking, it is worth defending.

14) Do not be afraid to admit an error in judgment if you are shown to be wrong

The board knows that you are forced to reply without any opportunity for careful consideration. Your answer may be demonstrably wrong. If so, admit it and get on with the interview.

15) Do not dwell at length on your present job

The opening question may relate to your present assignment. Answer the question but do not go into an extended discussion. You are being examined for a *new* job, not your present one. As a matter of fact, try to phrase ALL your answers in terms of the job for which you are being examined.

Basis of Rating

Probably you will forget most of these "do's" and "don'ts" when you walk into the oral interview room. Even remembering them all will not ensure you a passing grade. Perhaps you did not have the qualifications in the first place. But remembering them will help you to put your best foot forward, without treading on the toes of the board members.

Rumor and popular opinion to the contrary notwithstanding, an oral board wants you to make the best appearance possible. They know you are under pressure – but they also want to see how you respond to it as a guide to what your reaction would be under the pressures of the job you seek. They will be influenced by the degree of poise you display, the personal traits you show and the manner in which you respond.

ABOUT THIS BOOK

This book contains tests divided into Examination Sections. Go through each test, answering every question in the margin. We have also attached a sample answer sheet at the back of the book that can be removed and used. At the end of each test look at the answer key and check your answers. On the ones you got wrong, look at the right answer choice and learn. Do not fill in the answers first. Do not memorize the questions and answers, but understand the answer and principles involved. On your test, the questions will likely be different from the samples. Questions are changed and new ones added. If you understand these past questions you should have success with any changes that arise. Tests may consist of several types of questions. We have additional books on each subject should more study be advisable or necessary for you. Finally, the more you study, the better prepared you will be. This book is intended to be the last thing you study before you walk into the examination room. Prior study of relevant texts is also recommended. NLC publishes some of these in our Fundamental Series. Knowledge and good sense are important factors in passing your exam. Good luck also helps. So now study this Passbook, absorb the material contained within and take that knowledge into the examination. Then do your best to pass that exam.

EXAMINATION SECTION

EXAMINATION SECTION
TEST 1

DIRECTIONS: Each question or incomplete statement is followed by several suggested answers or completions. Select the one that BEST answers the question or completes the statement. *PRINT THE LETTER OF THE CORRECT ANSWER IN THE SPACE AT THE RIGHT.*

1. Physical and mental health are essential to the officer. According to this statement, the officer MUST be

   A. as wise as he is strong
   B. smarter than most people
   C. sound in mind and body
   D. stronger than the average criminal

2. Teamwork is the basis of successful law enforcement. The factor stressed by this statement is

   A. cooperation   B. determination
   C. initiative   D. pride

3. Legal procedure is a means, not an end. Its function is merely to accomplish the enforcement of legal rights. A litigant has no vested interest in the observance of the rules of procedure as such. All that he should be entitled to demand is that he be given an opportunity for a fair and impartial trial of his case. He should not be permitted to invoke the aid of technical rules merely to embarrass his adversary.
   According to this paragraph, it is MOST correct to state that

   A. observance of the rules of procedure guarantees a fair trial
   B. embarrassment of an adversary through technical rules does not make a fair trial
   C. a litigant is not interested in the observance of rules of procedure
   D. technical rules must not be used in a trial

4. One theory states that all criminal behavior is taught by a process of communication within small intimate groups. An individual engages in criminal behavior if the number of criminal patterns which he has acquired exceed the number of non-criminal patterns. This statement indicates that criminal behavior is

   A. learned   B. instinctive
   C. hereditary   D. reprehensible

5. The law enforcement staff of today requires training and mental qualities of a high order. The poorly or partially prepared staff member lowers the standard of work, retards his own earning power, and fails in a career meant to provide a livelihood and social improvement.
   According to this statement,

   A. an inefficient member of a law enforcement staff will still earn a good livelihood
   B. law enforcement officers move in good social circles
   C. many people fail in law enforcement careers
   D. persons of training and ability are essential to a law enforcement staff

6. In any state, no crime can occur unless there is a written law forbidding the act or the omission in question, and even though an act may not be exactly in harmony with public policy, such act is not a crime unless it is expressly forbidden by legislative enactment.
According to the above statement,

   A. a crime is committed with reference to a particular law
   B. acts not in harmony with public policy should be forbidden by law
   C. non-criminal activity will promote public welfare
   D. legislative enactments frequently forbid actions in harmony with public policy

7. The unrestricted sale of firearms is one of the main causes of our shameful crime record.
According to this statement, one of the causes of our crime record is

   A. development of firepower
   B. ease of securing weapons
   C. increased skill in using guns
   D. scientific perfection of firearms

8. Every person must be informed of the reason for his arrest unless he is arrested in the actual commission of a crime. Sufficient force to effect the arrest may be used, but the courts frown on brutal methods.
According to this statement, a person does NOT have to be informed of the reason for his arrest if

   A. brutal force was not used in effecting it
   B. the courts will later turn the defendant loose
   C. the person arrested knows force will be used if necessary
   D. the reason for it is clearly evident from the circumstances

9. An important duty of an officer is to keep order in the court.
On the basis of this statement, it is PROBABLY true that

   A. it is more important for an officer to be strong than it is for him to be smart
   B. people involved in court trials are noisy if not kept in check
   C. not every duty of an officer is important
   D. the maintenance of order is important for the proper conduct of court business

10. Ideally, a correctional system should include several types of institutions to provide different degrees of custody.
On the basis of this statement, one could MOST reasonably say that

    A. as the number of institutions in a correctional system increases, the efficiency of the system increases
    B. the difference in degree of custody for the inmate depends on the types of institutions in a correctional system
    C. the greater the variety of institutions, the stricter the degree of custody that can be maintained
    D. the same type of correctional institution is not desirable for the custody of all prisoners

11. The enforced idleness of a large percentage of adult men and women in our prisons is one of the direct causes of the tensions which burst forth in riot and disorder.
On the basis of this statement, a good reason why inmates should perform daily work of some kind is that

    A. better morale and discipline can be maintained when inmates are kept busy
    B. daily work is an effective way of punishing inmates for the crimes they have committed
    C. law-abiding citizens must work, therefore, labor should also be required of inmates
    D. products of inmates' labor will in part pay the cost of their maintenance

12. With industry invading rural areas, the use of the automobile, and the speed of modern communications and transportation, the problems of neglect and delinquency are no longer peculiar to cities but an established feature of everyday life.
This statement implies MOST directly that

    A. delinquents are moving from cities to rural areas
    B. delinquency and neglect are found in rural areas
    C. delinquency is not as much of a problem in rural areas as in cities
    D. rural areas now surpass cities in industry

13. Young men from minority groups, if unable to find employment, become discouraged and hopeless because of their economic position and may finally resort to any means of supplying their wants.
The MOST reasonable of the following conclusions that may be drawn from this statement only is that

    A. discouragement sometimes leads to crime
    B. in general, young men from minority groups are criminals
    C. unemployment turns young men from crime
    D. young men from minority groups are seldom employed

14. To prevent crime, we must deal with the possible criminal long before he reaches the prison. Our aim should be not merely to reform the law breakers but to strike at the roots of crime: neglectful parents, bad companions, unsatisfactory homes, selfishness, disregard for the rights of others, and bad social conditions.
The above statement recommends

    A. abolition of prisons   B. better reformatories
    C. compulsory education   D. general social reform

15. There is evidence which shows that comic books which glorify the criminal and criminal acts have a distinct influence in producing young criminals.
According to this statement,

    A. comic books affect the development of criminal careers
    B. comic books specialize in reporting criminal acts
    C. young criminals read comic books exclusively
    D. young criminals should not be permitted to read comic books

16. Suppose a study shows that juvenile delinquents are equal in intelligence but three school grades behind juvenile non-delinquents.
    On the basis of this information only, it is MOST reasonable to say that

    A. a delinquent usually progresses to the educational limit set by his intelligence
    B. educational achievement depends on intelligence only
    C. educational achievement is closely associated with delinquency
    D. lack of intelligence is closely associated with delinquency

17. There is no proof today that the experience of a prison sentence makes a better citizen of an adult. On the contrary, there seems some evidence that the experience is an unwholesome one that frequently confirms the criminality of the inmate.
    From the above paragraph only, it may be BEST concluded that

    A. prison sentences tend to punish rather than rehabilitate
    B. all criminals should be given prison sentences
    C. we should abandon our penal institutions
    D. penal institutions are effective in rehabilitating criminals

18. Some courts are referred to as *criminal* courts while others are known as *civil* courts. This distinction in name is MOST probably based on the

    A. historical origin of the court
    B. link between the court and the police
    C. manner in which the judges are chosen
    D. type of cases tried there

19. Many children who are exposed to contacts and experiences of a delinquent nature become educated and trained in crime in the course of participating in the daily life of the neighborhood.
    From this statement only, we may reasonably conclude that

    A. delinquency passes from parent to child
    B. neighborhood influences are usually bad
    C. schools are training grounds for delinquents
    D. none of the above conclusions is reasonable

20. Old age insurance, for whose benefits a quarter of a million city employees may elect to become eligible, is one feature of the Social Security Act that is wholly administered by the Federal government.
    On the basis of this paragraph only, it may MOST reasonably be inferred that

    A. a quarter of a million city employees are drawing old age insurance
    B. a quarter of a million city employees have elected to become eligible for old age insurance
    C. the city has no part in administering Social Security old age insurance
    D. only the Federal government administers the Social Security Act

21. An officer's revolver is a defensive, and not offensive, weapon.
    On the basis of this statement only, an officer should BEST draw his revolver to

    A. fire at an unarmed burglar
    B. force a suspect to confess
    C. frighten a juvenile delinquent
    D. protect his own life

22. Prevention of crime is of greater value to the community than the punishment of crime. 22.____
 If this statement is accepted as true, GREATEST emphasis should be placed on

 A. malingering B. medication
 C. imprisonment D. rehabilitation

23. The criminal is rarely or never reformed. 23.____
 Acceptance of this statement as true would mean that GREATEST emphasis should be placed on

 A. imprisonment B. parole
 C. probation D. malingering

24. The MOST accurate of the following statements about persons convicted of crimes is 24.____
 that

 A. their criminal behavior is almost invariably the result of low intelligence
 B. they are almost invariably legally insane
 C. they are more likely to come from underprivileged groups than from other groups
 D. they have certain facial characteristics which distinguish them from non-criminals

25. Suppose a study shows that the I.Q. (Intelligence Quotient) of prison inmates is 95 as 25.____
 opposed to an I.Q. of 100 for a numerically equivalent civilian group.
 A claim, on the basis of this study, that criminals have a lower I.Q. than non-criminals would be

 A. *improper;* prison inmates are criminals who have been caught
 B. *proper;* the study was numerically well done
 C. *improper;* the sample was inadequate
 D. *proper;* even misdemeanors are sometimes penalized by prison sentences

Questions 26-45.

DIRECTIONS: Select the letter of the word or expression that MOST NEARLY expresses the meaning of the capitalized word in the group.

26. ABDUCT 26.____

 A. lead B. kidnap C. sudden D. worthless

27. BIAS 27.____

 A. ability B. envy C. prejudice D. privilege

28. COERCE 28.____

 A. cancel B. force C. rescind D. rugged

29. CONDONE 29.____

 A. combine B. pardon C. revive D. spice

30. CONSISTENCY 30.____

 A. bravery B. readiness C. strain D. uniformity

31. CREDENCE
    A. belief   B. devotion   C. resemblance   D. tempo

32. CURRENT
    A. backward   B. brave   C. prevailing   D. wary

33. CUSTODY
    A. advisement   B. belligerence
    C. guardianship   D. suspicion

34. DEBILITY
    A. deceitfulness   B. decency
    C. strength   D. weakness

35. DEPLETE
    A. beg   B. empty   C. excuse   D. fold

36. ENUMERATE
    A. name one by one   B. disappear
    C. get rid of   D. pretend

37. FEIGN
    A. allow   B. incur   C. pretend   D. weaken

38. INSTIGATE
    A. analyze   B. coordinate   C. oppose   D. provoke

39. LIABLE
    A. careless   B. growing   C. mistaken   D. responsible

40. PONDER
    A. attack   B. heavy   C. meditate   D. solicit

41. PUGILIST
    A. farmer   B. politician
    C. prize fighter   D. stage actor

42. QUELL
    A. explode   B. inform   C. shake   D. suppress

43. RECIPROCAL
    A. mutual   B. organized   C. redundant   D. thoughtful

44. RUSE
    A. burn   B. impolite   C. rot   D. trick

45. STEALTHY 45.____

    A. crazed   B. flowing   C. sly   D. wicked

Questions 46-50.

DIRECTIONS: Each of the sentences numbered 46 to 50 may be classified under one of the following four categories:
    A faulty because of incorrect grammar
    B faulty because of incorrect punctuation
    C faulty because of incorrect capitalization or incorrect spelling
    D correct

Examine each sentence carefully to determine under which of the above four options it is best classified. Then, in the corresponding space at the right, write the letter preceding the option which is the BEST of the four suggested above. Each faulty sentence contains but one type of error. Consider a sentence to be correct if it contains none of the types of errors mentioned, even though there may be other correct ways of expressing the same thought.

46. They told both he and I that the prisoner had escaped. 46.____

47. Any superior officer, who, disregards the just complaints of his subordinates, is remiss in the performance of his duty. 47.____

48. Only those members of the national organization who resided in the Middle west attended the conference in Chicago. 48.____

49. We told him to give the investigation assignment to whoever was available. 49.____

50. Please do not disappoint and embarass us by not appearing in court. 50.____

KEY (CORRECT ANSWERS)

1. C	11. A	21. D	31. A	41. C
2. A	12. B	22. D	32. C	42. D
3. B	13. A	23. A	33. C	43. A
4. A	14. D	24. C	34. D	44. D
5. D	15. A	25. A	35. B	45. C
6. A	16. C	26. B	36. A	46. A
7. B	17. A	27. C	37. C	47. B
8. D	18. D	28. B	38. D	48. C
9. D	19. D	29. B	39. D	49. D
10. D	20. C	30. D	40. C	50. C

TEST 2

DIRECTIONS: Each question or incomplete statement is followed by several suggested answers or completions. Select the one that BEST answers the question or completes the statement. *PRINT THE LETTER OF THE CORRECT ANSWER IN THE SPACE AT THE RIGHT.*

1. Suppose a man falls from a two-story high scaffold and is unconscious. You should
    A. call for medical assistance and avoid moving the man
    B. get someone to help you move him indoors to a bed
    C. have someone help you walk him around until he revives
    D. hold his head up and pour a stimulant down his throat

2. For proper first aid treatment, a person who has fainted should be
    A. doused with cold water and then warmly covered
    B. given artificial respiration until he is revived
    C. laid down with his head lower than the rest of his body
    D. slapped on the face until he is revived

3. If you are called on to give first aid to a person who is suffering from shock, you should
    A. apply cold towels   B. give him a stimulant
    C. keep him awake   D. wrap him warmly

4. Artificial respiration would NOT be proper first aid for a person suffering from
    A. drowning   B. electric shock
    C. external bleeding   D. suffocation

5. Suppose you are called on to give first aid to several victims of an accident. FIRST attention should be given to the one who is
    A. bleeding severely   B. groaning loudly
    C. unconscious   D. vomiting

6. If an officer's weekly salary is increased from $400.00 to $450.00, then the percent of increase is _____ percent.
    A. 10   B. 11 1/9   C. 12 1/2   D. 20

7. Suppose that one-half the officers in a department have served for more than ten years, and one-third have served for more than 15 years.
Then, the fraction of officers who have served between ten and fifteen years is
    A. 1/3   B. 1/5   C. 1/6   D. 1/12

8. In a city prison, there are four floors on which prisoners are housed. The top floor houses one-quarter of the inmates, the bottom floor houses one-sixth of the inmates, one-third are housed on the second floor. The rest of the inmates are housed on the third floor. If there are 90 inmates housed on the third floor, the total number of inmates housed on all four floors together is
    A. 270   B. 360   C. 450   D. 540

9. Suppose that ten percent of those who commit serious crimes are convicted and that fifteen percent of those convicted are sentenced for more than 3 years.
   The percentage of those committing serious crimes who are sentenced for more than 3 years is _____ percent.

   A. 15   B. 1.5   C. .15   D. .015

10. Assume that there are 1,100 employees in a city agency. Of these, 15 percent are officers, 80 percent of whom are attorneys; of the attorneys, two-fifths have been with the agency over five years.
    Then the number of officers who are attorneys and have over five years' experience with the agency is MOST NEARLY

    A. 45   B. 53   C. 132   D. 165

11. An employee who has 500 cartons of supplies to pack can pack them at the rate of 50 an hour. After this employee has worked for half an hour, he is jointed by another employee who can pack 45 cartons an hour.
    Assuming that both employees can maintain their respective rates of speed, the total number of hours required to pack all the cartons is

    A. 4 1/2   B. 5   C. 5 1/2   D. 6 1/2

12. Thirty-six officers can complete an assignment in 22 days. Assuming that all officers work at the same rate of speed, the number of officers that would be needed to complete this assignment in 12 days is

    A. 42   B. 54   C. 66   D. 72

Questions 13-15.

DIRECTIONS: Questions 13 through 15, inclusive, are to be answered on the basis of the table below. Data for certain categories have been omitted from the You are to calculate the missing numbers if needed to answer the questions.

	2007	2008	Numerical Increase
Correction Officers	1,226	1,347	
Court Officers		529	34
Deputy Sheriffs	38	40	
Supervisors			
	2,180	2,414	—

13. The number in the *Supervisors* group in 2007 was MOST NEARLY

    A. 500   B. 475   C. 450   D. 425

14. The LARGEST percentage increase from 2007 to 2008 was in the group of

    A. Correction officers   B. Court officers
    C. Deputy sheriffs   D. Supervisors

15. In 2008, the ratio of the number of Correction Officers to the total of the other three categories of employees was MOST NEARLY

    A. 1:1   B. 2:1   C. 3:1   D. 4:1

16. A directed verdict is made by a court when

   A. the facts are not disputed
   B. the defendant's motion for a directed verdict has been denied
   C. there is no question of law involved
   D. neither party has moved for a directed verdict

17. Papers on appeal of a criminal case do NOT include one of the following:

   A. Summons
   B. Minutes of trial
   C. Complaint
   D. Intermediate motion papers

18. A pleading titled *Smith vs. Jones, et al.* indicates

   A. two plaintiffs
   B. two defendants
   C. more than two defendants
   D. unknown defendants

19. A District Attorney makes a *prima facie* case when

   A. there is proof of guilt beyond a reasonable doubt
   B. the evidence is sufficient to convict in the absence of rebutting evidence
   C. the prosecution presents more evidence than the defense
   D. the defendant fails to take the stand

20. A person is NOT qualified to act as a trial juror in a criminal action if he or she

   A. has been convicted previously of a misdemeanor
   B. is under 18 years of age
   C. has scruples against the death penalty
   D. does not own property of a value at least $500

21. A court clerk who falsifies a court record commits a(n)

   A. misdemeanor
   B. offense
   C. felony
   D. no crime, but automatically forfeits his tenure

22. Insolent and contemptuous behavior to a judge during a court of record proceeding is punishable as

   A. civil contempt
   B. criminal contempt
   C. disorderly conduct
   D. a disorderly person

23. Offering a bribe to a court clerk would not constitute a crime UNLESS the

   A. court clerk accepted the bribe
   B. bribe consisted of money
   C. bribe was given with intent to influence the court clerk in his official functions
   D. court was actually in session

24. A defendant comes to trial in the same court in which he had previously been defendant in a similar case.
The court officer should

   A. tell him, *Knew we'd be seeing you again*
   B. tell newspaper reporters what he knows of the previous action

C. treat him the same as he would any other defendant
D. warn the judge that the man had previously been a defendant

25. Suppose in conversation with you, an attorney strongly criticizes a ruling of the judge, and you believe the attorney to be correct.
You should

   A. assure him you feel the same way
   B. tell him the judge knows the law
   C. tell him to ask for an exception
   D. refuse to discuss the matter

26. Suppose a doorman refuses to admit you to an apartment house in which you are attempting to serve a process on a tenant.
Of the following, the BEST action for you to take is to

   A. bribe the doorman to admit you
   B. discard the process since it cannot be served
   C. gain entrance by force
   D. report the matter to your superior

27. False arrest is an offense for which the deputy sheriff may be held liable.
Therefore, before making an arrest, the deputy sheriff should

   A. be sure a witness is present
   B. be sure it is legal
   C. seek assistance from a patrolman
   D. deputize a private citizen

28. An arrested person should not be transported upon a public conveyance such as a streetcar, subway, or bus, except in an extreme emergency.
The reason for this regulation is MOST probably the

   A. danger of escape   B. embarrassment to the prisoner
   C. expense involved   D. possible delays

29. Except in rare emergencies, a deputy should not attempt to make an arrest without a partner.
The BEST reason for this is that the partner may be needed to

   A. arbitrate the matter
   B. lend prestige to the sheriff's office
   C. overcome resistance
   D. provide company for the deputy

30. At the end of each month, the deputy sheriff must submit to his superior officer an activity report covering the status of his assignments and the extent of his activities in the service of process during the month.
It is MOST important that such report be

   A. accurate   B. brief
   C. grammatically correct   D. lengthy

31. Deputies are required to hold seized chattels for three days after service of the replevin papers. This means three full 24-hour days, exclusive of the day of service, and the property should not be turned over earlier than 12:01 A.M. on the fourth day. When one day of the period falls on a Sunday or a public holiday, that day is excluded and an additional day must be added to make up the three.
According to this statement only, if service of replevin papers is made on Thursday, June 23rd, the property should be turned over on

    A. Sunday, June 26th
    B. Monday, June 27th
    C. Tuesday, June 28th
    D. Wednesday, June 29th

32. Certain property is declared by law to be exempt from seizure to satisfy a debt because it is of importance to the comfort of the family, although of small money On the basis of this law, which of the following would you MOST expect to be exempt from seizure?

    A. Broadloom rug
    B. Dining table
    C. Marble statuette
    D. Modern painting

33. As a general rule, a deputy sheriff is justified in refusing to seize an article which differs from the description in the replevin papers, unless the difference is clearly unimportant in the light of other identifying facts. According to this statement, which of the following would a deputy sheriff BEST be justified in seizing where there is a difference from the description in the papers?
A(n)

    A. automobile corresponding in make, year, model, and engine number, but differing in color
    B. sofa corresponding in upholstery material, color, width, and height, but differing in length
    C. television set corresponding in year, model, and size of screen, but differing in number of tubes required
    D. typewriter corresponding in year, model, size of type, and color, but differing in name of manufacturer

34. The legal aspect of the sheriff's duties is emphasized by his unique personal liability, not only for his own acts and omissions, but also for those of any deputy or employee in his office.
According to the foregoing quotation, it would be MOST correct to state that the sheriff

    A. and his employees have unique legal duties to perform
    B. is held responsible for actions taken by his subordinates
    C. is liable for the acts of his employees only under unique circumstances
    D. must personally serve many legal papers

35. Which one of the following descriptions of a defendant would help MOST in identifying him?

    A. Age - 31 years; weight - 168 pounds
    B. At time of escape was wearing gray hat, dark overcoat
    C. Deep scar running from left ear to chin
    D. Height - 5 feet, 9 inches; complexion - sallow

36. Which of the following could a deputy sheriff BEST accept as proof of a man's identity?

    A. A personal letter
    B. Automobile driver's license
    C. Automobile registration certificate
    D. Social security card

37. It was formerly the practice to require someone who knew the defendant by sight to accompany the deputy sheriff. It has been learned through experience that the value of such identification is over-rated.
    From this paragraph only, it may be BEST inferred that

    A. circumstantial evidence is not reliable
    B. identifications are sometimes inaccurate
    C. people are usually for the underdog
    D. testimony is often contradictory

38. The depositions must set forth the facts tending to establish that an illegal act was committed and that the defendant is guilty.
    According to this statement only, the one of the following which need NOT be included in a deposition is evidence that establishes the

    A. fact that an illegal act was committed
    B. fact that defendant committed the illegal act
    C. guilt of the defendant
    D. method of commission of the illegal act

39. Each deputy sheriff should understand how his own work helps to accomplish the purpose of the entire agency.
    This statement means MOST NEARLY that the deputy sheriff should understand the

    A. efficiency of a small agency
    B. importance of his own job
    C. necessity for initiative
    D. value of a large organization

40. When X is accused of having cheated Y of a sum of money and Y is proven to have been deprived of the money, there is an additional requirement for a verdict against X.
    The additional requirement is to prove that

    A. the money was stolen from Y
    B. X had the money after Y had it
    C. X had the money before Y had it
    D. X cheated Y of the money

41. To gain a verdict against X in a trial, it was necessary to show that he could have been at Y Street at 5 P.M.
    It was proven that he was seen at Z Street at 4:45 P.M. The question that MUST be answered to show whether X is guilty is:

    A. How long does it take to get from Z Street to Y Street?
    B. In what sort of neighborhood is Z Street located?
    C. Was X acting suspiciously on the day in question?
    D. Who was with X when he was seen at Z Street at 4:45 P.M.?

42. The deputy sheriff must give the defendant reasonable time to secure the bail fixed in the process before confining him to jail.
    The CHIEF purpose of bail is to

    A. permit personnel to act as bondsmen
    B. permit the defendant his liberty while assuring his presence at the trial
    C. raise additional money for the general fund of the city treasury
    D. relieve the city of the necessity of bringing the defendant before a judge

43. When a jury is selected, the attorney for each side has a right to refuse to accept a certain number of prospective jurors without giving any reason therefor.
    The reason for this is MAINLY that

    A. attorneys can exclude persons likely to be biased even though no prejudice is admitted
    B. persons who will suffer economically by being summoned for jury duty can be excused forthwith
    C. relatives of the litigants can be excused, thus insuring a fair trial for each side
    D. there will be a greater number of people from which the jury can be selected, thus insuring better quality

44. Suppose a deputy sheriff, feeling that the verdict against a judgment debtor was unfair, permits him to escape.
    On the basis of this information only, it is safe to assume that the

    A. judge passing sentence was unduly harsh
    B. judgment debtor had possession of a large sum of money
    C. deputy sheriff was recently appointed
    D. deputy sheriff used poor judgment

45. A deputy sheriff shall not receive a gift from any defendant or other person on the defendant's behalf.
    The BEST explanation for this departmental rule is that

    A. acceptance of a gift has no significance
    B. favors may be expected in return
    C. gifts are only an expression of good will
    D. litigants cannot usually afford gifts

46. All concerned are MOST likely to recognize the deputy sheriff's authority and cooperate with him if he conveys by his manner a complete confidence that they will do so. According to this statement only, a deputy sheriff should display

    A. arrogance   B. agitation   C. assurance   D. excitement

47. Since he is a city employee, a deputy sheriff who refuses to waive immunity from prosecution when called on to testify in court automatically terminates his employment.
    From this statement only, it may be BEST inferred that

    A. a deputy sheriff is a city employee
    B. all city employees are deputy sheriffs
    C. city employees may be fired only for malfeasance
    D. deputy sheriffs who waive immunity may not be prosecuted

48. In one case, a mistrial was declared because the indictment used the pronoun *he* instead of *she*.
    The MOST useful information a deputy sheriff can derive from this statement is that

    A. accuracy is important
    B. mistrial is a legal term
    C. one must always use good grammar
    D. to misrepresent is felonious

49. It is desirable that a deputy sheriff acquire a knowledge of the procedures of the division to which he is assigned MAINLY because such knowledge will help him

    A. become familiar with anti-social behavior
    B. discharge his duties properly
    C. gain insight into causes of crime
    D. in any personal legal proceeding

50. It is a frequent misconception that deputy sheriffs can be recruited from those registers established for the recruitment of police officers or firefighters. While it is true that many common qualifications are found in all of these, specific standards for a sheriff's work are indicated, varying with the size, geographical location and policies of the office.
    According to this paragraph only, it may BEST be inferred that

    A. a successful deputy sheriff must have some qualifications not required of a policeman or fireman
    B. qualifications which make a successful patrolman will also make a successful fireman
    C. the same qualifications are required of a deputy sheriff regardless of the office to which he is assigned
    D. the successful deputy sheriff is required to be both more intelligent and stronger than a fireman

KEY (CORRECT ANSWERS

1. A	11. C	21. C	31. C	41. A
2. C	12. C	22. B	32. B	42. B
3. D	13. D	23. C	33. A	43. A
4. C	14. D	24. C	34. B	44. D
5. A	15. A	25. D	35. C	45. B
6. C	16. A	26. D	36. B	46. C
7. C	17. D	27. B	37. B	47. A
8. B	18. C	28. A	38. D	48. A
9. B	19. B	29. C	39. B	49. B
10. B	20. B	30. A	40. D	50. A

SOLUTIONS TO PROBLEMS

6. CORRECT ANSWER: C

$$\frac{50}{400} = \frac{1}{8} = 12\frac{1}{2}\%$$

7. CORRECT ANSWER: C

   $1/2 + 1/3 = 3/6 + 2/6 = 5/6$

   $\therefore 1 - 5/6 = 1/6$

8. CORRECT ANSWER: B

   $1/4 + 1/6 + 1/3 = 3/12 + 2/12 + 4/12 = 9/12 = 3/4$

   $\therefore 1 - 3/4 = 1/4$ (rest of inmates housed on the third floor) Since 90 = 1/4, therefore, 4/4 (or 1) = 360.

9. CORRECT ANSWER: B

   $.10 \times .15 = .0150 = 1.5\%$

10. CORRECT ANSWER: B

    Step (1)   1100
              x.15
              ────
              5500
              1100
              ──────
              165.00 (peace officers)

    Step (2)   165
               x.80
               ─────
               132.00 (attorneys)

    Step (3) $132 \times 2/5 = 264/5 = 52.8$ (peace officers who are attorneys and have over five years' experience with the agency)

11. CORRECT ANSWER: C

    Since the first employee worked for 1/2 hour, he packed 25 cartons (50 ÷ 2). This leaves 475 cartons to be packed. This first employee packs at the rate of 50 an hour. The second employee, who joins him after 1/2 hour, packs at the rate of 45 an hour. 50 + 45 = 95 (rate of both employees together)

    $\therefore$ 475 ÷ 95 = 5 hours (time it takes both employees together) 5 hours + 1/2 hour = 5 1/2 hours

12. CORRECT ANSWER: C

    $x : 36 = 22 : 12$

    $12 \times x = 36 \times 22$

    $12x = 792$

    $x = 66$

EXAMINATION SECTION
TEST 1

DIRECTIONS: Each question or incomplete statement is followed by several suggested answers or completions. Select the one that BEST answers the question or completes the statement. *PRINT THE LETTER OF THE CORRECT ANSWER IN THE SPACE AT THE RIGHT.*

1. An order of civil arrest is signed by the Supreme Court, New York County, on September 24, 2012. On September 28, 2012, a deputy sheriff duly arrests the defendant on Queens Blvd. in the County of Queens. If the defendant is not released on bail, the defendant will thereafter be brought for a hearing in Supreme Court

    A. New York County
    B. Queens County
    C. of any county in New York City
    D. of any county in New York State

2. In the preceding Question 1, the hearing must be held NO LATER THAN _____, 2008.

    A. September 28
    B. September 29
    C. September 30
    D. October 10

3. In the preceding Question 1, the sheriff's office must notify the plaintiff or his attorney about the hearing NOT LATER THAN _____ the hearing.

    A. twenty-four hours before
    B. forty-eight hours before
    C. thirty-six hours before
    D. the morning of

4. John Doe has been held in contempt for his refusal to call off an illegal strike against his employer. Doe has been arrested and is lodged in the civil jail. Doe may be kept in jail

    A. not more than three months
    B. not more than six months
    C. until he posts bail
    D. until he calls off the strike

5. In the preceding Question 4, assume that upon being arrested Doe has a change of heart and agrees to call off the strike. The deputy's BEST course of action would be to

    A. accompany Doe to an appropriate place to insure that Doe keeps his word
    B. release Doe immediately
    C. contact the attorney for the employer and seek his instructions
    D. accept cash bail from Doe and not arrest him

6. A warrant of arrest has been properly issued to insure the presence of John Roe as a witness at a departmental trial in a city agency. The warrant is issued on June 1. The trial is scheduled for June 4. The MOST appropriate day to make the arrest would be

    A. as soon as possible after June 1
    B. on June 4, if possible
    C. on June 3, if possible
    D. when it is most convenient for the sheriff's office

17

7. Upon receipt of an order of civil arrest, the deputy sheriff checked the office file and found that there was a prior order of arrest which had never been executed. Of the following, the one which would NOT be an appropriate course of action for the deputy is to

   A. execute the earlier order of arrest
   B. execute the later order of arrest
   C. execute the earlier order and file a detainer for the later one with the warden of the jail
   D. call counsel for the plaintiff in that action to ascertain the status of the earlier order

8. In executing an order of civil arrest, the LEAST desirable place to make the arrest is

   A. the defendant's place of business
   B. in a public place
   C. on the street outside the defendant's home
   D. the defendant's home

9. An order of civil arrest has been issued for an orthodox Jew. On which of the following days is he immune from arrest?

   A. Only on Saturday
   B. Only on Sunday
   C. On both Saturday and Sunday
   D. Neither on Saturday nor on Sunday

10. Of the following persons, the one who is NOT immune from civil arrest is a(n)

    A. ordained clergyman
    B. maid who works at the French Ambassador's home
    C. fireman on duty
    D. marine on active duty

11. An order for the civil arrest of John P. Doe is delivered to the sheriff's office. A photograph of Mr. Doe accompanies the papers. Upon arriving at the home of Mr. Doe, the deputy sheriff finds that there are two men living together: John P. Doe and John Q. Doe. The photograph is that of John Q. Doe. Which of the following is the LEAST appropriate course of action for the deputy to follow?

    A. Arrest John Q. Doe
    B. Take no immediate arrest, but call the attorney for the plaintiff for instructions
    C. Suggest that both men accompany him to the sheriff's office, if they are willing to clarify the situation
    D. Arrest both men

12. Executing an order of civil arrest, the deputy sheriff is told by the defendant's wife that the defendant is recuperating from a severe heart attack and is, therefore, too ill to be moved. The FIRST step which should be taken is to

    A. arrest the defendant
    B. communicate with the attorney for the plaintiff and tell him the facts
    C. call a local hospital and request that a doctor come over and examine the defendant
    D. postpone the execution of the order of arrest for seventy-two hours

13. After an order of civil arrest has been signed, it

    A. may not be withdrawn without a court order
    B. must be executed within ten days
    C. must be filed in the county clerk's office
    D. may be withdrawn by the plaintiff's attorney anytime before it is executed

14. A deputy sheriff has a proper order for the civil arrest of John Doe. To effect the arrest, the deputy is authorized to

    A. break into Doe's home, if he is certain that Doe is there
    B. break into a warehouse where Doe is working
    C. shoot Doe if, after being arrested, Doe breaks away from the deputy
    D. chase Doe down the street and if Doe gets inside his house, to break in and arrest Doe in the house

15. While taking Baker to the civil jail, New York City deputy sheriff Doe negligently injures Baker. The following are liable to Baker for the negligence of Doe:

    A. Doe and the State of New York
    B. Doe and the sheriff of the City of New York
    C. only the sheriff of the City of New York
    D. only Doe

16. An attorney delivers to the sheriff's office an income execution which states the name of the judgment debtor's employer, but does not state how much money the judgment debtor earns from that employer. The MOST appropriate action which the sheriff's office should take is to

    A. serve the income execution upon the judgment debtor with a direction that he is expected to pay 10% of his wages to the sheriff, as those wages are earned
    B. serve the income execution upon the judgment debtor's employer with a direction that he must withhold from the debtor's wages 10% thereof and remit the money to the sheriff
    C. apprise the judgment creditor's attorney that the income execution is defective in form and suggest that the attorney include therein the amount of money which the judgment debtor is expected to earn
    D. ignore the income execution as defective in form and wait for an inquiry from the attorney as to why it has not been served

17. Armed with a proper order of civil arrest and all other necessary papers for the arrest of John Doe, a deputy sheriff enters Doe's apartment with the permission of Mrs. Doe. A man, believed by the deputy to be John Doe, is asleep on the couch in the living room. The deputy states to Mrs. Doe: *I have an order for the arrest of your husband. Consider him under arrest.* Mrs. Doe replies: *That man on the couch is my brother, Richard. My husband John is not here.*
    Which of the following persons now has a cause of action for false arrest?

    A. John Doe   B. Richard
    C. Mrs. Doe   D. None of the above

18. An order of civil arrest, which states that it is issued in an action for fraud and deceit, is signed for the arrest of *Alex Smith*. The only identification which the deputy sheriff has is a badly faded picture of Alex Smith. Taking it to the home of Alex Smith, the deputy sheriff knocks on the door. A woman answers and identifies herself as Alex Smith. Which of the following is NOT an appropriate course of action for the deputy to take?

    A. The deputy, upon assuring himself that the woman is Alex Smith intended to be named in the order, may arrest her.
    B. The deputy may contact the attorney for the plaintiff to ascertain who Alex Smith is.
    C. If the attorney for the plaintiff is unavailable, the deputy may contact the plaintiff himself to ascertain who Alex Smith is.
    D. If it is too late to contact anyone, the deputy may leave without arresting anyone.

19. An order of civil arrest in an action for conversion may be signed

    A. only after final judgment
    B. only before the summons is served
    C. at any time before the action is commenced and up until final judgment
    D. before or after final judgment

20. P has a judgment against D. X owes D a debt. The deputy sheriff has properly served an execution on X, but X refuses to pay. To compel payment, P should

    A. make a motion in the original action to compel payment
    B. make a motion in the original action to punish X for contempt
    C. commence a special proceeding to compel payment of the debt
    D. commence a special proceeding to punish X for contempt

21. Even though the defendant is known to be in New York, the one of the following which need NOT be personally served upon him is

    A. an order preliminarily enjoining the defendant
    B. an order temporarily restraining the defendant
    C. a subpoena duces tecum commanding defenant to deliver books
    D. a summons

22. In an action to recover possession of an automobile, plaintiff, before commencing the action, has properly directed the sheriff by requisition to seize the chattel and restore immediate possession to the plaintiff. Under the C.P.L.R., the summons must be served

    A. within thirty days after the requisition is delivered to the sheriff or else the sheriff may not seize the chattel
    B. when the sheriff seizes the chattel from the defendant
    C. within thirty days after the sheriff seizes the chattel
    D. within three days after the sheriff seizes the chattel

23. The provisional remedy of civil arrest is available in an action for

    A. trespass to a chattel
    B. ejectment
    C. specific performance of a contract to convey land located outside New York
    D. specific performance of a contract to convey land located in New York

24. In which of the following provisional remedies, granted before a summons is served, must jurisdiction be acquired over the defendant or his property within a certain time limit or else the provisional remedy becomes void? Attachment

    A. and arrest
    B. and lis pendens (notice of pendency)
    C. , arrest, and receivership
    D. , injunction, and lis pendens (notice of pendency)

25. In an action for damages based upon fraud, a defendant who has been arrested

    A. may be released upon bail only in the discretion of the court
    B. may be released upon bail only after he has served three days in jail
    C. may have the order of arrest vacated as unauthorized in an action for fraud
    D. has an absolute right to post bail for his release

KEY (CORRECT ANSWERS)

1.	B	11.	D
2.	C	12.	B
3.	A	13.	D
4.	D	14.	B
5.	C	15.	B
6.	B	16.	C
7.	B	17.	D
8.	D	18.	A
9.	C	19.	C
10.	A	20.	C

21. A
22. B
23. C
24. B
25. D

TEST 2

DIRECTIONS: Each question or incomplete statement is followed by several suggested answers or completions. Select the one that BEST answers the question or completes the statement. *PRINT THE LETTER OF THE CORRECT ANSWER IN THE SPACE AT THE RIGHT.*

1. The sheriff has properly delivered an income execution to D's employer. The employer has refused to honor the execution. The plaintiff's lawyer should now serve

    A. motion papers on the employer to punish him for contempt
    B. a notice of petition and a petition to obtain a judgment against the employer
    C. motion papers on the employer to obtain an order directing payment
    D. a subpoena upon the employer restraining him from paying D

2. An order of civil arrest has been signed against Doe in an action for fraud. The action has not yet been commenced. The summons must be served

    A. within 48 hours after Doe is arrested
    B. within 30 days after the arrest order is signed or the arrest order will become void
    C. at the time the deputy sheriff arrests Doe
    D. at a time not specified by any of the foregoing

3. The date on which a summons is prepared in a civil action

    A. is the date upon which the statute of limitations stops running
    B. is the date from which the defendant measures his time in which to appear
    C. must be typed on the face of the summons
    D. has no legal significance

4. An attorney has delivered an execution to the sheriff's office. A levy may thereafter be made under this execution within sixty days

    A. or else the execution becomes void and cannot be extended
    B. unless the period is extended (by a maximum of one sixty-day increment) in writing by the plaintiff's attorney
    C. unless the period is extended by court order
    D. unless the period is extended by successive sixty-day periods in writing by the plaintiff's attorney

5. John Doe works as a bank messenger for the Acme Bank in Manhattan. Doe lives in Nassau County. Peters has obtained a judgment against Doe in the Supreme Court, Queens County. Peters now delivers an income execution to the sheriff's office UNLESS

    A. Peters has already tried unsuccessfully to execute against personal property owned by Doe, the income execution is unauthorized
    B. Peters has already tried unsuccessfully to execute against real property owned by Doe, the income execution is unauthorized
    C. Doe earns in excess of thirty dollars per week, his salary is exempt from an income execution
    D. Doe earns in excess of eighty-five dollars per week, his salary is exempt from an income execution

6. In the preceding Question 5, the appropriate sheriff's office for Peters to deliver the income execution to would be located in

   A. Nassau County
   B. New York County
   C. either Nassau or New York County
   D. any county of the state

7. In the preceding Question 6, assuming the propriety of the income execution, the sheriff should INITIALLY serve it upon

   A. an official of the Acme Bank
   B. John Doe
   C. an official of the Acme Bank or John Doe, in the sheriff's discretion
   D. both John Doe and an official of the Acme Bank

Questions 8-13.

DIRECTIONS: In answering Questions 8 through 13, assume the following set of facts.

Abel commences an action against Dunn in the Supreme Court, Erie County, on January 10, 2008. Baker commences his action against Dunn in Supreme Court, Orange County, on January 20, 2008.

On January 30, 2008, Charles, who also intends to sue Dunn, obtains an order of attachment from the Supreme Court, Bronx County. The same day, levying under this order, a deputy sheriff (1) leaves a copy of the order of attachment and all necessary papers with Dunn's employer; and (2) leaves a copy of the order of attachment and all necessary papers with the person managing *Blackacre*, Dunn's palatial summer estate in Jefferson County.

On February 10, 2008, Dunn, who is a resident of Queens County, was properly served with a summons at his home in Charles' action.

On November 2, 2010, the jury in Baker's action returned a verdict in Baker's favor. On November 10, 2010, the jury in Charles' action returned a verdict in Charles' favor. On November 20, 2010, the jury in Abel's action returned a verdict in Abel's favor.

On December 1, 2010, Charles entered and docketed his judgment in the office of the clerk of Bronx County, and on the same afternoon docketed it by transcript in Queens County. On December 10, 2010, Abel entered and docketed his judgment in the office of the clerk of Erie County. On December 21, 2010, Baker entered and docketed his judgment in the office of the clerk of Orange County.

8. Who has first lien on Blackacre?

   A. Abel
   B. Baker
   C. Charles
   D. None of the above

9. With respect to Dunn's employer, Charles

   A. obtained a lien on January 30, 2008 on 10% of all income which Dunn would thereafter earn from his employer
   B. obtained no lien of any kind on the income which Dunn would earn from his employer

C. would have obtained a lien on 10% of Dunn's income if the deputy had delivered the order of attachment to Dunn instead of to the employer
D. has first lien on Dunn's income, but the lien becomes effective only on December 1, 2010

10. With respect to executing upon Charles' judgment of December 1, 2010, Charles' judgment may be satisfied

    A. by levying upon a car owned by Dunn and garaged in Manhattan
    B. only out of the sale of Blackacre
    C. only out of the income Dunn earns from his employer
    D. only out of the sale of Blackacre and the income Dunn earns

11. Without any further procedural steps, Abel may immediately deliver an execution to the sheriff of

    A. Queens County only
    B. Jefferson County only
    C. neither Queens County nor Jefferson County
    D. both Queens County and Jefferson County

12. Assume further that Abel dockets his judgment on August 1, 2011 in Jefferson County. Baker does the same on August 15, 2011, and Charles does it on September 1, 2011. If Charles then delivers an execution to the sheriff of Jefferson County on January 10, 2012 and if the sheriff notifies Abel and Baker who deliver similar executions to him on January 20, 2012, the proceeds of the sale of Blackacre will

    A. be prorated equally among Abel, Baker, and Charles
    B. go to Charles first, then to Abel; the balance to Baker
    C. go to Charles first; the balance to be prorated between Abel and Baker
    D. go to none of the above

13. If Dunn had sold Blackacre on October 1, 2010 to Y, a bona fide purchaser for value ignorant of the pending litigations, _____ could reach Blackacre on execution.

    A. Abel
    B. Baker
    C. both Abel and Baker
    D. neither Abel nor Baker

Questions 14-15.

DIRECTIONS: In Questions 14 and 15, select the BEST option.

14. Richard Roe lives and works in Manhattan, earning $300 a week in a brokerage house. Three judgments are entered against Roe by different plaintiffs, named A, B, and C. B delivers an income execution to the sheriff's office in New York County; then A does the same thing. A week later, C, who has a civil court judgment, delivers an income execution to a New York City marshal. In the circumstances,

A. if all three executions are thereafter served, A, B, and C will each be entitled to ten percent of Roe's salary
B. if C's income execution is the first one served upon Roe, C will have priority over A and B
C. B has priority over A and C
D. A has priority over B and C

15. In the preceding Question 14, assume that C, who has the civil court judgment, is the first to deliver the execution to a marshal and that B next delivers his execution to the sheriff, and, finally, that A delivers his execution to the sheriff. In the circumstances, 15._____

    A. C has priority over A and B
    B. the priority will depend upon which execution is thereafter served upon Roe
    C. the priority will depend upon which execution is thereafter served upon the brokerage house
    D. B has priority

16. An attorney delivers a property execution to the sheriff's office with a direction that it be immediately returned unsatisfied since the attorney has already ascertained that the judgment debtor has no property. The BEST course of action for the sheriff is to 16._____

    A. comply with the attorney's request
    B. mail the execution to the judgment debtor's home
    C. mail the execution to the judgment debtor's place of business
    D. make a bona fide attempt to locate the judgment debtor and demand that he pay the judgment

17. John Doe, a judgment debtor, has personal property stored in a warehouse owned by X. X has issued to Doe a negotiable warehouse receipt for the property. A PROPER way to levy upon this property is - 17._____

    A. to go to the warehouse and seize the property
    B. to seize the warehouse receipt from Doe
    C. to go to the warehouse and leave the execution with X
    D. none of the above

18. Pursuant to an order of attachment, a deputy sheriff has levied upon a Rolls-Royce automobile which, the plaintiff says, belongs to the defendant. Defendant denies that the automobile is his. The automobile has been stored in X's warehouse. Of the following courses of action, the one which would NOT be appropriate is to 18._____

    A. publish a notice in the New York Law Journal that the automobile is in storage and inviting the true owner to come forward
    B. get the plaintiff and X to agree that plaintiff will be solely responsible for the storage charges
    C. get the plaintiff's lawyer and X to agree that the lawyer will be solely responsible for the storage charges
    D. get an agreement from the plaintiff's lawyer that he will indemnify the sheriff in the event the sheriff is held responsible for the storage charges

19. Assume that in the preceding Question 18, the attorney agrees to advance the foreseeable storage charges. The recommended period of storage for which advance payment should be exacted is

    A. no more than three months
    B. no more than six months
    C. at least six months
    D. at least a year

20. An order of attachment has been issued against John Doe, a tailor who earns $500.00 a week in his own shop. A levy may be made by

    A. closing up the tailor shop over the objection of Doe
    B. seizing a number of customers' suits found on a rack in the tailor shop
    C. taking Doe's wedding ring
    D. physically removing a portable sewing machine from the tailor shop

21. Of the following, the property which is generally exempt from levy of execution is

    A. a Picasso painting that has been in the defendant's family for fifty years
    B. a television set
    C. property on the defendant's person
    D. the defendant's home, worth $50,000

22. A and B, two individuals, are partners in a finance company known as Ace Finance. A judgment has been entered against B for his negligence in driving his family automobile on a pleasure trip to Miami. This judgment may be executed by levying upon

    A. B's desk in the office of Ace Finance
    B. B's interest in the partnership
    C. a bank account maintained in the name of Ace Finance
    D. B's Timex watch, worth $25.00

23. A deputy sheriff, who has been levying under an order of attachment against John Doe, reads in a trade journal that Doe has filed a petition for bankruptcy. Of the following courses of action, the one which would NOT be appropriate is for the deputy to

    A. continue to levy upon Doe's assets as they are found
    B. call his superiors and notify them of the bankruptcy
    C. notify the plaintiff's attorney of the bankruptcy
    D. seek to determine whether the John Doe he read about is the same John Doe who is the defendant

24. Seeking to make a levy under an order of attachment, a deputy sheriff finds the defendant in possession of a 2008 Cadillac automobile, which the defendant asserts belongs to his brother. The defendant, however, has no registration for the automobile, asserting that the registration is with his brother. Of the following courses of action, the one which would NOT be appropriate is to

    A. drive with the defendant to his brother's house to check the registration
    B. obtain the consent of the plaintiff to let the defendant keep the automobile
    C. levy upon the automobile, if no immediate proof of ownership is available
    D. desist from levying on the auto if no immediate proof of ownership is available

25. In the preceding Question 24, assume that it is proven that the automobile belongs to the defendant, but there is a security interest filed by the Ace Finance Company. Then the automobile may   25._____

    A. not be levied on
    B. be levied upon and the purchaser at the eventual execution sale will obtain a clear and free title
    C. be levied upon and the purchaser at the eventual execution sale will obtain a title which is subject to the filed security interest of the Ace Finance Company
    D. be levied upon but the Ace Finance Company may not buy it at eventual execution sale

KEY (CORRECT ANSWERS)

1.	B	11.	D
2.	C	12.	D
3.	D	13.	D
4.	D	14.	C
5.	D	15.	A
6.	A	16.	D
7.	B	17.	B
8.	D	18.	A
9.	B	19.	C
10.	A	20.	D

21. C
22. B
23. A
24. D
25. C

TEST 3

DIRECTIONS: Each question or incomplete statement is followed by several suggested answers or completions. Select the one that BEST answers the question or completes the statement. *PRINT THE LETTER OF THE CORRECT ANSWER IN THE SPACE AT THE RIGHT.*

1. An execution against Doe has been delivered to the sheriff's office. Doe is found to possess a pawn ticket for a rare Stradivarius violin worth $2,500.00, which he pledged for $50.00.

    A. The court may permit the execution sale of the violin, even though it remains in the custody of the pawnbroker.
    B. The violin may not be sold upon execution unless it is first taken from the pawnbroker.
    C. If Doe is a professional violinist, the violin may NOT be sold upon execution.
    D. The violin may be sold upon execution only if the pawn ticket can be seized to prevent its negotiation.

2. A judgment has been obtained against John Doe, the president of a corporation. Although an income execution was properly served upon Doe, he has refused to pay any of his salary to the sheriff. A deputy has now been sent to serve the income execution upon the corporation. In the circumstances,

    A. the deputy must serve the execution upon John Doe as president of the corporation
    B. although the deputy may serve any officer of the corporation, the better practice is to serve John Doe as president
    C. if possible, the deputy should serve some other officer of the corporation
    D. preferred practice is simply to mail the income execution to the corporation

3. Peters obtains a judgment against Doe on June 1, 2012. On June 10, Peters learns that Doe, who has been in financial difficulties, intends to make an assignment for the benefit of creditors. On June 11, Peters delivers an execution to the sheriff. On June 15, Doe makes the assignment, in writing, to X for the benefit of all of Doe's creditors. In the circumstances, the

    A. sheriff may not levy under Peters' execution
    B. sheriff may levy under Peters' execution and sell Doe's property, but must hold the proceeds for the benefit of all Doe's creditors
    C. sheriff may levy under Peters' execution and sell the property for the benefit of Peters
    D. assignment for the benefit of creditors is void since no court approval was obtained for it

4. Before the commencement of an action by Peters against Doe, Doe transfers substantial amounts of stocks and bonds to his wife. This is done as a gift, though it is apparent that Doe did it to defeat any judgment which Peters might obtain. Doe continues to control the stocks and bonds. Peters has now obtained a judgment against Doe and has delivered an execution to the sheriff. In the circumstances,

A. the stocks and bonds may not be levied upon
B. the stocks and bonds may be levied upon, but only after a court has declared the transfer to Doe's wife to be fraudulent
C. if the deputy is convinced that the transfer was fraudulent, he should on his own authority proceed to levy on the stocks and bonds
D. if the deputy believes that the transfer was fraudulent, the better practice is to refer the question to his superior who may authorize the levy if there is convincing evidence that the transfer was fraudulent

5. An order of attachment has been signed in an action against Doe. Plaintiff's attorney notifies a deputy sheriff that Smith owes Doe $5,000 which Smith has borrowed from Doe. In the circumstances,

    A. Smith's debt may be levied upon by serving a copy of the order of attachment upon Smith
    B. Smith's debt to Doe may not be levied upon
    C. if Smith's debt is not presently due but is certain to become due within six months, it may not be levied upon
    D. Smith's debt may be levied upon ONLY if there is a negotiable instrument representing the debt

6. An order of attachment has been signed in an action against Doe. Investigation discloses that a friend of Doe named George has two automobiles belonging to Doe. On June 1, 2010, a deputy sheriff delivers a copy of the order of attachment to George. In the circumstances,

    A. no valid levy was made on June 1, 2010 because no automobile was physically seized
    B. no valid levy was made on June 1, 2010 unless a special order of the court was obtained to dispense the deputy sheriff from physically seizing the automobiles
    C. a valid levy was made on June 1, 2010 when the order of attachment and sheriff's Form S-30 were left with George
    D. a valid levy was made on June 1, 2010 and nothing further need be done to reduce the automobiles to possession until the lawsuit is over

7. In the preceding Question 6, assume that a proper levy was made on June 1, 2010. Assume further that another of Doe's automobiles is delivered to George thereafter. In the circumstances, the third automobile

    A. is subject to the levy of June 1, 2010 if the automobile comes into George's possession on or before November 1, 2010, even though George delivered the first two automobiles to the sheriff on July 1, 2010
    B. cannot be subjected to levy unless there is a new service of the order of attachment upon George
    C. is subject to the levy of June 1, 2010 if it comes into George's possession within 120 days after June 1, 2010.
    D. is subject to the levy of June 1, 2010 if it comes into George's possession within 90 days after June 1, 2010, and George still has undisputed possession of the first two automobiles

8. Doe is the life beneficiary, along with his three brothers, of a trust set up by his father. Doe receives $500.00 per month from the trust. The Acme Bank is serving as trustee. Peters has a judgment against Doe. The PROPER way in which to levy upon Doe's interest in the trust is to

   A. serve the appropriate papers upon Doe's three brothers
   B. serve the appropriate papers upon the Acme Bank
   C. serve the appropriate papers upon one of Doe's brothers
   D. file the papers with the State Department of Trusts

9. In the preceding Question 8,

   A. Doe has no interest in the trust which may be levied upon
   B. Doe's entire interest in the trust may be levied upon
   C. 10% of the income earned by Doe from the trust is exempt from levy
   D. 90% of the income earned by Doe from the trust is exempt from levy

10. An order of attachment has been signed in an action against Doe. Investigation reveals that Doe owns 500 shares of IBM stock. The stock certificates are in a safe deposit box in the Acme Bank. The stock may be levied upon by serving the appropriate papers upon

    A. Doe, although the stock certificates are in a safe deposit box in the Acme Bank
    B. the president of IBM Corporation
    C. the Acme Bank which has the certificates and then taking possession of the certificates
    D. the Secretary of State in Albany

11. An order of attachment has been signed in an action against Doe. A friend of Doe's is known to possess much valuable property belonging to Doe. The order of attachment and the other appropriate papers are served upon the friend on June 1, 2012. The friend must then serve upon the sheriff's office a statement of the property he possesses within _____ days.

    A. 10   B. 15   C. 30   D. 90

12. In the preceding Question 11, the sheriff's office will send the statement to

    A. the court where the action is pending
    B. the defendant
    C. the plaintiff's attorney
    D. other judgment creditors of Doe

13. In the preceding Question 11, which of the following would NOT be an appropriate course of action to follow in the 90-day period after June 1, 2012?
    The

    A. sheriff may seize all of Doe's property in the friend's possession
    B. plaintiff may obtain an order extending the 90-day period
    C. plaintiff may commence a special proceeding to compel the friend to deliver the property to the sheriff
    D. sheriff may commence a special proceeding to compel the friend to deliver the property to the sheriff

14. In which of the following cases may a deputy sheriff make a constructive seizure of property simply by leaving the appropriate papers with the person in possession of the property?
    When he is levying

    A. upon personal property capable of delivery, under a writ of execution
    B. upon personal property capable of delivery, under an order of attachment
    C. under a proper requisition to replevy
    D. under a writ of execution for the delivery of possession of a chattel

15. A deputy sheriff has been sent to a warehouse to actually seize property in execution of a judgment. Upon entering the warehouse, he is shown an office with a glass door inside of which is located the property the deputy wants. To make a PROPER levy, the deputy

    A. need only peer through the glass door
    B. does not have to enter the office but need only say: *That property is now subject to a levy*
    C. must enter the office and touch the property
    D. must enter the office, view the property, and have it under his immediate ability to control

16. Assuming that the deputy sheriff is certain that the defendant has property, in which of the following cases may the deputy break and enter in order to seize the property?

    A. When the property is in the defendant's home
    B. When the property is in the defendant's locker at work
    C. When the property is in a hotel room where the defendant has been living
    D. In none of the above cases

17. After an order of attachment is signed against Doe, a deputy sheriff learns that Doe's automobile is in Joe's Garage for repairs. Although the deputy presents the necessary attachment papers, Joe's Garage is reluctant to release the automobile until its repair bill is paid. Which of the following courses of action would be LEAST appropriate?
    The

    A. sheriff may seize and remove the car over the objection of Joe's Garage
    B. sheriff may persuade the plaintiff to pay the garage bill
    C. deputy may persuade the garage to surrender the automobile by advising the garage owner that his rights will be fully protected
    D. deputy may persuade the plaintiff's attorney to permit a constructive seizure of the car in the hope that the case may be settled within 90 days thereafter

18. After levying on a valuable book collection upon execution of a judgment against Doe, the sheriff is notified by an attorney that the collection belongs to the attorney's client, and not to the defendant. The book collection has not yet been sold in execution of the judgment. The PROPER course of action to be pursued by the attorney is to

    A. start an action for an injunction to enjoin the execution sale
    B. start an action against Doe to replevy the book collection
    C. start a special proceeding to determine his client's rights to the book collection
    D. issue a precept to the sheriff directing the return of the book collection to his client

19. An order of attachment has been signed in an action against Doe. The only asset which Doe has is an apartment house in Brooklyn. The PROPER way to levy upon the house is to

    A. serve the order of attachment upon Doe
    B. serve the order of attachment upon the person who manages the house
    C. serve the order of attachment upon any tenant, if the manager of the house cannot be found
    D. file a notice of attachment with the county clerk in Kings County

20. On September 1, 2003, Peters entered and docketed in Kings County a judgment against Doe. An execution was returned unsatisfied since Doe had no assets in Kings. In January 2011, Peters learns that Doe had inherited a house worth $60,000 in Kings upon the death of his father in 2009. Peters immediately sends an execution to the sheriff. Of the following, the MOST accurate statement is that the

    A. house may not be levied on and sold because Peters has no lien thereon
    B. sheriff may now proceed to sell the house
    C. sheriff must file with the clerk of Kings County a notice describing the judgment, the execution, and the house
    D. buyer at the execution sale will take whatever title and interest Doe had as of January 2011

21. John Doe bought a house for $50,000 by paying $20,000 in cash and by executing a bond and mortgage to the Acme Bank for $30,000. Eight years later, John Doe fell upon hard times and could not pay the mortgage. Acme Bank sued Doe on the bond and got a money judgment for $25,000, the amount then due on the bond and mortgage. Which of the following properties CANNOT be sold in execution of Acme's judgment?

    A. Doe's house
    B. Doe's interest in a joint bank account held with his wife
    C. Doe's automobile which he uses to get to and from work
    D. Doe's interest in a boat which he jointly owns with his brother

22. The Ace Finance Company intends to bring an action to replevy an automobile which it had sold to John Doe but upon which Doe had failed to make the necessary payments. On December 1, 2012, counsel for the finance company, without a court order, sends a requisition and the other appropriate papers to the sheriff's office directing the sheriff to seize the automobile before the action is commenced. The APPROPRIATE course of action for the sheriff's office to follow is to

    A. seize the car, but only if it can be found on a public street
    B. seize the car, no matter where it is found, if it can be done without breaking and entering
    C. seize the car, no matter where it is found, even if the sheriff has to break and enter to get the car
    D. apprise counsel for the finance company that a court order is required to authorize the seizure of the car

23. A properly issued requisition in a replevin case requires the sheriff to seize a Sony television set with a serial number Q-4289J. Upon arriving at the defendant's home, a Samsung television, with serial number Q-69452, is the only one found. Which of the following courses of action would be the LEAST appropriate?
To

   A. ascertain from the defendant whether he ever bought a television from the plaintiff and, if it appears that the Samsung television is the only set he ever bought from the plaintiff, to seize it
   B. call the plaintiff's attorney and ask for a clarification
   C. seize the Samsung television because that is the only one found on the premises
   D. leave the defendant's home and return the requisition to the plaintiff's attorney with an explanation as to why it was not executed

24. Defendant purchased a dishwasher from plaintiff and then installed it in his apartment in such a fashion that it became a fixture. It would require major carpentry to remove the dishwasher and to repair the area where the dishwasher had been installed. In an action of replevin, the sheriff is served with a properly issued requisition for the dishwasher. Upon arrival at defendant's home, a deputy discovers that the dishwasher has been installed as described. Which of the following courses of action would be MOST appropriate?

   A. The deputy may pull out the dishwasher and leave the defendant to repair the damage.
   B. Without checking with the plaintiff, the deputy may pull out the dishwasher and leave the plaintiff to pay the damage.
   C. The deputy may seal the dishwasher and direct the defendant to hold on to it *for the account of the plaintiff.*
   D. Refrain from seizure of the dishwasher since replevin does not lie for fixtures.

25. Plaintiff has commenced an action to replevy certain rare wood from the defendant. Pursuant to a properly issued requisition for the wood, a deputy sheriff arrives at defendant's home only to find that the defendant has used the wood to make a magnificent piano. Which of the following statements is TRUE?

   A. Plaintiff is NOT entitled to replevy the piano.
   B. Plaintiff may replevy the piano, but the deputy should not seize it pursuant to the requisition unless it is specifically described as a piano.
   C. The deputy should seize the piano, although the requisition mentions only wood.
   D. Wood is not the proper subject of a replevin action.

KEY (CORRECT ANSWERS)

1. A
2. C
3. C
4. D
5. A

6. C
7. D
8. B
9. D
10. C

11. A
12. C
13. D
14. B
15. D

16. B
17. A
18. C
19. D
20. B

21. A
22. D
23. C
24. D
25. B

TEST 4

DIRECTIONS: Each question or incomplete statement is followed by several suggested answers or completions. Select the one that BEST answers the question or completes the statement. *PRINT THE LETTER OF THE CORRECT ANSWER IN THE SPACE AT THE RIGHT.*

1. After the defendant has appeared in a replevin action, a proper set of papers is delivered to the sheriff requiring the seizure of the chattel. Unless the court orders otherwise, a set of all the papers must be served upon the

    A. defendant in the same manner as a summons
    B. defendant's attorney
    C. defendant's attorney, only if the attorney is in possession of the chattel being replevied
    D. defendant's attorney, only if the defendant is in possession of the chattel

2. Pursuant to a proper set of papers, a deputy sheriff seizes a chattel in a replevin action. The seizure occurs at 2:00 P.M. on Monday, December 14, 2012. Before he can deliver the chattel to the plaintiff, the sheriff must wait until _____, 2012.

    A. Friday, December 18   B. Thursday, December 17
    C. Wednesday, December 16   D. Tuesday, December 15

3. Pursuant to a proper order of attachment, defendant's automobile is levied upon while it is in a parking lot. The parking lot owner has been served with the correct papers. Which of the following statements is TRUE?

    A. The automobile must be removed from the parking lot within 60 days.
    B. The automobile may be left in the parking lot despite the objections of the parking lot owner, so long as the plaintiff agrees to pay the necessary expenses.
    C. With the consent of the parking lot owner, the car may be left in the parking lot and the plaintiff will pay the parking lot owner's fee.
    D. The automobile may NOT be left in the parking lot longer than it takes to find another place to store it.

4. When real property is to be sold in execution of a judgment, notice of the sale must be posted in at least three places at least _____ days prior to the sale.

    A. 60   B. 80   C. 46   D. 56

5. When personal property is to be sold in execution of a judgment, notice of the sale must be posted in at least three places at least _____ days prior to the sale.

    A. 6   B. 9   C. 30   D. 90

6. The sheriff intends to sell a parcel of land in execution of a money judgment against its owner. Which of the following is CORRECT?
The sheriff

    A. may negotiate a private sale to a customer to whom the land has peculiar value, so long as the sheriff receives a better price than a public auction would have yielded
    B. must sell only at a public auction
    C. may sell at either a public auction or a private negotiation, so long as he acts in good faith
    D. may sell at either a public auction or a private negotiation, so long as he has the permission of the plaintiff

Questions 7-12.

DIRECTIONS: In answering Questions 7 through 12, assume the following facts.

Judgments were entered and docketed against a defendant named X in the places and at the times indicated:
June 1, 2010: P-1 v. X in New York County
June 10, 2010: P-2 v. X in Bronx County
June 19, 2010: P-3 v. X in Queens County
June 30, 2010: P-4 v. X in New York County

X owns a Cadillac automobile which he keeps in Putnam County and a bank account with C-M Bank in Kings County. On June 25, 2010, X bought a parcel of land known as Blackacre, located in New York County, from Y, giving Y $60,000 in cash and executing a purchase money bond and mortgage to Y for $140,000.

Further assume, for question 7 only, that a restraining notice is served on X on behalf of P-4 on September 1, 2010; that an execution is delivered to the sheriff in Putnam County on behalf of P-2 on September 10, 2010; that an execution is delivered to the sheriff in Queens County on behalf of P-1 on September 15, 2010; that the sheriff in Queens County has now levied on the Cadillac which was moved from Putnam County to Queens County on September 12, 2010.

7. Who is entitled to the proceeds of the sale of the Cadillac?

   A. P-4 may obtain an order directing the sheriff in Queens to turn over the proceeds to him
   B. P-2 may obtain an order directing the sheriff in Queens to turn over the proceeds to him
   C. P-1 may obtain an order directing the sheriff in Queens to turn over the proceeds to him
   D. P-4, P-2, and P-1 share in proportion to their judgments

Further assume, for question 8 only, that a restraining notice and information subpoena are served on C-M Bank on behalf of P-4 on September 1, 2010; that a special proceeding is commenced on September 7, 2010 by P-3 to obtain a delivery order against C-M Bank; that P-2 delivers an execution to the sheriff in Kings County on September 10, 2010; that P-3 obtains and files his delivery order on September 21, 2010; and that the sheriff levies on the account on September 30, 2010.

8. Who is entitled to the account?

   A. P-4, P-3, and P-2 share in proportion to their judgments
   B. P-3
   C. P-2
   D. P-4

3 (#4)

Further assume, for question 9 only, that Y obtains a judgment of foreclosure on September 1, 2010; that P-3 and P-4 deliver executions to the sheriff in New York County on September 15, 2010; that P-1 delivers an execution to the sheriff in New York County on September 30, 2010; and that the land is properly sold thereafter.

9. Who is entitled to priority in the proceeds?   9._____

   A. Y
   B. P-3 and P-4 share in proportion to their judgments
   C. Y, P-3, and P-4 share in proportion to their judgments
   D. P-1

Further assume, for question 10 only, that P-2 delivers an execution to the sheriff in New York County on September 1, 2010; that P-3 delivers an execution to the same sheriff on September 4, 2010; that P-4 delivers an execution to the same sheriff on September 10, 2010; and that Blackacre is properly sold thereafter.

10. Who is entitled to priority in the proceeds?   10._____

    A. P-4
    B. P-3
    C. P-1
    D. P-1, P-2, and P-3 share in proportion to their judgments

11. In the preceding Question 10, the execution buyer takes   11._____

    A. title to Blackacre, free and clear of all encumbrances
    B. subject only to P-1's interest
    C. Blackacre subject only to Y's mortgage interest
    D. subject to P-1's and Y's interest

Further assume, for question 12 only, that P-4 delivers an execution to the sheriff in New York County on September 1, 2010; that P-2 delivers an execution to the same sheriff on September 10, 2010; that P-3 delivers an execution to the same sheriff on September 15, 2010; that P-I delivers an execution to the same sheriff on September 18, 2010; and that Blackacre is properly sold thereafter.

12. Who is entitled to priority in the proceeds?   12._____

    A. P-1, P-2, and P-3 share in the proceeds in proportion to their judgments
    B. P-4 is entitled to priority in the proceeds.
    C. P-1 is entitled to priority in the proceeds.
    D. P-1 and P-4 share the proceeds in proportion to their judgments.

13. Doe, a citizen and resident of the State of Maine, voluntarily agrees to testify in an action   13._____
    by A against B, pending in Supreme Court, New York County. A summons has been left with the sheriff by Peters for service on Doe. The sheriff now learns from Peters that Doe is in the Supreme Court building awaiting his turn to testify. A deputy sheriff serves Doe with the summons while Doe is standing around in the hallway of the courthouse. Doe has moved to set aside the service of the summons. The court should

    A. set aside service of process on the ground that Doe was immune from service
    B. set aside service on the ground that process may not be served in a courthouse

C. set aside service on the ground that, there being no unusual circumstances in the case, the sheriff's office should not have become involved in serving a summons
D. deny the motion

14. On June 1, 2012, a deputy sheriff makes a proper levy upon an automobile owned by Doe, a defendant in an action wherein an order of attachment has been signed. On July 1, 2012, the deputy makes a proper levy upon Doe's bank account. On October 15, 2012, Doe files a petition in bankruptcy. The trustee in bankruptcy is appointed on November 10, 2012. The bankruptcy court may properly compel the sheriff to turn over to the trustee

    A. the automobile
    B. the bank account
    C. both the automobile and the bank account
    D. neither the automobile nor the bank account

15. Real property has been sold to X in execution of a judgment in favor of the plaintiff. Which of the following statements is TRUE?
The defendant may

    A. redeem his property at any time by paying to X the same amount that X paid for the property plus interest
    B. redeem his property within one year after the sale by paying to X the same amount that X paid for the property plus interest
    C. redeem his property within one year after the sale by paying the full judgment to the plaintiff
    D. not redeem his property after the sheriff has delivered a sheriff's deed to X

16. With the statute of limitations due to expire on June 1, 2013, an attorney for the plaintiff delivers a summons on May 15, 2013 to the sheriff's office for service upon the defendant. The statute of limitations will NOT be a defense if the summons is served within _____ days after _____, 2013.

    A. 60; May 15   B. 60; June 1
    C. 90; May 15   D. 90; June 1

17. A deputy sheriff must serve a Supreme Court summons upon John Doe. Doe, a resident of New York, has carefully avoided being served. The deputy has learned that Doe is in a hotel room in Manhattan. The deputy goes to the hotel, calls from the lobby, and states that he is a former colleague of Doe's and would like to invite Doe for a drink. Doe comes down to the bar, where the deputy serves him. Doe now moves to set aside the service of process.
The court should

    A. *grant* the motion since the deputy was guilty of deception
    B. *grant* the motion since the deputy never actually touched Doe with the summons
    C. *grant* the motion since the deputy did not serve a complaint with the summons
    D. *deny* the motion since the service was valid

18. In the preceding Question 17, assume that John Doe was a citizen and resident of New Jersey who was in New York for a vacation. All other facts are the same. The court should

    A. *grant* the motion since the deputy was guilty of deception
    B. *grant* the motion since, as a nonresident, Doe was immune from service
    C. *deny* the motion since the service was valid
    D. *deny* the motion since a nonresident may be served anywhere in the state, anytime, including Sunday

18._____

19. In the preceding Question 18, assume that Doe was spotted on the street racing to his home. The deputy arrives at the home and is admitted peacefully by Doe's wife. Once in the house, the deputy goes from room to room, without express permission, locates Doe, and serves him.
    Of the following, the MOST accurate statement is that the

    A. service is void since the deputy committed an illegal search and seizure
    B. deputy could have broken into the house if he had been refused admittance
    C. service is valid
    D. deputy has a legal privilege to effectuate service and is never liable for trespass

19._____

20. A deputy sheriff is sent to the headquarters of Acme, Inc. to serve the corporation with a summons. Upon arriving there at 12:30 P.M., he is told by a building employee that everybody in the Acme office is out to lunch. The building employee volunteers to accept the summons and to redeliver it to the President of Acme when the latter returns from lunch.
    Of the following, the MOST accurate statement is that the

    A. service is void even if the building employee does redeliver the summons to the President of Acme, Inc.
    B. service is valid if the building employee does redeliver the summons to the President of Acme, Inc.
    C. service upon the building employee was itself a valid service upon Acme, Inc.
    D. deputy should have demanded access to the office of Acme, Inc. where he should have posted the summons in a conspicuous place

20._____

21. Service upon a partnership may be made by serving the summons on

    A. the managing agent of the partnership
    B. the director of the firm's legal department
    C. any partner at all
    D. only the partner who is designated by the firm to accept process

21._____

22. Before making substituted (nail and mail) service, the rule-of-thumb followed in the sheriff's office is that a deputy must have tried to make personal delivery of the summons at LEAST _____ times.

    A. 5   B. 4   C. 3   D. 2

22._____

23. Defendant John Doe lives in Queens and works for the Ace Company in Manhattan. After numerous unsuccessful attempts to deliver the summons personally to Doe, a deputy sheriff has been told by the plaintiff's attorney to try some other form of service.
    Of the following, the MOST accurate statement is that

23._____

A. the deputy may mail a copy of the summons to Doe's home in Queens and may leave another copy at the same place with Doe's wife
B. the deputy may mail a copy of the summons to Doe at the office of Ace Company and may leave another copy on Doe's desk at the Ace Company
C. the deputy may mail a copy of the summons to Doe at the office of the Ace Company and may affix another copy to the office door of the Ace Company
D. none of the above methods of service is valid

24. Poundage, in attachment cases, is allowed

   A. only if the sheriff actually reduces the property to physical custody
   B. on the value of the property levied upon, even though the property has never been reduced to physical custody
   C. at the rate of 3% on the first $10,000
   D. at the rate of 5% on the first $10,000

25. When the city issues an execution to the sheriff's office,

   A. the city must pay desk fees in advance
   B. a deputy should collect the desk fees from the defendant
   C. the city will pay the desk fees after the execution has been satisfied
   D. the desk fees may be used to reimburse a deputy sheriff for his use of his personal automobile on sheriff's business

KEY (CORRECT ANSWERS)

1.	B	11.	C
2.	A	12.	C
3.	C	13.	A
4.	D	14.	B
5.	A	15.	D
6.	B	16.	B
7.	B	17.	D
8.	B	18.	C
9.	A	19.	C
10.	A	20.	A

21.	C
22.	C
23.	A
24.	B
25.	B

EXAMINATION SECTION
TEST 1

DIRECTIONS: Each question or incomplete statement is followed by several suggested answers or completions. Select the one that BEST answers the question or completes the statement. *PRINT THE LETTER OF THE CORRECT ANSWER IN THE SPACE AT THE RIGHT.*

1. Identify the statements that contain clearly defined objectives:
   The objective
   I. in this section is to increase understanding of the principles of management
   II. of the literacy program is to teach prisoners to read
   III. of the work release program is to assist the prisoner in retaining his job and to keep him in the community
   IV. of jail programs is to rehabilitate the offender
   V. of the literacy program is to raise the reading level of the students to the fourth grade reading level

   The CORRECT answer is:

   A. I, III
   B. II, V
   C. III, V
   D. III, IV
   E. II, IV

2. The following are statements about the distinguishing characteristics of *line item* budgets, *performance* budgets, and *program* budgets.
   Indicate by writing the type of budget described in the space at the right.

   A. The focus is on the kinds and level of service performed.
   B. It deals with packages of commonly related activities.
   C. It focuses on specific problems and relevant policy issues.
   D. It is structured around identifiable units of service and their specific costs.
   E. How much is being spent and for what purpose.
   F. It focuses on the results of the performance of the service rather than on dollar costs.
   G. The budget reflects a concern for control.

3. Identify the kind of budget associated with the following questions:

   A. What services are being performed and what cost?
   B. What needs to be done, for whom, and how can it best be done?
   C. How much money did we spend in the past?

4. A significant characteristic of the program budget is that it lends itself to review and analysis.
   Why?

   A. The budget has a built-in accounting system that makes close control possible.
   B. The budget includes measurable objectives.
   C. It is possible to review performance based on units of service.
   D. All of the above

5. The advantages of program budgeting over line item and performance budgeting is:
   I. Tight, administrative control
   II. Forces the administrator to think through his total operation
   III. Measurable objectives
   IV. Simplicity of development
   V. Closer estimates of future costs

   The CORRECT answer is:

   A. I, II
   B. II, III, IV
   C. II, III, V
   D. III, IV, V
   E. II, IV

6. Indicate whether the following statements are true or false:

   A. High pay is more important as a factor in job satisfaction.
   B. When pay is low, increases in salary will increase job satisfaction, but only temporarily.
   C. An excellent method of improving morale of personnel is to assign to the jail, officers who can't make it in the field.
   D. Every officer should learn each post in the jail and can be expected to function equally well on every post.

7. List four methods of determining employee training needs.

   A. _____
   B. _____
   C. _____
   D. _____

8. Employee selection, probation, and training are closely related to each other. Select the statement that gives the BEST reason why this is true.
   They are

   A. related because they logically follow each other
   B. all a part of personnel administration
   C. related because each step supports the following step; but any one alone is not the most important
   D. practically the same

9. Sheriff D has hired his wife's third cousin, C, as jail officer. About a year later, he realizes that C is just not shaping up. He lacks interest, is slow to learn, and is forgetful. He cannot fire him, however, because C has passed his probationary period and is on permanent status. The jail staff now includes a marginal officer. Sheriff D feels, however, that the officer's performance can be improved through training.
   What do you think?

   A. Training can improve anyone's performance.
   B. The sheriff had better improve his selection process.
   C. Apparently, C needs motivational training.
   D. The sheriff cannot expect training to correct the mistakes that have been made in selection and orientation.

10. Indicate whether the following statements are true or false:

    A. A large number of security categories is an indication of an effective classification system.
    B. A classification system should have a simple procedure.
    C. The term trusty accurately describes this type of prisoner.
    D. Once classified, a prisoner need not be reviewed again.
    E. The objectives of classification are to evaluate the prisoner and determine the degree of supervision or control he requires.

11. One of the objectives of the jail is to ensure the safety of all prisoners.
    Identify the statements below that support this objective.
    I. Medical examination for all prisoners
    II. Permitting juveniles to be placed in cells with adult prisoners
    III. A classification system
    IV. Guidelines on admission of prisoners to the jail
    V. Treating all prisoners alike
    VI. Permitting trusties to supervise other prisoners
    The CORRECT answer is:

    A. I, II, III
    B. II, V, VI
    C. III, IV, V
    D. I, IV, V
    E. I, III, IV

12. Correspondence is permitted in order to maintain family and community ties.
    Identify the statements that support this objective.
    I. One letter a week is permitted.
    II. There is no mail censorship.
    III. The prisoner can write an unlimited number of letters.
    IV. The prisoner can write to his immediate family only.
    V. The prisoner may only write letters of one page.
    The CORRECT answer is:

    A. I, II
    B. II, III
    C. III, IV
    D. IV, V
    E. II, IV

13. Indicate whether the following statements are true or false:

    A. Censoring mail contributes to good security because it prevents prisoners from making escape plans.
    B. Requiring verification of persons to whom the prisoner wishes to write is a good idea because it provides valid identification of the correspondent.
    C. Limitations on mail are in reality a matter of administrative convenience.
    D. Packages keep prisoners happy and as a consequence discourage them from escape attempts.
    E. A prisoner's family should be permitted to send him food parcels in order to supplement his diet.

14. Indicate whether the following statements are true or false:

    A. Both long and short hair can be unsanitary.
    B. Women who have long hair do not have it cut when admitted to the jail.
    C. Length of hair is less important than its cleanliness.
    D. Cutting long hair for sanitary reasons ignores the fact that sanitation can be more easily achieved by washing.
    E. Both long and short hair clogs water drains.
    F. Long hair looks silly on men and, therefore, should not be allowed in the jail.

    14.___
    A.___
    B.___
    C.___
    D.___
    E.___
    F.___

15. Select the statement that achieves the objective of providing a sanitary jail and protects the health of prisoners.
    All prisoners will bathe

    A. on admission and regularly thereafter
    B. regularly, and all long hair will be cut
    C. regularly; hair will be washed regularly and kept combed. All prisoners with long hair must wear hair nets when assigned to the kitchen, laundry, or any other job near moving machinery.
    D. all of the above

    15.___

16. Indicate whether the following statements are true or false:

    A. A club carried by the officer in the jail must be considered a weapon.
    B. Weapons should be carried by jail personnel for their own protection.
    C. There is nothing wrong with carrying a derringer well concealed; it may save your life.
    D. Weapons carried in the jail do not provide any protection to the officer.
    E. Visiting law enforcement personnel should be permitted to carry their weapons in the jail since they are responsible persons.
    F. An officer who needs to carry a weapon in the jail should not be working in the jail.
    G. The best place for an armory is outside the jail.

    16.___
    A.___
    B.___
    C.___
    D.___
    E.___
    F.___
    G.___

KEY (CORRECT ANSWERS)

1. C
2. A. Performance
   B. Program
   C. Program
   D. Performance
   E. Line item
   F. Program
   G. Line item
3. A. Performance
   B. Program
   C. Line item
4. B
5. C

6. A. False
   B. True
   C. False
   D. False
7. A. Evaluation of employee performance
   B. Review of critical incidents
   C. Introduction of new procedures
   D. Surveying employees
8. C
9. D
10. A. False
    B. True
    C. False
    D. False
    E. True

11. E
12. B
13. A. False
    B. True
    C. False
    D. False
    E. True
14. A. True
    B. True
    C. True
    D. True
    E. True
    F. False
15. C

16. A. True
    B. False
    C. False
    D. True
    E. False
    F. True
    G. True

TEST 2

DIRECTIONS: Each question or incomplete statement is followed by several suggested answers or completions. Select the one that BEST answers the question or completes the statement. *PRINT THE LETTER OF THE CORRECT ANSWER IN THE SPACE AT THE RIGHT.*

1. Which of the following are APPROPRIATE methods of program development?
   I. Find out what other jails are doing and develop similar programs.
   II. An examination of the annual report will give sufficient information on prisoner needs to develop programs.
   III. A relatively wide range of data about the jail population will be needed.
   IV. There may be a need to develop both statistical
   V. studies and a testing program to get a clear picture of jail population needs.
   The CORRECT answer is:

   A. I, II B. II, III C. III, IV
   D. I, IV E. II, IV

   1.____

2. You are faced with the following situation:
   There is increasing pressure from the community to develop jail programs. A survey has been done of the jail population and the findings are as follows:

Education Level		Occupation		Residence	
0-4th Grade	75	General labor	90	Permanent residence	25
5-7th Grade	40	Construction labor	22	No permanent residence	114
8-12th Grade	20				
Over 12th	4	Skilled operators	6		139
	139	Clerical	21		
			139		

   Given the above figures, what would you do about program development?
   I. Start an illiteracy program, since a large number have a 4th grade education or less.
   II. Begin a work release program because there are 25 persons who have permanent residence.
   III. Test the 0-4th grade group to find out the level of literacy.
   IV. Develop a vocational training program for the general laborers.
   V. Although I might be interested in developing a work release program, I would want to know more about the group who claim permanent residence: such as marital status, job skills, and any kinds of problems they might have.
   VI. Set up a literacy program with volunteers from the community. Prisoners who need it will volunteer, and the participation from the community will solve the problems of criticism about a lack of programs in the jail.
   The CORRECT answer is:

   A. I, II, III B. III, IV, V C. II, III, V
   D. III, V E. III, VI

   2.____

3. Select the statements that are TRUE program objectives.
   I. It is the objective of the AA program to give the prisoner an understanding of his drinking problem.
   II. The objective of a work release program is to prevent job loss due to confinement.

   3.____

  III. The purpose of the AA program is to make help available to the problem drinker.
  IV. The objective of a literacy program is to raise the reading level of illiterate prisoners to the 5th grade reading level.
  V. The objective of the AA program is to have the prisoner recognize and admit his drinking problem.
  VI. The objective of jail programs is to rehabilitate prisoners.
  VII. The objective of a work release program is to restore the prisoner to the community.
  VIII. The objective of a literacy program is to teach prisoners to read.
The CORRECT answer is:

A. I, IV, V   B. I, II, III   C. VI, VII
D. IV, V   E. V, VI

4. Which of the following represents the PROPER sequence in program development?

 A. Funds, prisoner needs, program objectives, program selection, personnel
 B. Program selection, prisoner needs, program objectives, funds, personnel
 C. Prisoner needs, objectives, program selection, funds, personnel
 D. Objectives, prisoner needs, funds, program selection, personnel

5. Select the statements that MOST clearly express the characteristics of work release.
  I. It exposes the prisoner to many temptations - especially the alcoholic.
  II. It gives the prisoner an opportunity to contribute to the support of his family.
  III. It provides the prisoner with an opportunity to serve his sentence much more easily than if he were confined.
  IV. It provides cheap labor to local employers.
  V. The prisoner is faced with the problem of making decisions that he would not normally make if he were confined.
  VI. It gives the prisoner the opportunity to see his family more often.
  VII. It provides an opportunity for the prisoner to retain his ties in the community.
The CORRECT answer is:

A. I, II, III   B. II, III, IV   C. III, IV, V
D. V, VI, VII   E. II, V, VII

6. Which of the following kinds of prisoners should NOT be selected for work release?
  I. All alcoholics
  II. Persons with poor work records
  III. Persons with jobs in the community
  IV. Sex offenders
  V. Drunk drivers
  VI. Prisoners who do not have permanent residence in the
  VII. community
  VIII. The prisoner charged with assault and battery against his wife
The CORRECT answer is:

A. I, III   B. II, IV   C. III, V
D. IV, VI   E. V, VII

KEY (CORRECT ANSWERS)

1. C
2. D
3. D, E
4. C
5. E
6. D

TEST 3

DIRECTIONS: Each question or incomplete statement is followed by several suggested answers or completions. Select the one that BEST answers the question or completes the statement. *PRINT THE LETTER OF THE CORRECT ANSWER IN THE SPACE AT THE RIGHT.*

1. Select the statement that BEST defines the role of the jail administrator.　　　1._____

    A. The jail administrator is the person most knowledgeable about jails and is, therefore, one of the most important members of the planning committee.
    B. Although it is not necessary that the jail administrator be a member of the planning committee, he should appoint its members and approve the final report.
    C. The jail administrator is the initiator, coordinator, and consultant to the planning committee.
    D. All of the above

2. List the various kinds of data that are needed for a jail study. The main headings are given.　　　2._____
    Fill in the kinds of data which are included within those categories.

    A. Jail population studies (list six):
    1. _____ 2. _____
    3. _____ 4. _____
    5. _____ 6. _____
    B. Population forecasting (list three):
    1. _____
    2. _____
    3. _____

3. The jail is not an independent agency, and the activities of other branches of government influence jail population. List the two agencies that have the MOST immediate influence on the jail.　　　3._____

    A. _____
    B. _____

4. Sheriff D has been concerned about the conditions of his jail for some time. There has been an increase in the jail population which indicates to him the need for some expansion. A week ago, he was visited by a consultant from a steel company who helpfully surveyed the jail and recommended that the county needed a new jail.　　　4._____
    Do you feel this is the PROPER approach to jail planning?

    A. *No; the opinion of one man is not enough. The sheriff should consult with other experts.*
    B. *Yes; the consultant obviously knows his business. The sheriff should take his recommendations to the county governing board.*
    C. *No; having defined his problem as lack of space, the sheriff should propose an evaluation of the jail by a group of experts who can supply information that would support the sheriff's recommendation for a formal planning study.*
    D. *Yes; the sheriff is an expert on jails and can determine if the consultant's report is accurate.*

5. A number of problems will arise after a jail is built. What are the two MAIN problems, usually?

   A. _____
   B. _____

6. The planning group has submitted a report and specifications for a new jail to the county council. An architect has been selected and the specifications have been turned over to him to translate into building plans. The architect has designed three jails in the past five years and will not require any additional information than that contained in the report and specifications.
   Select the APPROPRIATE response to this situation.

   A. The architect's past experience will be very helpful in designing the new jail. He should not need any further information if the planning was done well.
   B. Although the architect is experienced in jail design, he will need assistance in translating specifications into operational realities. All jails are not the same and cannot be built as though they have similar functions and similar problems.
   C. Since the most important function of a jail is to hold prisoners, there is little reason for great variations in interior jail design.
   D. This architect is well suited for the job. He may be left to his own devices and predilections.

KEY (CORRECT ANSWERS)

1. C
2. A. (1) Daily average count
      (2) High and low admission rates
      (3) Seasonal population highs and lows
      (4) Age
      (5) Sex
      (6) Kinds of offenses
   B. (1) Projections of the community population
      (2) Present and projected arrest rates
      (3) Present and projected crime rates

3. A. Courts
   B. Police
4. C
5. A. Location - too far from the courts Police
   B. Not enough single cells
6. B

TEST 4

DIRECTIONS: Each question or incomplete statement is followed by several suggested answers or completions. Select the one that BEST answers the question or completes the statement. *PRINT THE LETTER OF THE CORRECT ANSWER IN THE SPACE AT THE RIGHT.*

1. Prisoner L was attacked and beaten by the prisoner who shared his two-man cell. He was hospitalized for internal injuries and a broken leg. Investigation revealed that his attacker, prisoner E, was mentally ill and had a long history of mental illness and assaultive behavior. The county and the sheriff were co-defendants in the suit that resulted from the investigation.
What step could have been taken to avoid this situation?

   A. Keep all prisoners in separate cells.
   B. Very little could be done. It is not possible to supervise prisoners all the time.
   C. A classification and evaluation procedure would have prevented this occurrence.
   D. The jail needed an evaluation and classification procedure, a trained admissions officer who could evaluate prisoners, and separate housing for dangerous prisoners.

1.____

2. Prisoner J reported to sick call with a black eye, three loose teeth, and bruises on his back. He claims that he was fined by a kangaroo court and beaten and robbed when he refused to pay. He threatens to sue the county and the sheriff for not providing him with protection from other prisoners.
How could this incident have been prevented?
   I.   Establish a rule against kangaroo courts
   II. Prisoner J was in a fight, but there is no evidence of a kangaroo court
   III. Improve supervisory procedures
   IV. Establish an evaluation program that will identify troublemakers
   V.   Very little can be done. It is impossible to prevent the formation of kangaroo courts.
   VI. Not permit money in the jail.
The CORRECT answer is:

   A. I, II
   B. II, III
   C. III, VI
   D. VI, VII
   E. III, V

2.____

3. The jail in an urban county is large and holds persons charged with a variety of crimes. There has been a history of sexual assaults, beatings, kangaroo courts, and escapes for a number of years. The last administrator was indicted for mismanagement and both he and the county have been successfully sued by prisoners who had suffered injuries while confined. The new administrator has been in office one year, but there has been no change in procedures. He and the county are being sued by a prisoner who was severely beaten and robbed by a kangaroo court.
According to past court decisions, which one of the following statements may be the APPROPRIATE finding of the court?

   A. Although these problems are of long standing, the sheriff has not had sufficient time to put into effect the appropriate procedures that would remedy the situation and prevent assaults such as this one from occurring

3.____

51

B. The sheriff has been well aware of the history of the jail and its problems. In fact, the assaults were a major feature of his campaign. Knowing the problems and aware of his responsibility for the safety of prisoners, he was in a position to anticipate danger but has taken no steps to prevent injury to prisoners
C. Both of the above
D. None of the above

4. Prisoner B suffered what apparently was a heart attack in his cell during the evening. It required a locksmith to get the door open. The key was worn and would not turn the lock. By the time the cell door was opened, Prisoner B was dead.
What step should have been taken to prevent this incident?

   A. Medical exam at admission would have discovered this condition.
   B. A key control system would have revealed the defective key.
   C. A procedure for responding to medical emergencies is needed.
   D. A duplicate key system with a key and lock inspection and reporting system

5. How do you feel the courts will rule in a case where a prisoner suffers injury or death because the cell door cannot be opened due to defective equipment?

   A. Probably find the sheriff not liable, because he has not shown malice or irresponsibility
   B. Probably find the sheriff liable because he should be aware of the condition of his jail and take the appropriate steps to protect his prisoners
   C. Both of the above
   D. None of the above

6. Prisoner W was found dead in his cell in the morning. Apparently, the head wound he had received prior to his arrest was much more serious than the jail staff had realized. The sheriff claims that he cannot be held liable for the death since he is required by law to accept all persons who are lawfully arrested.
How have courts ruled in cases similar to this?

   A. The courts have ruled that since the sheriff is required by law to accept lawfully arrested persons, he is powerless to reject those who may be in need of medical care. He, therefore, has no liability.
   B. The courts have ruled that the sheriff is bound to exercise ordinary and reasonable care for the preservation of a prisoner's life and health. He would, therefore, be liable, even though he was required by law to accept injured prisoners.
   C. Both of the above
   D. None of the above

7. The county jail has a new sheriff and a number of new deputies. There is no training program, and supervision of personnel is non-existent. The sheriff claims to know his deputies well since they are his friends. A prisoner is now suing the sheriff and the county claiming injuries received from a beating by one of the deputies. The prisoner claims that the deputy has a reputation in the community for a violent temper and has a history of numerous fights. He further claims that the sheriff is a close friend of the deputy and knows his reputation. If the prisoner's statements are accepted by the court as fact, how do you think the court will rule?

A. The court will not find the sheriff liable, because he cannot be held responsible for the official acts of his employees.
B. The court will find the sheriff liable. He has failed to exercise care in the selection of his employees and knew about the deputy's incompetence.
C. The court will not find the sheriff liable. Although he knew about his deputy's violent temper and history of fighting, he had no way of knowing that the deputy would assault prisoners. If he had known of his deputy's unfitness, and had not discharged him, he would be liable.
D. None of the above

8. Sheriff O consistently refuses to make any exceptions for attorney visits and insists that they conform to the regular visiting hours. Some attorneys have complained to him that this policy is causing undue hardship to both then and their clients. Today an attorney appeared at the jail at 6:00 P.M. and requested to visit with prisoner T. At this time of the evening, the prisoners have been fed and counted. The jail does not have any evening activities; it is not understaffed, and the prisoner is not an escape risk. Do you feel a visit should be permitted?

   A. *No.* The attorney can return the next day at a reasonable hour.
   B. *Yes.* There are no activities that might cause a scheduling conflict.
   C. *No.* Permitting a prisoner out of his cell at this time of night could be dangerous.
   D. *Yes.* This is an area of administrative discretion. In order to deny such visits, the sheriff must show good reason such as danger to the jail or interference with vital activities. The plea of inconvenience is not adequate as a reason for denying a visit.

9. Attorney B has written a strong letter to Sheriff F protesting the inspection of mail between him and his clients. He has stated in no uncertain terms that if this *censorship,* as he calls it, continues, he will take the sheriff to court for interfering with the attorney-client relationship.
What should the sheriff do?

   A. Change his policy and permit unrestricted and uninspected mail from this attorney to enter the jail
   B. Inform the attorney that there will be no change in mail inspection policy and the reasons why
   C. Avoid a court fight and change mail policy to permit mail between attorneys and their clients to enter the jail uninspected
   D. Ignore the letter; the attorney knows the law on these matters and is bluffing

10. Prisoner A has requested permission to purchase a law book from the publisher. Which of the following statements contains the PROPER decision?

    A. Deny. He has no appeal pending.
    B. Review his request and, if the book will be useful to him in preparing his case, approve the purchase.
    C. Deny. Rumor has it that the prisoner is doing legal work for other prisoners.
    D. Suggest that he consider hiring an attorney.
    E. Approve the request.

11. Prisoner K has been in the process of appealing his conviction. Unfortunately, he is illiterate and without funds. Furthermore, his *attorney,* Prisoner G, is now in segregation for writing documents for prisoners - he had been working on K's paper when he was caught in a cell inspection. You have an interview with K at his request. He insists that he has a reasonable chance of success in his appeal and complains that you have no right to block his legal activities by locking up the *jail house lawyer,* Prisoner G. He also threatens to write a letter of complaint to the court.
What should you do?

    A. Release G from segregation and avoid any censure from the court
    B. Give K a list of lawyers and let him select one
    C. Refer K to legal aid, even though you know this agency has no funds to handle appeals
    D. Since you cannot provide any reasonable alternative, it will be necessary to release G from segregation to help K with his appeal

12. Identify those conditions that would probably create an opportunity for court intervention in disciplinary matters.
    I. A policy that permits lower rank personnel to place prisoners in isolation or segregation without the administrator's approval
    II. Weekly review of all prisoners in isolation
    III. Reduction of food to two meals a day
    IV. Sleeping pad and blanket placed in cell every evening
    V. No lights
    VI. Regular use of washing and bathing facilities outside of cell

    The CORRECT answer is:

    A. I, II, III   B. II, III, IV   C. I, III, V
    D. III, V, VI   E. II, IV, VI

13. Prisoner V has been confined in isolation for 20 days. He is uncertain about when he will be returned to the population since he has not been interviewed since he was placed on punishment status. The cell is well lit, ventilated, and has a cot, mattress, and blanket. V is permitted to write and may have visits as long as he bathes and shaves regularly. While in isolation, he is not permitted any reading material; since he has very little opportunity for exercise, he is fed two meals a day.
Which one of the statements below CORRECTLY describes the conditions above?

    A. The conditions of isolation are above average and are within guidelines that will prevent court intervention.
    B. The conditions of segregation may be above average when compared to other jails. However, the standards of his confinement are lower than that of other prisoners because he is receiving two meals per day.
    C. Both of the above
    D. None of the above

14. Prisoner O claims to belong to some obscure and unusual religion. He claims that in order to practice his faith, he requires another person of similar faith to join him in prayer at least once a week for a two-hour period. He insists that he can eat only green vegetables and lamb. The sheriff has refused permission for a two-hour visit because he does not have staff to supervise, or the facilities, and will not authorize any special foods. O threatens to go to court because he claims the right to practice his religion. What should the sheriff do?

    A. O has the right under the Constitution to practice his religion. The sheriff should permit the two-hour visit. The diet request should be denied, however, because it would cause a hardship to the jail.
    B. O has the right to believe anything he wishes. However, he does not have an absolute right to practice his religion if it presents a danger to the community. In this instance, refusal of the two-hour visit is based on security and supervisory problems. Denial of food is proper since such a diet for one person would be extremely burdensome to the jail.
    C. Both of the above
    D. None of the above

15. Three youthful prisoners have been sentenced to the jail for 30 days each for disorderly conduct. They have made a request to have the local underground newspaper mailed to them. The sheriff has reviewed a copy of the paper and feels it is *dirty, revolutionary,* and *communist* and should not be permitted in the jail.
    Which statement below is a PROPER response to the sheriff's position?

    A. Underground papers fall into the same category as pornography and should be prohibited from entering the jail.
    B. The courts have upheld this kind of censorship. The sheriff is on safe ground in denying these prisoners the paper.
    C. The sheriff is voicing personal opinions. He has not shown that the paper will threaten the security or good order of the jail. A court may have to decide on this if the prisoners decide to press their case. It would be wise for the sheriff to re-examine the paper to determine if his objections are objective or personal.
    D. None of the above

KEY (CORRECT ANSWERS)

1. D	6. B	11. D
2. C	7. B	12. C
3. B	8. D	13. B
4. D	9. B	14. B
5. B	10. E	15. C

TEST 5

DIRECTIONS: Each question or incomplete statement is followed by several suggested answers or completions. Select the one that BEST answers the question or completes the statement. *PRINT THE LETTER OF THE CORRECT ANSWER IN THE SPACE AT THE RIGHT.*

1. Sheriff P has only recently been elected. As administrator of the jail, he feels a responsibility to the community for running an efficient operation. He is also interested in running for re-election in another two years. Today, two prisoners escaped from the jail.
How should he handle this situation so that he develops public confidence in his administration?

   A. Sheriff P should come up with an explanation for the escape that will not make him look incompetent. It is most important that he begin his term in office with as good an image as possible.
   B. Since he is newly elected, he can blame the escape on the old administration.
   C. He should give the facts about the escape, indicate how he intends to clear up the deficiencies that were the underlying cause and, if necessary, point out some of the problems that may contribute to further incidents. Blaming the past administration is hardly a positive approach.
   D. None of the above

1.____

2. Sheriff N is sincerely interested in operating a clean, efficient operation. He feels that it is important to let the community know about the jail. He, therefore, accepts numerous speaking engagements from businessmen, organizations, and fraternal orders. He is an excellent storyteller and entertains his audiences with descriptions of prisoners and the kinds of crimes they commit. He feels very strongly that his audiences are interested in prisoners and their crimes and that since he satisfies their interest, he is developing a good community relations program.
Do you agree?

   A. *No.* Stories about prisoners and their crimes have nothing to do with community relations.
   B. *Yes.* You can't have much of a call for speaking engagements if you aren't an interesting speaker.
   C. *Yes.* If he can keep the public interested in prisoners, they will remain interested in the jail.
   D. *No.* Telling interesting stories does not inform the public about the jail, nor is speechmaking the only component of a community relations program.

2.____

3. You are in the process of reviewing your jail operation as a step in improving your community relations program. There are a number of changes you can make that will make a good impression on the community without jeopardizing jail safety or security. At this time you are considering liberalizing correspondence and visiting.
Will this or will this not contribute to a community relations program?

   A. *No.* Only a small part of the community is represented by prisoners and their families.
   B. *No.* If you are going to liberalize correspondence and visiting, do it for a sensible reason.

3.____

56

C. *Yes.* You have determined that liberalizing this procedure will not endanger the security of the jail. You have also identified a significant public and are meeting their needs.
D. None of the above

4. Sheriff A has developed an excellent relationship with reporter B. Yesterday he took B through the jail for an inside story about an escape that had occurred that morning. Other news media were not notified until noon. As usual, B wrote an excellent story, much of it favorable to Sheriff A.
What do you think of Sheriff A's behavior?

   A. Poor press relations. He should not give any reporter an opportunity for a scoop.
   B. Poor policy. It is not good practice to become too friendly with reporters.
   C. Good press relations. Because he had a sympathetic reporter, he was given favorable publicity.
   D. None of the above

5. A jail is planning a formal graduation ceremony for those prisoners who have completed a literacy program. Sheriff A is debating on whether or not to invite prisoners' families and notify the news media.
What should he do?

   A. Notify the news media - it will be good publicity.
   B. Don't invite anyone. This is too small an event to be of interest to anyone.
   C. Invite only selected news media - too many would endanger the jail's security.
   D. Invite the news media but not the prisoners' families; they may create security and contraband problems.
   E. Invite both news media and immediate family members. The event is an excellent means of informing the community of a jail program. Family members and prisoners will realize the importance of the program by participating in a ceremony.

6. A newspaper sent a young reporter to cover the story about the escape of three prisoners. Although the story was essentially correct, the reporter made a few minor errors.
What action should the sheriff take?

   A. Call the editor and complain about the reporter's inaccuracies.
   B. Call the reporter and let him know that his story contained errors.
   C. Call the editor and advise him that any inaccuracies in the future and the reporter will not be allowed in the jail.
   D. Ignore the errors since they were minor.

7. The jail has admitted a prisoner who is accused of a double murder. Community interest is high, and the news media are all insisting on interviews with the jail administrator and with the accused. The jail is small and does not have facilities for many reporters.
What should the jail administrator do?

   A. Permit only a few reporters in at one time, until all have had an opportunity to conduct interviews.
   B. Meet with the reporters outside the jail and give them an interview. Refuse to allow interviews with the prisoner.

C. Have the reporters select representatives to conduct interviews in the jail.
D. Have the reporters select a representative to conduct interviews with the administrator. Do not permit any interviews with the prisoner unless he agrees and is accompanied by his attorney.

8. The jail has had a serious escape that was effected by sawing bars and picking locks. The chief jailer has been interviewed by the news media and maintains that the escape was caused by the incompetence of the officers on duty that night. The sheriff has also been interviewed and stated that the jail is old and needs to be replaced. Which statement below BEST describes this situation?

   A. The chief jailer is probably right. After all, he spent more time in the jail than the sheriff.
   B. The sheriff as the administrator has the responsibility for news releases.
   C. It is obvious that the sheriff has not given much thought to developing a procedure for giving news releases. If he had, responsibility for releasing information about the jail would be clearly assigned and there would not be an opportunity for conflicting statements.
   D. The chief jailer and the sheriff are probably both right about the causes of the escape.

8. _____

KEY (CORRECT ANSWERS)

1. C
2. D
3. C
4. A
5. E

6. D
7. D
8. C

EXAMINATION SECTION
TEST 1

DIRECTIONS: Each question or incomplete statement is followed by several suggested answers or completions. Select the one that BEST answers the question or completes the statement. *PRINT THE LETTER OF THE CORRECT ANSWER IN THE SPACE AT THE RIGHT.*

Questions 1-12.

DIRECTIONS: Questions 1 through 12 are based on the Criminal Procedure Law. Each question consists of two statements. Mark your answer.
- A. if only sentence I is correct
- B. if only sentence II is correct
- C. if sentences I and II are correct
- D. if neither sentence I nor II is correct

1.
    I. Except as otherwise provided in the Criminal Procedure Law, a prosecution for a misdemeanor must be commenced within three years after the commission thereof.
    II. Except as otherwise provided in the Criminal Procedure Law, a prosecution for a petty offense must be commenced within two years after the commission thereof.

2.
    I. A person may not be prosecuted twice for the same offense.
    II. A defendant may not be convicted of any offense upon the testimony of an accomplice unsupported by corroborative evidence tending to connect the defendant with the commission of such offense.

3.
    I. A defendant may testify in his own behalf, but his failure to do so is not a factor from which any inference unfavorable to him may be drawn.
    II. A child less than twelve years old may not testify under oath in a criminal proceeding in a court of law.

4.
    I. A person may be convicted of an offense solely upon evidence of a valid confession or admission made by him without additional proof that the offense charged has been committed.
    II. Evidence of a written or oral confession, admission, or other statement made by a defendant with respect to his participation or lack of participation in the offense charged may not be received in evidence against him in a criminal proceeding if such statement was involuntarily made.

5.
    I. A summons may be served by a police officer, or by a complainant at least eighteen years of age, or by any other person at least eighteen years old designated by the court.
    II. A summons may be served anywhere in the county of issuance or anywhere in an adjoining county in the state.

6.
    I. Any person may arrest another person for a felony anywhere in the state when the latter has in fact committed such felony.
    II. Any person may arrest another person for any offense other than a felony when the latter has in fact committed such offense in his presence, provided that the arrest is made only in the county in which such offense was committed.

7. I. A search warrant must be executed not more than three days after the date and time of issuance and it must thereafter be returned to the court without unnecessary delay.
   II. No search warrant may be executed unless the police officer gives notice of his authority and purpose to the occupant of the premises or vehicle to be searched. In addition, the police officer must serve a copy of the warrant upon the occupant of said premises or vehicle.

7.____

8. I. An appearance ticket may be issued by a police officer following an arrest without a warrant if the arrest was for a Class B misdemeanor but not if the arrest was for a Class A misdemeanor.
   II. An appearance ticket may, at the discretion of the police officer or other public servant authorized to issue appearance tickets, be served either personally or by registered or certified mail, return receipt requested.

8.____

9. I. Under the *Youthful Offender Treatment* article of the Criminal Procedure Law (Article 720), *youth* means a person charged with a crime who was at least sixteen years old and less than nineteen years old at the time of his alleged commission of such crime.
   II. When an individual has been adjudged eligible for youthful offender treatment, he may be found guilty by reason of a preponderance of the evidence rather than guilty based upon proof beyond a reasonable doubt.

9.____

10. I. A police officer may arrest a person without a warrant for any offense, other than for a petty offense, when he has reasonable cause to believe that such person has committed such offense, whether in his presence or otherwise.
    II. A police officer may arrest a person for a petty offense without a warrant when such offense was committed in the officer's presence, within the geographical area of such police officer's employment, and such arrest is made in the county where such offense was committed.

10.____

11. I. A police officer may stop a person in a public place located within the geographical area of such officer's employment when he reasonably suspects that such person is committing, has committed or is about to commit either (a) a felony or (b) any misdemeanor as defined in the penal law, and may demand of him his name, address, occupation, the name and address of his employer, and an explanation of his conduct.
    II. Whenever a police officer stops a person in a public place for temporary questioning, he may search such person for a deadly weapon or any instrument, article or substance readily capable of causing serious physical injury and of a sort not ordinarily carried in public places by law-abiding persons.

11.____

12. I. A defendant in any criminal action who is less than eighteen years old may refuse to permit himself to be fingerprinted unless accompanied by a parent or legal guardian.
    II. A police officer who is executing an arrest warrant need not have the warrant in his possession; if he has not, he must show it to the defendant upon request as soon after the arrest as possible.

12.____

Questions 13-24.

DIRECTIONS: Questions 13 through 24 are to be answered SOLELY on the basis of the Penal Law.

13. A person is guilty of grand larceny in the first degree when he steals property which

    A. consists of personal property valued at more than $1500
    B. is obtained by instilling in the victim a fear that that the victim's membership in a subversive organization will be revealed
    C. consists of goods valued in excess of $250
    D. is obtained by instilling in the victim a fear that an antique vase which he owns will be damaged

14. Using or threatening the immediate use of a dangerous instrument is an element of all of the following offenses EXCEPT _____ in the _____ degree.

    A. robbery; first
    B. burglary; first
    C. robbery; second
    D. burglary; second

15. Which of the following describes a person guilty of escape in the first degree?

    A. A person convicted of a felony escapes from a detention facility.
    B. A person just convicted of a misdemeanor escapes from a courtroom by impersonating a police officer.
    C. A person escapes from a police officer's custody by causing serious physical injury to the officer.
    D. After committing a felony, a person escapes from the scene of the crime by using or threatening the immediate use of a deadly weapon.

16. A person who wantonly and recklessly fires a rifle into a crowd of people without any specific intent to injure or kill would NOT be guilty of

    A. murder if death results
    B. assault in the first degree if serious physical injury results
    C. assault in the second degree if physical injury results
    D. reckless endangerment in the first degree if no injury results

17. Each of the following choices states an offense involving the forcible stealing of property, and certain additional facts.
    In which choice would the defendant be guilty of the offense stated, based SOLELY on the facts given in the choice? Robbery in the

    A. first degree - defendant robs a bank while carrying two sticks of dynamite, which cannot be seen under his jacket
    B. second degree - while defendant and his partner are fleeing from a store they have just robbed, the partner pushes a bystander to the ground, thereby causing a painful bruise to bystander's shoulder
    C. first degree - while robbing a bank, defendant threatens to kidnap and kill the manager's wife unless the manager gives him all the money in the vault
    D. second degree - defendant robs a jewelry store, while his partner waits in a getaway car parked around the corner

18. A person is ALWAYS guilty of a felony if he unlawfully possesses 18.____

    A. any loaded firearm in a vehicle
    B. any deadly weapon and is not a citizen of the United States
    C. any dagger or razor with intent to use the same unlawfully against another
    D. a shotgun in a building used for educational purposes

19. Knowing that Jones intends to rob a bank, Smith gives Jones a rifle to use during the 19.____
    robbery. However, the day before the robbery is supposed to occur, the police arrest
    Jones on an old charge, thereby preventing the robbery.
    Based on these facts, it would be CORRECT to state that Smith is

    A. *not guilty* of any crime
    B. *guilty* of conspiracy in the second degree and criminal facilitation in the second degree
    C. *guilty* of criminal facilitation in the second degree but is not guilty of conspiracy in the second degree
    D. *guilty* of conspiracy in the second degree but is not guilty of criminal facilitation in the second degree

20. Each of the following choices states an offense involving the death of a person, and certain additional facts. 20.____
    In which choice would the defendant NOT be guilty of the offense stated, based SOLELY on the facts given in the choice?

    A. Manslaughter in the second degree - when the defendant intentionally causes or aids another person to commit suicide
    B. Murder - when the defendant and two other persons attempt to commit escape in the second degree, and one of the participants causes the death of a person other than one of the participants
    C. Manslaughter in the first degree - when with intent to cause serious physical injury to another person, the defendant causes the death of a third person
    D. Murder - when the defendant engages in conduct which creates a grave risk of death of another person, and thereby causes the death of another person

21. Which of the following elements would raise the crime of custodial interference from the 21.____
    second degree to the first degree?

    A. The intent to hold a child permanently or for a protracted period
    B. Exposure of the person taken to a risk that his health will be materially impaired
    C. The taking of a child less than sixteen years old from his lawful custodian
    D. Enticement of an incompetent person from lawful custody

22. Which one of the following elements must ALWAYS be present for a person to be guilty of 22.____
    arson in the first degree?

    A. The presence in the building at the time of another person who is not a participant in the crime
    B. Intentional damage to a building caused by a fire
    C. Knowledge by the person that another person not a participant in the crime is present in the building
    D. Circumstances which render the presence in the building of another person not a participant in the crime a reasonable possibility

23. For which of the following crimes is it a necessary element that a person knowingly enter or remain unlawfully in a dwelling, as the word *dwelling* is defined in the Penal Law?

    A. Criminal trespass in the first and second degree
    B. Criminal trespass in the second degree and burglary in the first degree
    C. Criminal trespass in the first degree and burglary in the second degree
    D. Burglary in the first and second degree

24. Assume that the police stop a car in which three men are riding. Ward is the driver, and Jones and King are passengers. During a lawful search, the police find one-quarter ounce of morphine concealed in King's coat. Based SOLELY on these facts, it would be CORRECT to state that

    A. King, Jones, and Ward are all guilty of criminal possession of a dangerous drug
    B. a presumption of knowingly possessing the morphine applies to Ward but not to Jones
    C. King is guilty of criminal possession of a dangerous drug and Ward is guilty of conspiracy
    D. King is guilty of criminal possession of a dangerous drug but Ward and Jones are not

---

KEY (CORRECT ANSWERS)

1. D		11. D	
2. A		12. B	
3. C		13. D	
4. B		14. C	
5. C		15. A	
6. C		16. C	
7. D		17. B	
8. D		18. A	
9. A		19. A	
10. C		20. D	

21. B
22. A
23. B
24. D

TEST 2

DIRECTIONS: Each question or incomplete statement is followed by several suggested answers or completions. Select the one that BEST answers the question or completes the statement. *PRINT THE LETTER OF THE CORRECT ANSWER IN THE SPACE AT THE RIGHT.*

1. Which of the following statements is(are) CORRECT?
   The Criminal Procedure Law (CPL) applies to
   I. all criminal actions and proceedings commenced on or after September 1, 1971, and appeals and other post-judgment proceedings relating thereto.
   II. criminal actions and proceedings commenced before September 1, 1971 but pending thereafter
   III. appeals and other post-judgment proceedings commenced on or after September 1, 1971 which relate to criminal actions and proceedings commenced or concluded prior thereto, provided that, where application of CPL would not be feasible or would work injustice, the former Code of Criminal Procedure shall apply
   IV. criminal procedure matters occurring on or after September 1, 1971 which are not a part of any particular action or case

   The CORRECT answer is:

   A. All of the above
   B. I *only*
   C. I, II, III
   D. II, III, IV

2. Which of the following is hearsay?
   A(n)

   A. written statement by a person not present at the court hearing where the statement is submitted as proof of an occurrence
   B. oral statement in court by a witness of what he saw
   C. written statement of what he saw by a witness present in court
   D. re-enactment by a witness in court of what he saw

3. In a criminal case, a statement by a person not present in court is

   A. *acceptable* evidence if not objected to by the prosecutor
   B. *acceptable* evidence if not objected to by the defense lawyer
   C. *not acceptable* evidence except in certain well-settled circumstances
   D. *not acceptable* evidence under any circumstances

4. The rule on hearsay is founded on the belief that

   A. proving someone said an act occurred is not proof that the act did occur
   B. a person who has knowledge about a case should be willing to appear in court
   C. persons not present in court are likely to be unreliable witnesses
   D. permitting persons to testify without appearing in court will lead to a disrespect for law

5. One reason for the general rule that a witness in a criminal case MUST give his testimony in court is that

   A. a witness may be influenced by threats to make untrue statements
   B. the opposite side is then permitted to question him
   C. the court provides protection for a witness against unfair questioning
   D. the adversary system is designed to prevent a miscarriage of justice.

6. An appeal MAY be taken from a

   A. verdict
   B. judgment
   C. decision
   D. conviction

7. Jury trial commences

   A. with the selection of a jury
   B. when the defendant makes opening address
   C. when the first opening address is made
   D. when the first witness is sworn

8. Adjective criminal law is governed PRIMARILY by the

   A. Penal Law
   B. Civil Practice Law and Rules
   C. Criminal Procedure Law
   D. Code of Criminal Procedure

9. Which of the following contain(s) references included in the definition of *warrant of arrest?*

   I. Process of local criminal court to produce defendant for arraignment
   II. Produce defendant for arraignment upon filed accusatory instrument
   III. Addressed to peace officer to produce defendant for arraignment
   IV. Process of any criminal court requiring defendant to appear before it for arraignment on a prosecutor's information

   The CORRECT answer is:

   A. I, II, III, IV
   B. III *only*
   C. I, II, III
   D. I, II, IV

10. Superior courts have jurisdiction in the following areas:

    I. Unlimited trial jurisdiction of all offenses
    II. Exclusive trial jurisdiction of felonies
    III. Concurrent trial jurisdiction of misdemeanors
    IV. Preliminary jurisdiction of all offenses, exercised only through grand juries

    The CORRECT answer is:

    A. I *only*
    B. I, II
    C. I, II, III
    D. II, III, IV

11. Petty offense means

    A. all violations and traffic infractions
    B. some misdemeanors and all violations
    C. only conduct which is not a traffic infraction and is punishable by imprisonment for not more than 15 days
    D. a class B misdemeanor only

12. An offense committed near a boundary between two adjoining counties of this state may be prosecuted in either of such counties.
    The MAXIMUM distance from a county border is

    A. 1,000 feet   B. 1,000 yards   C. 500 feet   D. 500 yards

13. A felony is committed on the Hudson River south of the northern boundary of New York City.
    The county or counties having jurisdiction to try the case is(are)

    A. New York, Richmond, Bronx, Kings, and Queens Counties
    B. New York, Richmond, and Bronx Counties
    C. New York and Richmond Counties only
    D. New York County only

14. A crime is committed on a bus regularly carrying passengers from Nassau County to Manhattan by way of Queens. At the time of the occurrence, the bus is in Nassau on its way to its terminal point—Manhattan. The victim is a Queens resident. The alleged perpetrator is a resident of Manhattan.
    The county or counties having jurisdiction in this case is(are)

    A. Nassau or New York   B. Nassau or Queens
    C. Nassau, Queens, or Manhattan D. Nassau only

15. Prosecution of a crime MUST be commenced within

    A. one year after commission, for all misdemeanors and petty offenses
    B. two years after commission, for all misdemeanors and petty offenses
    C. 5 years after commission, for all felonies
    D. 5 years after commission, for some felonies

16. A private person in making an arrest is limited as follows:

    A. For an offense, at any hour of day or night
    B. For a crime only, at any hour of any day or night
    C. For a felony only, at any hour of any day or night
    D. All of the above

17. An appearance ticket directs a specific person to appear in a criminal court in connection with the alleged commission of a designated offense.
    This appearance ticket may be issued only by a

    A. local criminal court judge
    B. local criminal court judge or police officer
    C. police officer or authorized public servant
    D. police officer, authorized public servant, or local criminal court judge

18. An arrest by a private person without a warrant can PROPERLY be made in which one of the following situations?

    A. There is reasonable cause to believe that the person being arrested committed a felony.
    B. The person arrested for a felony has in fact committed the felony.
    C. The person arrested for a misdemeanor has in fact committed the misdemeanor.
    D. The person arrested for any offense has in fact committed the offense.

19. A peace officer, outside the geographical area of his employment, has reasonable cause to believe that a felony was committed in his presence.
    In the circumstances,

    A. he may make an arrest, without restriction
    B. he may make an arrest only on the same authority as that of a private person
    C. he may make an arrest during the commission of the felony, immediately thereafter or during immediate flight
    D. none of the above

    19.____

20. After making an arrest, a police officer must perform all required recording, fingerprinting, and other related duties.
    He MUST do so

    A. immediately
    B. without unnecessary delay
    C. within 24 hours
    D. within 8 hours

    20.____

21. A police officer, acting without a warrant, may arrest a person

    A. only in the geographical area of his employment
    B. outside the geographical area of his employment only for a felony
    C. without restriction, for a petty offense committed anywhere in the state
    D. for a crime committed anywhere in the state

    21.____

22. Summons is a process whose SOLE function is to

    A. commence a criminal action
    B. substitute for a warrant of arrest, where a warrant may not be issued
    C. produce defendant for arraignment upon a filed accusatory instrument
    D. inform defendant as to nature of the offenses charged

    22.____

23. A summons may be served by

    A. any person without restriction
    B. any person at least 18 years old
    C. a police officer, without restriction
    D. a peace officer, without restriction

    23.____

24. An arrest warrant is addressed to and can be executed by

    A. any adult person
    B. a police officer or classification of police officers
    C. a peace officer or classification of peace officers
    D. any person over the age of 18, not a party to the action

    24.____

25. Which of the following would invalidate an acknowledgment?

    A. Failure to say deponent is known to notary
    B. Seal is missing
    C. Acts done on Sunday
    D. Affiant misspells his name

    25.____

KEY (CORRECT ANSWERS)

1. A	11. A
2. A	12. D
3. C	13. A
4. A	14. A
5. B	15. D
6. B	16. A
7. A	17. C
8. C	18. B
9. D	19. C
10. D	20. B

21. D
22. C
23. C
24. B
25. A

TEST 3

DIRECTIONS: Each question or incomplete statement is followed by several suggested answers or completions. Select the one that BEST answers the question or completes the statement. *PRINT THE LETTER OF THE CORRECT ANSWER IN THE SPACE AT THE RIGHT.*

1. A warrant of arrest may be executed anywhere in the state   1._____

    A. without restriction, if it is issued by a city court
    B. in all cases, without restriction
    C. in all cases, provided it is appropriately endorsed by a local criminal court of the county where the arrest is to be made
    D. when issued by the city criminal court

2. A warrant of arrest may be executed on any day   2._____

    A. of the week, at any hour
    B. except Sunday, at any hour of the day; but on Sunday only between 9:00 A.M. and 6:00 P.M.
    C. including Sunday, provided it is so endorsed by the issuing court
    D. except Sunday

3. A police officer or court officer of a criminal court may stop a person, under specified circumstances, when he reasonably suspects that the person is committing, has committed, or is about to commit any felony   3._____

    A. or a Class A misdemeanor defined in the Penal Law
    B. or misdemeanor defined in the Penal Law
    C. or any misdemeanor only
    D. only

4. At a hearing on a felony complaint, defendant   4._____

    A. may testify in his own behalf within the discretion of the court, but he has a right to call witnesses
    B. has a right to testify in his own behalf, but he may call witnesses only within the discretion of the court
    C. has a right to testify in his own behalf and to call witnesses
    D. may testify in his own behalf, within the discretion of the court, and call witnesses in his behalf, within the discretion of the court

5. A grand jury, to be legally constituted, MUST consist of _____ members.   5._____

    A. not less than 16 and not more than 23
    B. not less than 12 and not more than 16
    C. not less than 12 and not more than 23
    D. at least 12

6. At a preliminary hearing on a felony complaint,   6._____
    I. the defendant must be present
    II. the defendant has a right to be present, but he may waive this right
    III. the defendant has a right to call witnesses in his behalf
    IV. all witnesses called may be cross-examined

The CORRECT answer is:

A. I, II   B. II, III   C. I, IV   D. II, IV

7. The number and term of grand juries empanelled for a court are determined generally by

    A. Supreme Court in the county, on application of the District Attorney showing the estimated need
    B. Rules of the court for which the grand jury is drawn
    C. Judicial Conference regulations
    D. Appellate Division rules

8. The quantum of proof required for a court to hold a defendant for grand jury action on a felony complaint is proof

    A. affording the court reasonable cause to believe
    B. sufficient for a reasonable man
    C. by a fair preponderance of the evidence
    D. beyond a reasonable doubt

9. The acting foreman of a grand jury is

    A. chosen by lot
    B. chosen by the court
    C. the second grand juror to be empanelled
    D. chosen by the grand jurors

10. When a grand jury requires legal advice, they may receive it

    A. only from the court, District Attorney, or an attorney designated by either
    B. either from the court or District Attorney, only
    C. only from the District Attorney
    D. only from the court

11. In all cases, when a motion is made for a change of venue, a(n)

    A. application for a stay, denied by a Supreme Court justice, may not thereafter be granted by a justice of the Appellate Division
    B. application for a stay, denied by a Supreme Court justice, may be reviewed and granted by a justice of the Appellate Division
    C. stay may be granted only by any Supreme Court justice in the judicial district
    D. stay may be granted by any superior court judge in the judicial district

12. Evidence of mental disease or defect as a trial defense excluding criminal responsibility is admissible

    A. only as to a defendant who has previously been examined under court order by two qualified psychiatrists
    B. provided the defendant has served and filed timely written notice of intention to rely thereon
    C. provided the People have served a demand on the defendant to give notice of this defense
    D. in all cases without restriction

13. On a defense of alibi,

    A. the People in all cases are entitled on trial to an adjournment not in excess of 3 days
    B. a court may receive testimony as in D below but on application must grant an adjournment of not less than 7 days
    C. a court may not receive testimony as in D below
    D. a court may receive testimony, in its discretion, from a witness who was not included in defendant's notice of alibi

14. Which of the following statements are CORRECT?
    I. The People, having the burden of proof, address the jury before defendant at all stages.
    II. A closing address to the jury by the prosecution is required.
    III. A closing address to the jury by both sides is discretionary.
    IV. An opening address to the jury by both sides is discretionary.
    V. The People in all cases must make an opening address to the jury.

    The CORRECT answer is:

    A. I, II, III
    B. II, III, IV
    C. I, II, IV
    D. I, II, V

15. In selecting a jury, the MAXIMUM total number of challenges to alternate jurors that may be exercised by BOTH parties is

    A. 16   B. 8   C. 4   D. 2

16. A grand jury witness may be called only on request of the

    A. court, District Attorney, or grand jury
    B. court
    C. District Attorney or the grand jury
    D. grand jury

17. A prospective defendant in a grand jury proceeding who wishes the grand jury to hear a witness in his behalf is limited by the fact that

    A. the grand jury, in its discretion, may hear the witness if the defendant makes an oral or written request
    B. the grand jury must hear the witness if the defendant makes an oral or written request
    C. the grand jury must hear the witness only if the defendant makes a written request
    D. there may be no legal basis for such a request

18. When a charge has been dismissed by a grand jury following its consideration of the matter, which of the following is CORRECT?

    A. It may be resubmitted to successive grand juries by court order, without limitation.
    B. It may be resubmitted to a grand jury if a court so authorizes, but no further submission thereafter is permissible.
    C. Without court order, it may be considered by another grand jury, but not by the same grand jury.
    D. It may again be considered by the same grand jury, without court order.

19. An indictment MUST contain
    I. endorsement, *A True Bill,* signed by the district attorney
    II. applicable section number of the statute allegedly violated
    III. date or period when alleged conduct occurred
    IV. statement in each court that the grand jury accuses the defendant of a designated offense

    The CORRECT answer is:

    A. I, II, IV
    B. III, IV
    C. II, III, IV
    D. I, II, III, IV

20. With respect to an offense raised to higher grade by reason solely of a previous conviction, which of the following statements is CORRECT?

    A. Under no circumstances is a jury permitted to know of the previous conviction.
    B. The order of trial is in this instance substantially the same as in other cases, except for arraignment on a special information.
    C. Before any proceeding to establish defendant's identity and previous conviction, he must be advised of the privilege against self-incrimination.
    D. The defendant's conviction of the predicate case may be established at any time before the case goes to the jury.

21. The term *petty offense* includes

    A. no misdemeanors, some violations, all traffic infractions
    B. no misdemeanors, but all violations and traffic infractions
    C. some misdemeanors, all violations and traffic infractions
    D. all misdemeanors, violations, and traffic infractions

22. Conviction, as defined in CPL, means

    A. entry of guilty plea, or guilty verdict
    B. serving of sentence
    C. entry of final judgment
    D. imposition and entry of sentence

23. With regard to a non-jury trial, which of the following is CORRECT?

    A. Trial commences when both parties appear, are ready, and the court announces that the case is on trial. The court's determination as to guilt or innocence is properly termed a verdict.
    B. If there is no opening address, trial commences when the first witness is sworn, and the court's determination as to guilt or innocence is properly termed a verdict.
    C. An opening address, if made, commences the trial, and the court's determination of guilt or innocence is properly termed a decision.
    D. There must be an opening address to the court; this commences the trial; and the court's determination of guilt or innocence is properly termed a decision.

24. In relation to double jeopardy, a person may not be twice prosecuted for the same offense.
    Assuming the same offense, which of the following does NOT relate to double jeopardy under CPL?

    A. Defendant is found not guilty after trial in one jurisdiction
    B. An accusatory instrument is filed in a court of another country
    C. An accusatory instrument is filed in a Federal court
    D. An accusatory instrument is filed in a state other than New York

25. Which of the following is NOT applicable to a warrant of arrest? 25.____

    A. Its function is to produce defendant for arraignment.
    B. It commences a criminal action.
    C. It is issued only by a local criminal court.
    D. It is addressed to a police officer.

KEY (CORRECT ANSWERS)

1.	D	11.	A
2.	A	12.	B
3.	A	13.	D
4.	B	14.	D
5.	A	15.	A
6.	D	16.	C
7.	D	17.	A
8.	A	18.	B
9.	B	19.	B
10.	B	20.	B

21. B
22. A
23. B
24. B
25. B

READING COMPREHENSION
UNDERSTANDING AND INTERPRETING WRITTEN MATERIAL
EXAMINATION SECTION
TEST 1

DIRECTIONS: Each question or incomplete statement is followed by several suggested answers or completions. Select the one that BEST answers the question or completes the statement. *PRINT THE LETTER OF THE CORRECT ANSWER IN THE SPACE AT THE RIGHT.*

Questions 1-4.

DIRECTIONS: Questions 1 through 4 are to be answered SOLELY on the basis of the following passage.

Morally, there is no basis for the assertion that the commission of a social offense allows society to strip a human being of all his rights except those which, through some sort of *natural law* concept, he needs to survive. Rather, society is justified in punishing offenders only to the extent that it needs to protect itself; excessive retribution is *immoral*. Thus, unless society can demonstrate that a specific deprivation is necessary to its self-preservation, or to its reassertion of authority over the individual offender, it should not be entitled to enforce the deprivation. To place the burden on the prisoner to demonstrate that he should not be deprived of a particular right appears to be unfair and unjustified for two reasons: (1) the resources and skills are unequally distributed in society's favor, and (2) the concept of *proportionality* as a rudimentary value is rejected by such an approach, which even theories of retribution and vengeance do not support.

Pragmatically, too, prisoners should be viewed and treated as human beings. Ninety-five percent of all those incarcerated in prisons are returned to the free world. It violates common sense to expect a man who has been treated at best as a cipher while in prison to be enamored of a society which has not only enchained him but also has increased his torment while he is confined. When he is released, his action is likely to be antisocial rather than social. Additionally, the imposition of excessive suffering on offenders permeates society's attitudes toward others in its midst. Just as we are now realizing that violence abroad erodes the barriers against domestic violence, official hostility toward some human beings tends to add an aura of authority to hostility toward and among others. Disinclination to cherish humanity at one point in society leads to total abdication of humanity at another.

1. In the above passage, it is pointed out that

   A. it is a practical approach to treatment to take away all but the basic rights of a prisoner
   B. it is proper to remove an inmate's rights within a system of rewards and punishments
   C. incarceration should not be used for revenge against one who has offended society
   D. the inmate ought to play a primary role in determining treatment methods

1.____

2. According to the above passage,
   A. inmates who are treated badly are apt to resort to antisocial behavior when they are returned to society
   B. there is a tendency among inmates to join organizations dedicated to achieving civil rights for the victims of society
   C. society generally sees all inmates as being equal, despite inconsistent observation of prisoners' rights
   D. recidivism is a serious problem for the majority of prisoners who are released on parole

3. While criticizing the kind of treatment prisoners receive in our institutions, the above passage implies that
   A. the mistreatment of prisoners is an outcome of society's benign attitude toward the law-abiding citizen
   B. cruelty begets cruelty, and that humane treatment will make better citizens of those entrusted to our care
   C. when violence in this country spreads, it increases all over the world
   D. an aura of authority has replaced official hostility in correctional institutions

4. According to the above passage, penal authorities are justified in depriving prisoners of rights
   A. in order to satisfy society's desire for retribution against criminal offenders
   B. until prisoners can demonstrate that particular deprivations are unjustified
   C. whenever the preservation of order within the institution will be facilitated
   D. only when it is necessary to protect society or maintain control over the inmate

Questions 5-8.

DIRECTIONS: Questions 5 through 8 are to be answered SOLELY on the basis of the following excerpt from a memo circulated by a correction official for comments.

Some bargaining is virtually inevitable between those charged with enforcing institutional regulations and inmates who are supposed to be regulated for the simple reason that administrators rarely have sufficient resources to gain complete conformity to all the rules. An insufficient number of guards and cells and inadequately threatening punishments create an environment in which institutional rules are often ignored. At the same time, the attempt to impose order upon individuals deprived of normal amenities, who often lack opportunities for adequate recreation or privacy, tends to produce violent disorder. Toleration by correctional administrators and officers of constant violation of institutional rules results even if confined to a level considered by administrators to be neither very visible nor very serious. Recurring contact between guards and inmates creates ample opportunity for an ongoing informal bargaining.

Although some form of bargaining has long been recognized as a basic process of control within prisons and other total institutions, it is not clear whether a system of control which relies on private, particularized bargains between staff and inmates contributes to the goals of rehabilitation, order, or protection from arbitrary punishment. In fact, within the daily bargaining process, often the only goal sought to be achieved by the institution is short term surface order - the semblance that everything is running smoothly with no official (or public) cause for alarm.

5. According to the above passage, all of the following conditions contribute to the existence of bargaining EXCEPT

   A. difficulty in getting inmates to conform to the rules
   B. the scarcity of guards and cells
   C. the scarcity of administrators
   D. the pressures of confinement brought on by prison conditions

6. According to the above passage, which one of the following is MOST likely to create a climate for bargaining between inmates and staff?

   A. Lack of privacy
   B. Lack of opportunities for recreation
   C. Frequent interaction between guards and inmates
   D. Desires of guards to avoid enforcement of rules

7. The author IMPLIES that the practice of bargaining in institutions is a process which

   A. is not generally recognized outside institutions
   B. eliminates violent disorders among inmates
   C. should be utilized more frequently
   D. has been in existence for a long time

8. According to the above passage, which one of the following statements concerning bargaining is MOST NEARLY correct?
   It

   A. contributes to the goals of the institution because it protects inmates from arbitrary punishment
   B. impedes rehabilitation since it weakens respect for correctional personnel
   C. is a method of reducing the visibility of inmate rule violations
   D. detracts from the smooth operation of the institution because it is an ineffective system of control

Questions 9-12.

DIRECTIONS: Questions 9 through 12 are to be answered on the basis of the following portion of a report submitted by a Tour Commander to the appropriate superior about an unusual occurrence in a Detention Dormitory. The portion of the report consists of 21 numbered sentences, some of which may or may not follow the principles of good report writing.

1. Following is a report of an altercation between inmate John Doe, #441-77-9375, and inmate Henry Green, #441-77-1656.
2. At approximately 6:15 A.M. on June 15, an alarm was received in the Control Room from Officer Arthur Kinney #6214 of the 7M dormitory (General Population).
3. Captain Ronald Doaks #529 and Officer Henry James #7654 responded immediately to determine the cause of the alarm.
4. Captain Doaks reports that, upon arrival, he observed inmate John Doe, #441-77-9375, on the officer's bridge bleeding from the mouth.

5. The institutional doctor also found a stab wound in the left arm.
6. The Captain observed inmate Henry Green, #441-77-1656, locked behind the *B* gate, heard him shouting obscenities and threatening further harm to Officer Kinney.
7. He noticed a large group of inmates standing quietly in the day room.
8. Officer Kinney, who was on post alone, reports he heard a commotion in the rear of the dormitory while sitting at his desk reading the Departmental Rules and Regulations.
9. He could not see what was going on because of a large crowd of inmates.
10. He reports that inmate Doe suddenly broke through the crowd screaming toward the *B* gate.
11. Doe was being pursued by inmate Green.
12. Officer Kinney states that he sounded the alarm and allowed inmate Doe onto the bridge.
13. Since inmate Doe was bleeding from the mouth, Captain Doaks ordered Officer James to escort him to the clinic for immediate examination and treatment by Dr. James White, who subsequently suspected a broken jaw and also discovered a puncture wound in the left bicep.
14. Dr. White ordered his transfer to Harmony Hospital for x-ray of the jaw.
15. Inmate Green, who appeared free of injury, stated to the Captain that he and Doe argued over the telephone, agreed to *take it to the back* and fight.
16. Green would make no further statements.
17. No other inmate in the dormitory would admit seeing anything.
18. Inmate Green received an infraction and was transferred to the Administrative Area pending further investigation.
19. The housing area was then restored to order and normal operations were resumed.
20. Prior to his transfer to the hospital, inmate Doe stated to the Captain that he was assaulted by inmate Green for no apparent reason.
21. He was told that he has an infraction and, upon return from the hospital, would be transferred to another housing unit pending investigation.

9. Of the following, which sentence is MOST likely to be out of sequence?

   A. 2   B. 5   C. 8   D. 14

10. Of the following, which sentence indicates the GREATEST need for further clarification by the Tour Commander submitting the report?

    A. 4   B. 6   C. 9   D. 17

11. Which one of the following sentences BEST indicates the possibility of potential danger remaining in 7M because of the omission of a necessary procedure?

    A. 3   B. 14   C. 19   D. 21

12. Which one of the following sentences is LEAST significant to the report?

    A. 4   B. 7   C. 11   D. 17

Questions 13-16.

DIRECTIONS: Questions 13 through 16 are to be answered SOLELY on the basis of the following fictitious directive which may or may not conform with actual policy and procedure of the Department of Correction.

<u>DIRECTIVE NO. 15</u>   Dated March 1

Guidelines for Members of the Department when accepting packages for inmates being held in custody of the City Department of Correction.

1. <u>Receipt and Distribution of Packages</u>

All packages delivered by the postal authorities must bear the name and address of the sender. All packages regardless of whether received through the mail or delivered by an individual, during visiting hours only, must be in a cardboard box with tape sealing same so as to prevent access to contents of package. When package is received by mail, it is to be placed in the mailroom of the institution concerned by the staff member assigned to picking up the mail. In addition, the officer delivering the package to mailroom officer will get a receipt for all packages. The mailroom officer shall prepare Form P-103 in duplicate, which will document the time and description of all packages received, including the contents thereof, as well as the name and address of the sender. Packages must be weighed and weight noted on Form P-103, as no inmate is to receive an excess of 40 lbs. in packages in a six-month period. Log is to be maintained of all packages received, distributed, and returned to sender, including the weights for packages received and accepted. When a package is brought to the institution by an individual, during visiting hours only, it is to bear the name and address of person who is responsible for articles in package, who must be the individual who is delivering the package. Form P-103 is to remain with package until signed by inmate, since original of Form P-103 is the institutional record and substantiation that inmate has received his/her package.

As soon as practicable, all packages are to be searched for contraband and appropriate actions taken. If package is determined to be acceptable, inmate concerned shall be called to mailroom and shall inspect package, sign Form P-103 in duplicate, receive the duplicate copy of Form P-103, and remove package to his/her respective cell. If the inmate is not available when called for, package is to be secured in a locked closet or room and key so secured that only authorized personnel have access to area. If mailroom officer is not on duty when package is brought to institution by an individual, officer assigned to visits is to be responsible for handling and safekeeping of package according to this directive.

2. <u>Acceptability of Articles</u>

Suitable clothing may be accepted in all packages according to guidelines determined by the head of each institution. However, the institutional clothing card must be referred to so excess clothing is not accumulated and in order to maintain a strict control over same. Food and snacks are also acceptable items - no alcoholic beverages, nor glass containers are to be accepted. Sharp instruments are not to be accepted nor any item that may create a hazard or breach of security within the institution. Shaving utensils are to be distributed by the institution and are not to be accepted in packages. Under no circumstances is money or jewelry to be accepted in packages. No medications are to be accepted when included in packages or otherwise, but, when the occasion arises, inmate must be instructed that all medications are dispensed through the medical staff assigned to that institution. Prescription eyeglasses can be accepted, but must be inspected and approved by the institutional physician before distribution to inmate. Under no circumstances are cigarettes to be accepted in packages since they must be purchased through each institutional commissary.

3. Appropriate Areas For Use

Food received in packages cannot be removed from the housing area. Under no circumstances should an inmate bring food to the main dining room as a substitution or addition to the departmental menu. Books and magazines cannot be removed from the housing areas. Under no condition should any inmate's library privileges be cancelled or modified because he has received publications from another source. All eatable items are to be consumed either in the inmate's cell or the day room of the housing area he/she is assigned to. Any inmate who has received special permission to receive an item of clothing for sporting or athletic purposes may use said clothing only in the gymnasium of the institution, said clothing is to remain in the gymnasium, and a system for laundering determined and controlled by the Recreation Director.

4. A. Safeguarding Undelivered Packages

All undelivered packages will be secured in a locked closet of the mailroom or the mailroom itself. The mailroom shall be secured whenever a custodial member is not in attendance. The key to the mailroom must be secured so that only authorized personnel have access to the area. The schedule for the use of the mailroom must be arranged to create accountability for the safekeeping of all packages received for any inmate of the Department. Every effort must be made to deliver packages to inmates as soon as is practicable. However, if after ten days, the package is not delivered, it must be returned to the sender with an appropriate notation - under no condition may a package remain undelivered for more than ten days.

B. Ensuring that Unacceptable Packages or Unacceptable Items Are Returned to Sender

All unacceptable packages or unacceptable items must be returned to sender immediately upon being determined unacceptable. The inmate must be notified of any article or package that is being returned, but not necessarily before the items have been mailed. Upon mailing any unacceptable items to the sender, no items shall be returned which would violate postal regulations. Whenever articles are returned to sender, a return receipt must be requested of the postal authorities.

5. Procedure for the Prosecution of Persons Violating the Postal Regulations or Prison Contraband Law

Whenever serious contraband is found in a package received by mail at an institution of the Department, the supervisor investigating the incident will notify the postal authorities, cooperating with them whenever possible. The officer who actually finds contraband must be witness to any criminal proceedings that would follow. If contraband is delivered to the institution by an individual, the Police Department shall be notified, and the supervisor investigating said incident will cooperate fully with the Police Department. The officer who actually finds contraband will be a witness if any criminal proceeding is instituted. All serious contraband will be turned over to the Police Department and a voucher received for same. The supervisor will conduct a complete investigation of all discoveries of serious contraband received in packages, and submit proper reports to the head of the institution.

6. System of Appeals for Those Inmates Denied Packages or Contents Thereof

Any inmate who has been denied a package or any article included in a package and has been informed of this by the mailroom officer may request Form P-111, fill out same, and return it to the mailroom officer. This is a form of appeal and must be forwarded to the A/D/W-A/D/S in charge of security, who will investigate the complaint and render a decision on the complaint. The inmate must be interviewed by the A/D/W or A/D/S or a designated person, who will inform him/her of the reason for the denial, and the security Deputy's decision. If the inmate tells the security Deputy he/she wishes to appeal, a copy of the decision and Form P-111 will be forwarded to the D/S or D/W for a final decision. If no appeal is requested after the interview and rendering of the A/D/W-A/D/S - decision, or at the conclusion or final decision by the D/W - D/S, Form P-111 and the written copy of the decision will be filed in the inmate's folder.

7. Procedure for Receiving Special Permission for Items or Articles Not Generally Allowed the Institutional Population, Before the Package is Received

An inmate wishing to receive a specific item who has a legitimate need, may write to the head of the institution stating the need, if the item is not generally allowed in the institution. When determined necessary by the head of the institution, the inmate will be asked to submit a professional opinion substantiating the need. The request and substantiation will be submitted to a review board and their determination will be forwarded to the head of the institution for his/her approval. Only upon receipt of the approval of the head of the institution will special permission be given for possession of a specific item or article.

13. According to the above directive, which one of the following is NOT a condition for receiving a package in an institution of the Department?   13.____

   A. All packages must be weighed and logged in an effort to control the aggregate weight of packages received by each inmate at an institution.
   B. Packages may be brought to the institution by individuals during visiting hours only.
   C. If a package has been determined acceptable by a custodial officer, the inmate shall inspect the package, sign for it, and take possession of it.
   D. The log maintained by the mailroom officer is the institutional substantiation that the inmate has received the package.

14. According to the above directive, which one of the following is NOT a valid statement regarding acceptability of items in packages received for inmates in institutions of the Department?   14.____

   A. Money, jewelry, and medications are not to be accepted in packages.
   B. Prescription eyeglasses can be accepted by the institution before they are approved and inspected by the institutional physician.
   C. Shaving utensils which meet the guidelines established by the head of the institution may be acceptable when received in packages.
   D. The institutional clothing card must be consulted when determining whether to accept clothing in packages.

15. According to the above directive, which one of the following statements is NOT valid concerning actions to be taken when postal regulations or prison contraband laws are violated while sending or delivering packages to an institution?

    A. The officer who discovers serious contraband in a package, whether delivered to an institution by an individual or mailed through the postal authorities, is a witness as far as the Department is concerned.
    B. The supervisor responsible for investigating the discovery of serious contraband in a package brought to the institution by a visitor must notify the Director of Operations immediately.
    C. All serious contraband must be turned over to the Police Department and vouchered, whether or not criminal proceedings are instituted.
    D. The supervisor responsible for investigating the discovery of serious contraband in a package brought to the institution must submit his/her report to the head of the institution.

16. According to the above directive, which one of the following is a VALID statement concerning an application for special permission to receive an article not generally allowed in an institution?

    A. A professional opinion substantiating the need for the item requested must accompany the application for special permission to receive said item.
    B. A review board, upon receipt of the application and professional opinion substantiating the need for the item, will render a final decision.
    C. An inmate wishing to receive a special item, for any reason, may write to the head of the institution.
    D. The head of the institution may approve, for use by a specific inmate, a specific item or article which is not generally permitted in the institution.

Questions 17-19.

DIRECTIONS: Questions 17 through 19 are to be answered SOLELY on the basis of the following passage.

In collaboration with operating staff and research social scientists, the statistician should be responsible for installing standard measures of achievement in the information system. Reliability of measurements used by the system should be reviewed periodically. This review will be especially important if predictive devices are installed to facilitate comparison of expectations with observed outcomes.

This evaluation technique is well suited to standardized use by information systems. A standard base expectancy table is established to predict results of programs for groups, using criteria such as recidivism or completion of training. Such a device will be capable of assigning any given subject to a class of like subjects grouped by the statistical weighting of aggregated characteristics. Group expectancy for success or failure as determined by recidivism or other criteria can be expressed in percentiles.

Use of base expectancies for comparison with observed outcomes may be thought of as a *soft* method of evaluation. But its economy, in comparison with the classical control group procedure, is considerable. It eliminates the need for routine management of research controls over extended periods. Comparison of predicted with observed outcome affords a rough estimate of program effectiveness. For example, if the average expected recidivism of a group of offenders exposed to a behavior modification program is 50 percent, but the observed outcome is 25 percent, a *prima facie* indication of program effectiveness is established.

Such an indication affords the administrator some assurance that a program seriously subjected to a controlled evaluation with similar results is continuing to be effective. It may also provide a rough estimate of the value of a program that has not been evaluated under the control group method. This kind of evaluation has many limitations. A predictive device is valid only to the extent that the group observed is typical of the population used as the basis for the standard. A second objection to the use of predictive devices in evaluation rests on the tendency of the predictive bases to deteriorate. The applicability of a prediction under circumstances prevailing in year one will not necessarily be the same circumstance prevailing in year ten. Accordingly, it is good practice to audit the accuracy of the predictive device at least every five years to assure that the circumstances are the same. A final objection is that predictive devices can be used only for global indications of program effectiveness.

17. Of the following, the KEY element in the traditional approach to program evaluation that would NOT be used in the approach described in the passage is 17.____

    A. computers
    B. recidivism rates
    C. standard populations
    D. control groups

18. Of the following, the MOST appropriate title for the above passage is 18.____

    A. HOW TO PREDICT THE RESULTS OF PROGRAM EVALUATIONS
    B. A *SOFT* METHOD OF PROGRAM EVALUATION
    C. THE USE OF PREDICTIVE DEVICES IN PROGRAM EVALUATION
    D. COOPERATION BETWEEN THE STATISTICIAN AND OPERATING STAFF

19. All of the following statements describe limitations of using predictive devices to evaluate programs for the first time EXCEPT: 19.____

    A. The group under study must be typical of the group used to develop the predictive device.
    B. Predictive devices can be used only for global indications of program effectiveness.
    C. Predictive devices are more expensive to use than classical control group procedure.
    D. The circumstances prevailing in the year of the study must be the same as in the year the predictive device was developed.

Questions 20-25.

DIRECTIONS: Questions 20 through 25 are to be answered SOLELY on the basis of the following passage.

At present, in State X, whole classes of offenders are retained at unnecessarily close and expensive levels of confinement and supervision because the various decision-makers involved are required to make predictions about the future behavior of offenders which cannot, given the present state of social science, be made accurately. Items such as social and psychological history, changes in attitude, estimates of institutional progress, and anticipation of constructive responses to parole supervision are particularly useless as evaluative criteria in the disposition of offenders because such subjective evaluations are rooted in the attitudes of the appraiser and in the constructive tendencies of bureaucracies.

The result has been that while probation is used extensively (chiefly because institutions are overcrowded) parole board policy has become increasingly cautious and expensive. Although the initial choice between probation and commitment to prison is often arbitrary, the offender thus committed tends to remain incarcerated for long periods. Because the absence of a clear, positive, and legislatively authorized parole policy is a fundamental obstacle to the reallocation of funds, and because the decision problems involved are repeated at each level of the correctional system, the Committee on Criminal Penalties examined the state parole policy. It then presented model legislation which required that offenders committed to prison be automatically released to parole at expiration of the statutory minimum parole-eligible period (often only six months under present law), unless their individual histories contained substantial evidence of past serious violence. The resulting institutional savings were to be devoted chiefly to improving parole services and subsidies for improvements in local law enforcement agencies.

The basic intent of the legislation was to substitute clearly defined statutory ineligibility for release criteria based on the past actions of offenders for the present administratively defined eligibility criteria that necessarily rely on predictive data of highly questionable validity. By requiring the early release of any offender not shown to be clearly ineligible, the act would essentially remove responsibility for the disposition of doubtful cases from the parole authorities and return it to the courts.

20. Of the following, the MOST suitable title for the above passage is

   A. THE REASONS FOR GRANTING PAROLE
   B. THE COMMITTEE ON CRIMINAL PENALTIES
   C. DECISION PROBLEMS IN CORRECTIONS
   D. A NEW APPROACH IN PAROLE POLICY

21. According to the above passage, which of the following is NOT a true statement about the present correctional system in State X?

   A. Many offenders are retained at unnecessarily close and expensive levels of confinement and supervision.
   B. The offenders committed to prison tend to remain incarcerated for long periods.
   C. Probation has become more and more extensive in application chiefly because institutions are overcrowded.
   D. When reviewing cases, parole authorities often use objective criteria like the social and psychological history of inmates.

22. According to the above passage, one change from the present system of parole which would result from the enactment of the proposed system of parole is that

   A. criminals could be paroled after the minimum parole eligibility period
   B. offenders who committed serious violent acts would automatically be paroled after a specified amount of time
   C. institutions would become overcrowded
   D. responsibility for parole in doubtful cases would essentially be given to the court rather than the parole authorities

23. According to the proposed method of determining parole, an inmate would be paroled after a specified period

    A. unless ineligible by administrative criteria
    B. unless ineligible by specific legislative criteria
    C. if eligible according to administrative criteria
    D. if eligible according to specific legislative criteria

24. Under the proposed method of determining parole, parole would be granted or denied depending on the inmate's

    A. past actions
    B. present behavior
    C. present psychological adjustment
    D. probable future actions

25. According to the above passage, the one of the following that is NOT a primary reason why the Committee on Criminal Penalties presented the legislation described above was to

    A. set objective criteria for parole
    B. expedite the reallocation of funds
    C. eliminate arbitrary commitment to prison
    D. prevent overlong commitment of many inmates

KEY (CORRECT ANSWERS)

1.	C	11.	C
2.	A	12.	B
3.	B	13.	D
4.	D	14.	C
5.	C	15.	B
6.	C	16.	D
7.	D	17.	D
8.	C	18.	C
9.	B	19.	C
10.	B	20.	D

21. D
22. D
23. B
24. A
25. C

PREPARING WRITTEN MATERIAL
EXAMINATION SECTION
TEST 1

Questions 1-15.

DIRECTIONS: For each of Questions 1 through 15, select from the options given below the MOST applicable choice, and mark your answer accordingly.
    A. The sentence is correct.
    B. The sentence contains a spelling error only.
    C. The sentence contains an English grammar error only.
    D. The sentence contains both a spelling error and an English grammar error.

1. He is a very dependible person whom we expect will be an asset to this division. 1.____

2. An investigator often finds it necessary to be very diplomatic when conducting an interview. 2.____

3. Accurate detail is especially important if court action results from an investigation. 3.____

4. The report was signed by him and I since we conducted the investigation jointly. 4.____

5. Upon receipt of the complaint, an inquiry was begun. 5.____

6. An employee has to organize his time so that he can handle his workload efficiantly. 6.____

7. It was not apparent that anyone was living at the address given by the client. 7.____

8. According to regulations, there is to be at least three attempts made to locate the client. 8.____

9. Neither the inmate nor the correction officer was willing to sign a formal statement. 9.____

10. It is our opinion that one of the persons interviewed were lying. 10.____

11. We interviewed both clients and departmental personel in the course of this investigation. 11.____

12. It is concievable that further research might produce additional evidence. 12.____

13. There are too many occurences of this nature to ignore. 13.____

87

14. We cannot accede to the candidate's request.   14._____

15. The submission of overdue reports is the reason that there was a delay in completion of this investigation.   15._____

Questions 16-25.

DIRECTIONS: Each of Questions 16 through 25 may be classified under one of the following four categories:
    A. Faulty because of incorrect grammar or sentence structure.
    B. Faulty because of incorrect punctuation.
    C. Faulty because of incorrect spelling.
    D. Correct

Examine each sentence carefully to determine under which of the above four options it is best classified. Then, in the space at the right, write the letter preceding the option which is the BEST of the four suggested above. Each incorrect sentence contains but one type of error. Consider a sentence to be correct if it contains none of the types of errors mentioned, even though there may be other correct ways of expressing the same thought.

16. Although the department's supply of scratch pads and stationary have diminished considerably, the allotment for our division has not been reduced.   16._____

17. You have not told us whom you wish to designate as your secretary.   17._____

18. Upon reading the minutes of the last meeting, the new proposal was taken up for consideration.   18._____

19. Before beginning the discussion, we locked the door as a precautionery measure.   19._____

20. The supervisor remarked, "Only those clerks, who perform routine work, are permitted to take a rest period."   20._____

21. Not only will this duplicating machine make accurate copies, but it will also produce a quantity of work equal to fifteen transcribing typists.   21._____

22. "Mr. Jones," said the supervisor, "we regret our inability to grant you an extention of your leave of absence.   22._____

23. Although the employees find the work monotonous and fatigueing, they rarely complain.   23._____

24. We completed the tabulation of the receipts on time despite the fact that Miss Smith our fastest operator was absent for over a week.   24._____

25. The reaction of the employees who attended the meeting, as well as the reaction of those who did not attend, indicates clearly that the schedule is satisfactory to everyone concerned.

25._____

KEY (CORRECT ANSWERS)

1.	D		11.	B
2.	A		12.	B
3.	A		13.	B
4.	C		14.	A
5.	A		15.	C
6.	B		16.	A
7.	B		17.	D
8.	C		18.	A
9.	A		19.	C
10.	C		20.	B

21. A
22. C
23. C
24. B
25. D

TEST 2

Questions 1-15.

DIRECTIONS: Questions 1 through 15 consist of two sentences. Some are correct according to ordinary formal English usage. Others are incorrect because they contain errors in English usage, spelling, or punctuation. Consider a sentence correct if it contains no errors in English usage, spelling, or punctuation, even if there may be other ways of writing the sentence correctly. Mark your answer:
    A. If only sentence I is correct.
    B. If only sentence II is correct.
    C. If sentences 1 and II are correct.
    D. If neither sentence I nor II is correct.

1. I. The influence of recruitment efficiency upon administrative standards is readily apparant.
   II. Rapid and accurate thinking are an essential quality of the police officer.

2. I. The administrator of a police department is constantly confronted by the demands of subordinates for increased personnel in their respective units.
   II. Since a chief executive must work within well-defined fiscal limits, he must weigh the relative importance of various requests.

3. I. The two men whom the police arrested for a parking violation were wanted for robbery in three states.
   II. Strong executive control from the top to the bottom of the enterprise is one of the basic principals of police administration.

4. I. When he gave testimony unfavorable to the defendant loyalty seemed to mean very little.
   II. Having run off the road while passing a car, the patrolman gave the driver a traffic ticket.

5. I. The judge ruled that the defendant's conversation with his doctor was a privileged communication.
   II. The importance of our training program is widely recognized; however, fiscal difficulties limit the program's effectiveness.

6. I. Despite an increase in patrol coverage, there were less arrests for crimes against property this year.
   II. The investigators could hardly have expected greater cooperation from the public.

7. I. Neither the patrolman nor the witness could identify the defendant as the driver of the car.
   II. Each of the officers in the class received their certificates at the completion of the course.

8. I. The new commander made it clear that those kind of procedures would no longer be permitted.
    II. Giving some weight to performance records is more advisable than making promotions solely on the basis of test scores.

9. I. A deputy sheriff must ascertain whether the debtor, has any property.
    II. A good deputy sheriff does not cause histerical excitement when he executes a process.

10. I. Having learned that he has been assigned a judgment debtor, the deputy sheriff should call upon him.
    II. The deputy sheriff may seize and remove property without requiring a bond.

11. I. If legal procedures are not observed, the resulting contract is not enforseable.
    II. If the directions from the creditor's attorney are not in writing, the deputy sheriff should request a letter of instructions from the attorney.

12. I. The deputy sheriff may confer with the defendant and enter this defendants' place of business.
    II. A deputy sheriff must ascertain from the creditor's attorney whether the debtor has any property against which he may proceede.

13. I. The sheriff has a right to do whatever is necessary for the purpose of executing the order of the court.
    II. The written order of the court gives the sheriff general authority and he is governed in his acts by a very simple principal.

14. I. Either the patrolman or his sergeant are always ready to help the public.
    II. The sergeant asked the patrolman when he would finish the report.

15. I. The injured man could not hardly talk.
    II. Every officer had ought to had in their reports on time.

Questions 16-26.

DIRECTIONS: For each of the sentences given below, numbered 16 through 25, select from the following choices the MOST correct choice and print your choice in the space at the right. Select as your answer:
- A. If the statement contains an unnecessary word or expression
- B. If the statement contains a slang term or expression ordinarily not acceptable in government report writing.
- C. If the statement contains an old-fashioned word or expression, where a concrete, plain term would be more useful.
- D. If the statement contains no major faults.

16. Every one of us should try harder.

17. Yours of the first instant has been received.

18. We will have to do a real snow job on him. 18.____
19. I shall contact him next Thursday. 19.____
20. None of us were invited to the meeting with the community. 20.____
21. We got this here job to do. 21.____
22. She could not help but see the mistake in the checkbook. 22.____
23. Don't bug the Director about the report. 23.____
24. I beg to inform you that your letter has been received. 24.____
25. This project is all screwed up. 25.____

KEY (CORRECT ANSWERS)

1.	D		11.	B
2.	C		12.	D
3.	A		13.	A
4.	D		14.	D
5.	B		15.	D
6.	B		16.	D
7.	A		17.	C
8.	D		18.	B
9.	D		19.	D
10.	C		20.	D

21.	B
22.	D
23.	B
24.	C
25.	B

TEST 3

DIRECTIONS: Questions 1 through 25 are sentences taken from reports. Some are correct according to ordinary English usage. Others are incorrect because they contain errors in English usage, spelling, or punctuation. Consider a sentence correct if it contains no errors in English usage, spelling, or punctuation, even if there may be other ways of writing the sentence correctly. Mark your answer:
- A. If only sentence I is correct
- B. If only sentence II is correct
- C. If sentences I and II are correct
- D. If neither sentence I nor II is correct

1.
   I. The Neighborhood Police Team Commander and Team Patrolmen are encouraged to give to the public the widest possible verbal and written disemination of information regarding the existence and purposes of the program.
   II. The police must be vitally interelated with every segment of the public they serve.

2.
   I. If social gambling, prostitution, and other vices are to be prohibited, the law makers should provide the manpower and method for enforcement.
   II. In addition to checking on possible crime locations such as hallways, roofs yards and other similar locations, Team Patrolmen are encouraged to make known their presence to members of the community.

3.
   I. The Neighborhood Police Team Commander is authorized to secure, the cooperation of local publications, as well as public and private agencies, to further the goals of the program.
   II. Recruitment from social minorities is essential to effective police work among minorities and meaningful relations with them.

4.
   I. The Neighborhood Police Team Commander and his men have the responsibility for providing patrol service within the sector territory on a twenty-four hour basis.
   II. While the patrolman was walking his beat at midnight he noticed that the clothing stores' door was partly open.

5.
   I. Authority is granted to the Neighborhood Police Team to device tactics for coping with the crime in the sector.
   II. Before leaving the scene of the accident, the patrolman drew a map showing the positions of the automobiles and indicated the time of the accident as 10 M. in the morning.

6.
   I. The Neighborhood Police Team Commander and his men must be kept apprised of conditions effecting their sector.
   II. Clear, continuous communication with every segment of the public served based on the realization of mutual need and founded on trust and confidence is the basis for effective law enforcement.

7. I. The irony is that the police are blamed for the laws they enforce when they are doing their duty.
    II. The Neighborhood Police Team Commander is authorized to prepare and distribute literature with pertinent information telling the public whom to contact for assistance.

8. I. The day is not far distant when major parts of the entire police compliment will need extensive college training or degrees.
    II. Although driving under the influence of alcohol is a specific charge in making arrests, drunkeness is basically a health and social problem.

9. I. If a deputy sheriff finds that property he has to attach is located on a ship, he should notify his supervisor.
    II. Any contract that tends to interfere with the administration of justice is illegal.

10. I. A mandate or official order of the court to the sheriff or other officer directs it to take into possession property of the judgment debtor.
    II. Tenancies from month-to-month, week-to-week, and sometimes year-to-year are termenable.

11. I. A civil arrest is an arrest pursuant to an order issued by a court in civil litigation.
    II. In a criminal arrest, a defendant is arrested for a crime he is alleged to have committed.

12. I. Having taken a defendant into custody, there is a complete restraint of personal liberty.
    II. Actual force is unnecessary when a deputy sheriff makes an arrest.

13. I. When a husband breaches a separation agreement by failing to supply to the wife the amount of money to be paid to her periodically under the agreement, the same legal steps may be taken to enforce his compliance as in any other breach of contract.
    II. Having obtained the writ of attachment, the plaintiff is then in the advantageous position of selling the very property that has been held for him by the sheriff while he was obtaining a judgment.

14. I. Being locked in his desk, the investigator felt sure that the records would be safe.
    II. The reason why the witness changed his statement was because he had been threatened.

15. I. The investigation had just began then an important witness disappeared.
    II. The check that had been missing was located and returned to its owner, Harry Morgan, a resident of Suffolk County, New York.

16. I. A supervisor will find that the establishment of standard procedures enables his staff to work more efficiently.
    II. An investigator hadn't ought to give any recommendations in his report if he is in doubt.

16.____

17. I. Neither the investigator nor his supervisor is ready to interview the witness.
    II. Interviewing has been and always will be an important asset in investigation.

17.____

18. I. One of the investigator's reports has been forwarded to the wrong person.
    II. The investigator stated that he was not familiar with those kind of cases.

18.____

19. I. Approaching the victim of the assault, two large bruises were noticed by me.
    II. The prisoner was arrested for assault, resisting arrest, and use of a deadly weapon.

19.____

20. I. A copy of the orders, which had been prepared by the captain, was given to each patrolman.
    II. It's always necessary to inform an arrested person of his constitutional rights before asking him any questions.

20.____

21. I. To prevent further bleeding, I applied a tourniquet to the wound.
    II. John Rano a senior officer was on duty at the time of the accident.

21.____

22. I. Limiting the term "property" to tangible property, in the criminal mischief setting, accords with prior case law holding that only tangible property came within the purview of the offense of malicious mischief.
    II. Thus, a person who intentionally destroys the property of another, but under an honest belief that he has title to such property, cannot be convicted of criminal mischief under the Revised Penal Law.

22.____

23. I. Very early in it's history, New York enacted statutes from time to time punishing, either as a felony or as a misdemeanor, malicious injuries to various kinds of property: piers, boos, dams, bridges, etc.
    II. The application of the statute is necessarily restricted to trespassory takings with larcenous intent: namely with intent permanently or virtually permanently to "appropriate" property or "deprive" the owner of its use.

23.____

24. I. Since the former Penal Law did not define the instruments of forgery in a general fashion, its crime of forgery was held to be narrower than the common law offense in this respect and to embrace only those instruments explicitly specified in the substantive provisions.
    II. After entering the barn through an open door for the purpose of stealing, it was closed by the defendants.

24.____

25. I. The use of fire or explosives to destroy tangible property is proscribed by the criminal mischief provisions of the Revised Penal Law.
    II. The defendant's taking of a taxicab for the immediate purpose of affecting his escape did not constitute grand larceny.

25.____

KEY (CORRECT ANSWERS)

1.	D	11.	C
2.	D	12.	B
3.	B	13.	C
4.	A	14.	D
5.	D	15.	B
6.	D	16.	A
7.	C	17.	C
8.	D	18.	A
9.	C	19.	B
10.	D	20.	C

21.	A
22.	C
23.	B
24.	A
25.	A

TEST 4

Questions 1-4.

DIRECTIONS: Each of the two sentences in Questions 1 through 4 may be correct or may contain errors in punctuation, capitalization, or grammar. Mark your answer:
- A. If there is an error only in sentence I
- B. If there is an error only in sentence II
- C. If there is an error in both sentences I and II
- D. If both sentences are correct.

1. I. It is very annoying to have a pencil sharpener, which is not in working order.
   II. Patrolman Blake checked the door of Joe's Restaurant and found that the lock has been jammed.

2. I. When you are studying a good textbook is important.
   II. He said he would divide the money equally between you and me.

3. I. Since he went on the city council a year ago, one of his primary concerns has been safety in the streets.
   II. After waiting in the doorway for about 15 minutes, a black sedan appeared.

Questions 4-8.

DIRECTIONS: Each of the sentences in Questions 4 through 8 may be classified under one of the following four categories:
- A. Faulty because of incorrect grammar
- B. Faulty because of incorrect punctuation
- C. Faulty because of incorrect capitalization or incorrect spelling
- D. Correct

Examine each sentence carefully to determine under which of the above four options it is BEST classified. Then, in the space at the right, print the capitalized letter preceding the option which is the BEST of the four suggested above. Each faulty sentence contains but one type of error. Consider a sentence to be correct if it contains none of the types of errors mentioned, even though there may be other correct ways of expressing the same thought.

4. They told both he and I that the prisoner had escaped.

5. Any superior officer, who, disregards the just complaints of his subordinates, is remiss in the performance of his duty.

6. Only those members of the national organization who resided in the Middle west attended the conference in Chicago.

7. We told him to give the investigation assignment to whoever was available.

8. Please do not disappoint and embarass us by not appearing in court.

Questions 9-13

DIRECTIONS: Each of Questions 9 through 13 consists of three sentences lettered A, B, and C. In each of these questions, one of the sentences may contain an error in grammar, sentence structure, or punctuation, or all three sentences may be correct. If one of the sentence in a question contains an error in grammar, sentence structure, or punctuation, print in the space at the right the capital letter preceding the sentence which contains the error. If all three sentences are correct, print the letter D.

9. A. Mr. Smith appears to be less competent than I in performing these duties.
   B. The supervisor spoke to the employee, who had made the error, but did not reprimand him.
   C. When he found the book lying on the table, he immediately notified the owner.

9._____

10. A. Being locked in the desk, we were certain that the papers would not be taken.
    B. It wasn't I who dictated the telegram; I believe it was Eleanor.
    C. You should interview whoever comes to the office today.

10._____

11. A. The clerk was instructed to set the machine on the table before summoning the manager.
    B. He said that he was not familiar with those kind of activities.
    C. A box of pencils, in addition to erasers and blotters, was included in the shipment of supplies.

11._____

12. A. The supervisor remarked, "Assigning an employee to the proper type of work is not always easy."
    B. The employer found that each of the applicants were qualified to perform the duties of the position.
    C. Any competent student is permitted to take this course if he obtains the consent of the instructor.

12._____

13. A. The prize was awarded to the employee whom the judges believed to be most deserving.
    B. Since the instructor believes his book is the better of the two, he is recommending it for use in the school.
    C. It was obvious to the employees that the completion of the task by the scheduled date would require their working overtime.

13._____

Questions 14-20.

DIRECTIONS: In answering Questions 14 through 20, choose the sentence which is BEST from the point of view of English usage suitable for a business report.

14. A. The client's receiving of public assistance checks at two different addresses were disclosed by the investigation.
    B. The investigation disclosed that the client was receiving public assistance checks at two different addresses.
    C. The client was found out by the investigation to be receiving public assistance checks at two different addresses.
    D. The client has been receiving public assistance checks at two different addresses, disclosed the investigation.

    14.____

15. A. The investigation of complaints are usually handled by this unit, which deals with internal security problems in the department.
    B. This unit deals with internal security problems in the department usually investigating complaints.
    C. Investigating complaints is this unit's job, being that it handles internal security problems in the department.
    D. This unit deals with internal security problems in the department and usually investigates complaints.

    15.____

16. A. The delay in completing this investigation was caused by difficulty in obtaining the required documents from the candidate.
    B. Because of difficulty in obtaining the required documents from the candidate is the reason that there was a delay in completing this investigation.
    C. Having had difficulty in obtaining the required documents from the candidate, there was a delay in completing this investigation.
    D. Difficulty in obtaining the required documents from the candidate had the affect of delaying the completion of this investigation.

    16.____

17. A. This report, together with documents supporting our recommendation, are being submitted for your approval.
    B. Documents supporting our recommendation is being submitted with the report for your approval.
    C. This report, together with documents supporting our recommendation, is being submitted for your approval.
    D. The report and documents supporting our recommendation is being submitted for your approval.

    17.____

18. A. The chairman himself, rather than his aides, has reviewed the report.
    B. The chairman himself, rather than his aides, have reviewed the report.
    C. The chairmen, not the aide, has reviewed the report.
    D. The aide, not the chairmen, have reviewed the report.

    18.____

19. A. Various proposals were submitted but the decision is not been made.
    B. Various proposals has been submitted but the decision has not been made.
    C. Various proposals were submitted but the decision is not been made.
    D. Various proposals have been submitted but the decision has not been made.

19.____

20. A. Everyone were rewarded for his successful attempt.
    B. They were successful in their attempts and each of them was rewarded.
    C. Each of them are rewarded for their successful attempts.
    D. The reward for their successful attempts were made to each of them.

20.____

21. The following is a paragraph from a request for departmental recognition consisting of five numbered sentences submitted to a Captain for review. These sentences may or may not have errors in spelling, grammar, and punctuation:
    (1) The officers observed the subject Mills surreptitiously remove a wallet from the woman's handbag and entered his automobile. (2) As they approached Mills, he looked in their direction and drove away. (3) The officers pursued in their car. (4) Mills executed a series of complicated manuvers to evade the pursuing officers. (5) At the corner of Broome and Elizabeth Streets, Mills stopped the car, got out, raised his hands and surrendered to the officers. Which one of the following BEST classifies the above with regard to spelling, grammar, and punctuation?
    A. 1, 2, and 3 are correct, but 4 and 5 have errors.
    B. 2, 3, and 5 are correct, but 1 and 4 have errors.
    C. 3, 4, and 5 are correct, but 1 and 2 have errors.
    D. 1, 2, 3, and 5 are correct, but 4 has errors.

21.____

22. The one of the following sentences which is grammatically PREFERABLE to the others is:
    A. Our engineers will go over your blueprints so that you may have no problems in construction.
    B. For a long time he had been arguing that we, not he, are to blame for the confusion.
    C. I worked on his automobile for two hours and still cannot find out what is wrong with it.
    D. Accustomed to all kinds of hardships, fatigue seldom bothers veteran policemen.

22.____

23. The MOST accurate of the following sentences is:
    A. The commissioner, as well as his deputy and various bureau heads, were present.
    B. A new organization of employers and employees have been formed.
    C. One or the other of these men have been selected.
    D. The number of pages in the book is enough to discourage a reader.

23.____

24. The MOST accurate of the following sentences is:
 A. Between you and me, I think he is the better man.
 B. He was believed to be me.
 C. Is it us that you wish to see?
 D. The winners are him and her.

24.____

KEY (CORRECT ANSWERS)

1.	C	11.	B
2.	A	12.	B
3.	C	13.	D
4.	A	14.	B
5.	B	15.	D
6.	C	16.	A
7.	D	17.	C
8.	C	18.	A
9.	B	19.	D
10.	A	20.	B

21. B
22. A
23. D
24. A

EXAMINATION SECTION
TEST 1

DIRECTIONS: Each question or incomplete statement is followed by several suggested answers or completions. Select the one that BEST answers the question or completes the statement. *PRINT THE LETTER OF THE CORRECT ANSWER IN THE SPACE AT THE RIGHT.*

1. In general, the one of the following which an officer should NOT do in delegating decision-making authority is to

    A. insure that the activities of his subordinates conform to patterns of behavior consistent with organizational needs
    B. assume that his decisions may not be so good as those of his subordinates
    C. permit his subordinates to undertake whatever action they consider appropriate
    D. set the goals and let his subordinates decide how to achieve them

1.____

2. Assume that, in order to motivate his subordinates and promote efficiency in his command, a supervisor uses a strong *no nonsense* approach and deliberately puts pressure on his men to achieve goals much higher than he can reasonably expect them to meet. Of the following, the MOST likely result of the supervisor's approach is that the men will

    A. concentrate heavily on long-range tasks at the expense of those more immediately at hand
    B. become frustrated and be motivated to band together to *beat the system*
    C. begin to set for themselves and achieve even higher goals than those set by the supervisor
    D. perform their tasks more efficiently than routine housekeeping or maintenance work

2.____

3. *Filtering of information* occurs when information is changed as one individual communicates it to another. Filtering often occurs when a subordinate passes on information to his superior. This generally occurs because the subordinate desires to please his boss. Which one of the following states BOTH whether or not filtering is an advantage or disadvantage and also the best reason therefor? It is a(n)

    A. *advantage* because it keeps a superior from bogging down with too much information
    B. *advantage* because it helps the superior to judge his subordinate's powers of discrimination
    C. *disadvantage* because an officer may inadvertently filter out information that is important for his superior to have
    D. *disadvantage* because it places too much responsibility on a subordinate to be aware of what pleases his superior

3.____

4. Which one of the following abilities MOST differentiates a supervisor who is an effective leader from one who is not an effective leader?
The ability to

    A. exercise his authority fairly
    B. establish strong personal relationships with subordinates

4.____

C. consider the job related problems of his men as his most important problem
D. fulfill the individual needs of his subordinates in addition to fulfilling the department's goals

5. Which one of the following BEST states the most appropriate attitude for a supervisor to take with regard to the individual personal goals of his subordinates?
The supervisor should

   A. not be concerned with the individual personal goals of his subordinates under any circumstances
   B. support only those individual personal goals of his subordinates which are job related in nature
   C. support individual personal goals of his subordinates as long as they do not interfere with the overall objectives of the department
   D. not be concerned with the individual personal goals of his subordinates unless they clearly conflict with the overall objectives of the department

6. *The supervisor who is responsible to several superiors is in an advantageous position since he has the benefit of intimate contacts with more people in higher positions.* This statement is GENERALLY

   A. *false* because a supervisor should not normally be directly responsible to more than one superior at the same time
   B. *true* since the supervisor is in a position to learn more about the overall operation of the agency
   C. *false* because there is a tendency in such a case for the supervisor to lose touch with his own subordinates
   D. *true* since he can sometimes receive more favorable treatment for his subordinates by judicious use of such contacts

7. In his supervisory relations with newly-appointed men, the superior would *generally* be acting MOST properly when he

   A. avoids pointing out specific errors in performance and makes only general and constructive criticism
   B. quickly corrects every error made by the employee as soon as he observes the error
   C. compliments the employee for specific acts rather than for overall good work
   D. withholds correction of all but the most serious errors of job performance until the employee is more experienced and better able to accept and evaluate such corrections

8. The factor which makes the supervisory activity of the second-line supervisor more difficult than that of the first-line supervisor is that the second-line supervisor

   A. usually is required to establish uniform practices and coordinate work functions of several units
   B. must initiate disciplinary procedures more often
   C. is less aware of the training needs of those at the operating level
   D. is answerable to those of higher rank in the organizational hierarchy

9. Of the following possible reasons why a subordinate may be reluctant to accept additional delegated authority, the one which is MOST subject to effective solution by a supervisory officer's efforts is that the subordinate

   A. does not have the necessary information to do a good job
   B. finds it easier to ask his supervisor than to decide for himself how to handle a problem
   C. has a fear of being criticized by his superior when he has made a mistake
   D. is lacking in self-confidence

10. The number of subordinates who can be supervised DIRECTLY and MOST EFFECTIVELY by one supervisor tends to

    A. *decrease* as the number and difficulty of tasks performed by subordinates *increase*
    B. *increase* as the leadership ability of the supervisor *decreases*
    C. *decrease* as the job knowledge and experience of subordinates *increase*
    D. *increase* as the distance separating the supervisor's work location from the work locations of his subordinates *increases*

11. In handling any problem, experts recommend that a supervisor use the following four-step procedure in reaching a sound decision, but not in the order given:
    I. Take action
    II. Get all the facts
    III. Weigh and decide
    IV. Recognize the problem

    Which one of the following choices indicates the CORRECT order of the above four procedural steps in handling any problem?

    A. II, IV, I, III
    B. IV, II, III, I
    C. I, IV, II, III
    D. II, III, IV, I

12. Which of the following statements expresses a PROPER supervisory technique for dealing with mistakes made by subordinates?

    A. When you catch a mistake, let the subordinate know you are really angry immediately.
    B. Make sure the subordinate understands just what he did that was wrong and what he should have done instead.
    C. It does not hurt to exaggerate the seriousness of the error you are criticizing in order to make sure your point sinks in.
    D. Hold your criticism until you see whether the subordinate can correct the situation himself; if he doesn't, then you will have several complaints to hit him with.

13. There are many lines of work, particularly in administration, where measuring production is thought to be inapplicable because of the nature of the work.
    For the authority, this is, in general,

    A. *true;* the authority was established primarily to render a service and is not concerned with making a profit
    B. *false;* work standards can be established wherever organization charts can be prepared

C. *true;* the work of the authority fluctuates widely with the seasons of the year, days of the week, and the time of day
D. *false;* the activities of the authority lend themselves rather well to the setting of performance standards

14. Official memoranda set forth an outline of the grievance procedure and also establish time limits within which action must be taken by various supervisory levels on specific grievance cases.
Such time limits are desirable MAINLY because they

   A. give more latitude to the employee in the actual presentation of his grievance to management
   B. make unlikely the use of the grievance machinery for the adjudication of petty or imagined grievances
   C. permit management to prepare a more precise answer to the employee who has a grievance
   D. recognize the importance of settling employee grievances without undue delay

15. An estimate of employee morale could LEAST effectively be appraised by

   A. checking accident and absenteeism records
   B. determining the attitudes of employees toward their job
   C. examining the number of requests for emergency leaves of absence
   D. observing general housekeeping practices

16. Hearing and grievance boards require specific evidence of offenses and infractions with full particulars as to times, dates, and places.
In addition, such boards most importantly desire assurance that the supervisor instituting the charges has FIRST

   A. assured himself that the offender is guilty beyond a reasonable doubt
   B. brought charges against the offender after long and serious reflection
   C. considered the consequences of finding the offender guilty as charged
   D. taken appropriate steps in an attempt to help the offender change his conduct

17. When discussing supervisory or administrative matters, references may be made to *span of control.*
The term *span of control* means MOST NEARLY the

   A. control exercised by the highest policy-making individual or group in an organization
   B. effectiveness of disciplinary procedures in achieving a high work standard
   C. maximum physical distance at which subordinates can be located and still be controlled effectively by a central headquarters office
   D. number of subordinates who can be effectively supervised by one supervisor

18. The one of the following statements which is LEAST accurate with respect to the role of the supervisor is that the supervisor

   A. helps carry out policies which are usually formulated at a higher level
   B. is an element of the supervisory structure closest to the employee

C. is given responsibilities for carrying out definite orders
D. is properly considered a representative of his subordinates but not a part of the management team

19. An obvious display of authority should

    A. be considered a function of the executive or the administrator rather than of the supervisor
    B. be used frequently to develop the supervisor-subordinate relationship
    C. be used when other efforts to secure cooperation have failed
    D. never be used as a method of supervision

20. The one of the following which is LEAST justified as a reason for a supervisor to attempt to help a subordinate in the solution of a very personal problem is that such a personal problem may

    A. be leading to serious disciplinary action for the correction of its consequences
    B. be similar to one experienced by the supervisor himself in the recent past
    C. have affected his work
    D. have affected the morale of the other officers

21. When time is NOT a factor, a supervisor enhances both initiative and cooperation by using which one of the following orders?

    A. Command
    B. Plea
    C. Detailed written instructions
    D. Suggestion

22. The development of a *grapevine* or a *rumor clinic* in an institution is USUALLY the result of

    A. the constant provocation of gossip by a few problem individuals
    B. unofficial approval of this employee activity
    C. lack of adequate communication through official channels
    D. employees' disapproval of the administration

23. Appraisal of an employee during his probationary period by an immediate supervisor who happens to be a personal friend of the employee is

    A. *unacceptable* because familiarity results in favoritism
    B. *unacceptable* because people on probation should not be evaluated by immediate supervisors
    C. *acceptable* because it encourages other employees to perform their duties in a manner satisfactory to the appraiser
    D. *acceptable* because the familiarity of the appraiser helps in a complete evaluation

24. In planning the weekly work routine, it is MOST important for a supervisor to

    A. ask employees which assignments they would prefer
    B. ask for volunteers to perform routine tasks
    C. indicate the daily anticipated attendance
    D. list areas of priority interest

25. Of the following, which is NOT a recommended practice of a supervisor?

    A. Giving reasons for emergency assignments or overtime work
    B. Attempting to detect a deep neurosis by examination of work habits or observation of behavior
    C. Taking corrective disciplinary action when an employee fails to improve his attendance following a corrective interview
    D. Consulting with employees as to the best way of getting a job done

26. When there is general and intentional violation of an official rule of conduct by employees, attention should be focused MOST directly upon finding out what is wrong with the

    A. rule itself
    B. employees violating the rule
    C. organizational objectives
    D. informal channels of communication

27. Of the following statements, which one does NOT express a recognized principle of effective supervision?

    A. Every supervisor should be delegated authority in accordance with his responsibility.
    B. Every supervisor should give his men detailed and frequent instructions whenever he gives them assignments.
    C. Every employee should be treated as an individual.
    D. Each employee at any one time should have one, and only one, immediate supervisor.

28. The following four numbered steps are recognized techniques in job training:
    I. Explain and demonstrate how to do the operation
    II. Let the learner try doing the operation on his own
    III. Explain the purpose and importance of the operation
    IV. Correct errors and omissions as the learner makes them

    Which one of the following choices CORRECTLY indicates the order in which the above four training steps should be performed?

    A. I, III, II, IV
    B. III, I, II, IV
    C. III, II, IV, I
    D. II, I, III, IV

29. In hearings involving employees charged with violations of the department's Code of Discipline, one of the main breaches of discipline is failing to obey orders.
    The CHIEF implication this should have for the officer is that he should

    A. issue orders in writing whenever this is practicable
    B. make assignments to *teams* of men as often as possible so that the men in a team can check each other
    C. make sure his orders are understood and check on their implementation as soon as possible
    D. take disciplinary action promptly for failure to obey orders

30. Suppose that work by your men in the field is sometimes delayed because they wait for you to arrive to make certain decisions before continuing with their work.
As an officer, this should indicate to you the need for

    A. breaking up job assignments into smaller units
    B. developing more initiative in your men
    C. having the men select someone to be in charge if you are not there
    D. issuing complete instructions if you know you are going to be awa

30._____

KEY (CORRECT ANSWERS)

1.	C	16.	D
2.	B	17.	D
3.	C	18.	D
4.	D	19.	C
5.	C	20.	B
6.	A	21.	D
7.	C	22.	C
8.	A	23.	A
9.	A	24.	D
10.	A	25.	B
11.	B	26.	A
12.	B	27.	B
13.	D	28.	B
14.	D	29.	C
15.	C	30.	B

TEST 2

DIRECTIONS: Each question or incomplete statement is followed by several suggested answers or completions. Select the one that BEST answers the question or completes the statement. *PRINT THE LETTER OF THE CORRECT ANSWER IN THE SPACE AT THE RIGHT.*

1. Disciplinary action will in most instances be initiated by the immediate superior of the person to be disciplined. This is so MAINLY because   1.____

    A. it permits the higher superiors to be able to devote most of their attention and effort to broader and more generalized problems of administration
    B. it helps to develop a forceful image of the immediate superior which will serve to prevent other overt acts of misconduct by other subordinates
    C. the immediate superior is the one most qualified to make recommendations as to the severity of punishment to be applied
    D. the immediate superior is usually in the best position to observe derelictions of duty requiring some kind of corrective action

2. The repeated use by a superior officer of a call for volunteers to get a job done is objectionable MAINLY because   2.____

    A. it may create a feeling of animosity between the volunteers and the non-volunteers
    B. it may indicate that the superior is avoiding responsibility for making assignments which will be most productive
    C. it is an indication that the superior is not familiar with the individual capabilities of his men
    D. it is unfair to men who, for valid reasons, do not or cannot volunteer

3. It is a generally accepted principle of supervision that disciplinary action should be taken quickly when it needs to be taken.   3.____
The one of the following statements which BEST supports the taking of prompt disciplinary action is that

    A. the accuracy of official disciplinary records will thereby be insured
    B. the offender is more likely to feel that the disciplinary action will be severe
    C. the supervisor is more likely to remember the details surrounding the offender's breach of discipline
    D. there is an avoidance of the prolonged aggravation caused by later disposition of the case

4. Which one of the following is NOT a recognized guideline for helping supervising officers to become good listeners in face-to-face communications?   4.____

    A. Anticipating what the speaker is going to say before he says it
    B. Recognizing and allowing for the supervisor's own prejudices
    C. Removing sources of distraction as much as possible
    D. Facing and watching the speaker while he talks before answering

5. An employee's performance should be evaluated quarterly during the probationary period and at least once a year after the probationary period.
Of the following, the CHIEF justification for the less frequent formal evaluation of employee performance after the probationary period is that

   A. oversupervision of experienced employees is unnecessary and undesirable and may create resentment on the part of the employee
   B. the employee has already proven himself satisfactory by passing his probationary period
   C. the older employee reacts more quickly and responsive-ly to supervision
   D. the supervisor has already achieved a considerable degree of familiarity with the employee's capabilities, performance, and need for further training

6. Of the following, the MOST important reason why supervisors should give careful consideration to the techniques they utilize for assignment of employees to specific jobs is that

   A. an opportunity is thus offered the supervisor for periodic evaluation of the qualifications and work performance of all employees
   B. efficiency of employees is dependent in part on the techniques used by supervisory officers for selection of employees for assignments
   C. requests of employees for change in work assignments may indicate dissatisfaction with present conditions
   D. standardized techniques for the selection of employees for specific job assignments have not yet been developed

7. A superior officer, investigating why an order had not been carried out, was told by the officers concerned that they had not realized that what the superior officer intended as an order.
This incident illustrates MOST directly an order that was not

   A. concise
   B. possible of performance
   C. recognizable as an order
   D. reviewed after issuance of the order

8. Which of the following is MOST important in correcting unsatisfactory employee behavior?

   A. Assigning the employee to work closely with a more experienced employee
   B. Letting the employee know the most severe penalties for continued unsatisfactory behavior
   C. Getting the employee to admit that there is need for improvement in his behavior
   D. Conducting corrective interviews in groups so that discussions can be uninhibited

9. Which of the following is the KEY to effective decision-making?

   A. Information analysis   B. Operations research
   C. Planning   D. Review

10. Scheduling the work of his group is one of the responsibilities of a supervisor.
The one of the following which is NOT a proper principle of work scheduling is

   A. assigning all the difficult jobs to the better workers
   B. keeping work related by time, space, or function together

C. making sure that all workers have sufficient work to achieve a meaningful day's work
D. assigning a variety of work to teach employees

11. There are four classic stages of teaching a job.
    Of the following, the one which is NOT a classic stage of teaching a job is

    A. application or performance
    B. gradation or progression
    C. preparation or introduction
    D. presentation or demonstration

12. Which of the following statements INCORRECTLY describes the role of a supervisor?

    A. A supervisor communicates to management the weaknesses in existing practices and recommends changes to meet actual conditions.
    B. A supervisor carefully avoids critically appraising the work output of subordinates because to do so would adversely affect morale.
    C. The supervisor accepts responsibility for the work output of subordinates.
    D. The supervisor is the middleman of an organization.

13. Trust, confidence, and respect by employees for their supervisors are built up by actions taken by the supervisor.
    Which one of the following supervisors conducts himself in a way that would PROBABLY be approved?
    Supervisor

    A. *A* is most comfortable when he is paternalistic. He freely gives advice on personal matters and is very interested in his employees' personal problems. He makes it a practice to chat frequently with his people on social subjects.
    B. *B* provides little supervision. He has formed a particularly close friendship with one of his employees who tells him about everything which goes on in the unit.
    C. *C* radiates self-confidence and positiveness. He takes no interest in employee problems. He dislikes employees who complain. Once he makes up his mind, he does not change his views.
    D. *D* is willing to admit his personal inadequacies. He is willing to be frank about existing problems and existing working conditions. His philosophy is that to get you must give.

14. Which of the following statements BEST describes a view of what constitutes discipline?

    A. Discipline is a conditioner which rewards acceptable behavior and punishes unacceptable actions. It is a training procedure up to the point where diminishing results indicate further training is worthless.
    B. Discipline may be viewed as an internal regulating mechanism which constantly scans the various procedural alternatives available in the work situation. The selection of less than the perfect solution should be followed promptly by corrective action.
    C. Discipline may best be described as a subjective procedure. Discipline should not be undertaken without consultation with one's superior.
    D. Plainly described, discipline is a procedure for insuring that departmental rules and regulations are carried out to the letter.

15. With respect to the training function, which of the following CORRECTLY states the position? 15.____

    A. Employee training can be handled very effectively as part of the supervisor-supervised relationship with the supervisor doing the training.
    B. On-the-job training can never be as effective as classroom training because employee supervisors are generally not conscientious listeners.
    C. Supervisors occasionally make effective trainers provided that they receive formal instruction in training techniques and can discipline themselves not to look down upon those who require training.
    D. The major point to be made in favor of training by supervisors is that such training gives supervisors an opportunity to review their own procedures.

16. Assume that a situation arises in your department which will require a considerable amount of overtime work which will be paid for in cash or in time off at the employee's option. One employee has financial problems and wants all the overtime he can get; another states he can work late only two days a week because of social plans; a third employee who is unmarried does not want to work overtime. 16.____
    The principle to be kept in mind in assigning employees to work overtime is that

    A. a discreet assessment must be made of each individual's situation, with overtime being assigned to those in greatest need
    B. if a man cannot work overtime in an agency responsible for the administration of justice, he belongs in another job
    C. it is a poor supervisory practice to ask an employee to work overtime when he does not wish to do so, so long as there is another employee willing to report for duty
    D. whenever overtime may be compensated for in cash, the supervisor should view this as an additional opportunity to reward those who by their loyalty and efficiency have earned the right to overtime work

17. The lecture method of training employees is 17.____

    A. of considerable value in refresher training but otherwise has more disadvantages than advantages
    B. probably the most valuable technique of teaching, provided that the lecturer has a dynamic rapid-fire method of presenting the material
    C. suitable only for training entry-level employees
    D. a one-way communication process that does not attempt to evaluate whether the student understands the lecture

18. Assume that a certain agency makes it a practice to penalize an employee who is late in reporting for duty. If he is late a second time in a particular month, his penalty is more severe. If he is late a third time in the month, the penalty is still more severe. 18.____
    An employee will USUALLY view this type of agency policy of increasing penalties as

    A. *bad;* fairness requires that there should be no penalty the first time an employee is guilty of an infraction
    B. *bad;* the commission of an infraction by an employee is usually unintentional
    C. *good;* more severe sanctions for repeated infractions are just
    D. *good;* sanctions are nearly always less severe than the circumstances warrant

19. The view on employee morale is that

    A. a supervisor develops the highest state of employee morale by the *carrot and stick* philosophy of rewarding good behavior and punishing bad behavior
    B. every person's morale is low in a unit where the chuckling loafer gets paid as much as the disgruntled *high-pressure* producer
    C. it is necessary to constantly maintain an equilibrium within the organization in which all members of the work group can obtain satisfaction
    D. high morale is rarely, if ever, possible in positions involving the administration of justice because the *client* population tends to be resistive and resentful

20. A characteristic of the EFFECTIVE leader-supervisor is

    A. a desire to become thoroughly familiar with the latest studies in his field
    B. a willingness to engage in risk-taking behavior
    C. complete familiarity with his departmental rules and regulations
    D. the courage to mete out swift punishment for infractions

21. Effective communication requires a *climate of acceptance.* In order to achieve this *climate of acceptance,* the supervisor SHOULD

    A. cheerfully accept the blame for errors innocently made by subordinates
    B. conduct himself in a way which leads his subordinates to regard him as trustworthy
    C. maintain a personal notebook in which he keeps a record of the orders he has issued
    D. never issue an order without giving a supporting reason for the order

22. It is a generally accepted supervisory principle that, so far as possible, no subordinate should have more than one immediate supervisor.
    Even in situations where orders from two supervisors, at different times, direct a subordinate to perform the same job, it may confuse the subordinate because

    A. each of the supervisors may want the job performed in a different manner
    B. he is not given an opportunity to express his views on how the job should be performed
    C. each of the supervisors may claim credit for a good job performed by the subordinate
    D. he is uncertain as to which supervisor has the most precise knowledge of the job

23. There must be an opportunity for subordinates at all levels to offer constructive criticism about the manner in which operations are carried on.
    Of the following, the PRINCIPAL reason why such criticism by subordinates of the manner in which operations are carried on is sometimes of limited value is that subordinates

    A. do not normally possess sufficient knowledge of agency-wide problems
    B. fail to realize that agency-wide operations are dynamic and not static
    C. lack the motivation to offer criticism of matters above their level of operation
    D. who offer such criticism create discord among fellow subordinates who resent an overly critical individual in their midst

24. The best training results come from a plan which touches on all phases of an employee's work in a general manner. This statement is GENERALLY

    A. *false;* such training will probably result in the imparting of superficial knowledge
    B. *true;* training cannot reasonably be expected to embrace all parts of the job in a thorough manner
    C. *false;* such training could best be accomplished by a very careful reading of the rules and regulations
    D. *true;* any other method would necessarily involve that too much unproductive time be devoted to training

25. Of the following, the MOST important reason for planning work schedules for subordinates is that

    A. coverage of essential operations is more likely to be assured
    B. emergency situations can be handled more expeditiously
    C. it enhances the authority of the supervisor and, therefore, contributes to the effective carrying out of orders
    D. subordinates are more likely to be satisfied with their assignments

KEY (CORRECT ANSWERS)

1.	D	11.	B
2.	B	12.	B
3.	D	13.	D
4.	A	14.	A
5.	D	15.	A
6.	B	16.	C
7.	C	17.	D
8.	C	18.	C
9.	D	19.	C
10.	A	20.	B

21.	B
22.	A
23.	A
24.	A
25.	A

EXAMINATION SECTION
TEST 1

DIRECTIONS: Each question or incomplete statement is followed by several suggested answers or completions. Select the one that BEST answers the question or completes the statement. *PRINT THE LETTER OF THE CORRECT ANSWER IN THE SPACE AT THE RIGHT.*

1. One of the basic characteristics of a good police supervisor is the courage to accept his supervisory responsibilities and to avoid making excuses and explanations. Of the following, the MOST valid deduction to make from this statement is that the supervisor should

    A. hold subordinates strictly to account so that he is not unjustly blamed
    B. not be required to assume responsibility for the error of a subordinate
    C. not seek to evade blame by referring to the inadequacies of his subordinates
    D. not accept excuses or explanations from his subordinates if they do not perform their duties properly

1.____

2. A rather complex change is to be made in patrol procedures. As a supervising officer, it is your responsibility to make sure that your subordinates are informed of this change. The one of the following courses of action which is MOST likely to result in good performance is for you to

    A. assign one of your best officers to explain the order
    B. distribute an exact copy of the new order as soon as it becomes available
    C. explain the new procedure after your subordinates have had some experience with it
    D. explain the new procedure carefully before it is adopted

2.____

3. As a supervising police officer, you have noticed that, upon the issuance of verbal orders by you to officers, there are seldom any questions asked by them seeking clarification of such orders. You have also noticed that, upon questioning the officers while on patrol, few of them have really understood your orders.
Of the following courses of action, the one which constitutes the BEST solution to this problem is for you to

    A. question the officers immediately following the issuance of your orders
    B. take disciplinary action against those who are not able to understand your orders
    C. issue your orders in written form so that they may be understood more readily
    D. request that your commanding officer issue the orders

3.____

4. A certain officer has a habit of issuing orders and giving directions to other officers on his own responsibility without having received the permission of the supervising officer to do so. Sometimes this occurs in the presence of the supervising officer whose silence on these occasions is interpreted as approval.
This practice is

    A. *bad;* it must result in poorer performance by the other officers
    B. *good;* it helps develop leadership qualities in particular officers who indicate a willingness to accept responsibility

4.____

117

C. *bad;* it creates an uncertainty in the minds of the other officers about whether a particular order should be obeyed
D. *good;* it makes the work of the supervising officer easier

5. As a supervising police officer, you have observed in your subordinates a consistent lack of attention to several minor patrol duties.
The BEST of the following actions for you to take FIRST is to

   A. attempt to perform these minor duties yourself
   B. take no action on the situation unless this lack of attention spreads to important duties
   C. instruct your subordinates concerning the necessity for performing all duties
   D. request the Chief to speak to your subordinates concerning the situation

6. As a supervising police officer, you have directed a subordinate to follow a specific route while on patrol. You later discover the subordinate patrolling an area outside the designated route.
The one of the following which is the BEST course of action for you to take FIRST is to

   A. explain to the subordinate your reasons for assigning him to the designated route
   B. question the subordinate concerning his reason for not following the designated route
   C. send him back to the designated route immediately
   D. take disciplinary action against the subordinate

7. A newly appointed supervising police officer has decided that he will give equal supervisory attention to each of his subordinates. Such a decision by this supervising officer is

   A. *wise;* all of the subordinates are thereby assured of fair and impartial treatment
   B. *unwise;* the amount of supervisory attention should be varied according to the needs of individual subordinates
   C. *wise;* such a decision will permit the supervising officer to devote more of time to actual patrol
   D. *unwise;* such a decision should be postponed until the Chief can be consulted

8. The one of the following which does NOT constitute an acceptable purpose of the disciplinary process in a police organization is to

   A. improve and maintain the morale of the department
   B. improve the individual whose work falls below defined standards of job performance
   C. provide a strict system of equal punishments for similar offenses
   D. raise or maintain the prestige of the department in the community

9. One of the officers under your supervision has suddenly become very careless in his personal appearance, and his job performance has fallen below the required standard. Questioning of the officer reveals that this condition is due to a serious personal problem.
For you to assist in the solving of this problem is

   A. *improper;* your police background and training make it unlikely that you could provide any real assistance
   B. *proper;* all personal problems of your officers should be your concern

C. *improper;* you would be intruding upon the officer's right to privacy in personal matters
D. *proper;* the officer's personal problem has seriously affected his work

10. A community resident has asked an officer to recommend a good television repairman. For the officer to make such a recommendation would be

    A. *proper;* the officer is performing a service that will help a community resident
    B. *improper;* the officer is not qualified to know a good television repairman from a poor one
    C. *proper;* the officer can thus prevent the community resident from being victimized
    D. *improper;* the officer would be doing something that might affect his effectiveness as a law enforcement officer

11. It is a generally accepted principle of supervision that disciplinary action should be taken quickly when it needs to be taken.
    The one of the following statements which BEST supports the taking of prompt disciplinary action is that

    A. the accuracy of official disciplinary records will thereby be insured
    B. the offender is more likely to feel that the disciplinary action will be severe
    C. the supervisor is more likely to remember the details surrounding the offender's breach of discipline
    D. there is an avoidance of the prolonged aggravation caused by later disposition of the case

12. A supervising police officer has been informed by a certain officer under his supervision that he will soon resign his job and accept employment elsewhere.
    In this situation, the BEST course of action for the supervising officer is to

    A. assign him to the most difficult tasks and tours in order to favor the men remaining
    B. avoid giving him new types of assignments
    C. find out what his new job is and then try to persuade him to remain
    D. refrain from assigning him to work involving any responsibility

13. Officer X has complained to you that Officer Y generally is favored by getting the more desirable assignments. For you, as a supervising police officer, to attempt to explain to Officer X the reason for these assignments of Officer Y would be

    A. *proper;* it is likely to lessen Officer X's objection
    B. *improper;* your authority as a supervisor would be weakened
    C. *proper;* it is needed in order to protect Officer Y from Officer X's resentment and jealousy
    D. *improper;* as a supervisor, there is no need for you to explain the assignments which you make

14. A community resident has complained to the supervising police officer that a certain officer makes a habit of asking him and other residents to buy tickets for dances. An investigation reveals that this is, so.
    Of the following, the BEST course of action for the supervising officer is to

    A. advise the resident that he is under no obligation to buy any such tickets
    B. forbid the officer to sell these tickets, briefly explaining why

C. permit the sale of these tickets only if other groups are allowed equal opportunity to sell tickets to their affairs
D. tell the officer to use discretion in asking people to buy tickets and to avoid asking those who might complain

15. An officer has reprimanded a young boy for playing on the grass in a project. The boy's mother tells the officer that he should be more concerned with arresting criminals than with reprimanding children for petty violations.
Of the following, the BEST answer for the officer to make to this woman is that

   A. children must be taught good conduct by all those concerned for their welfare
   B. damage to public property means higher rents and higher taxes
   C. serious criminals often begin their careers with minor violations
   D. the police force does its best to enforce all laws and regulations

16. In view of the fact that police patrol activity is not able to eliminate all opportunities for criminal behavior, the one of the following procedures which is generally regarded as MOST desirable is for the patrol force to

   A. assign the entire available patrol force to those areas which have the greatest incidence of crime
   B. attempt to give an impression of omnipresence at every hour and in all sections of the community
   C. devote its major efforts to the creation of wholesome influences in a community
   D. keep a substantial patrol force in reserve to answer specific complaints received from the public

17. Although the system of three eight-hour shifts is generally employed by police departments, it would be MORE suitable to provide for overlapping shifts when

   A. an average work load for one shift is substantially less than the other shifts
   B. an hourly work load on one shift fluctuates widely from the average of the shift
   C. the average work load for one shift is substantially greater than the other shifts
   D. the hourly work loads in each of the shifts is almost the same as the average of that shift

18. The highest quality of patrol service results from the permanent assignment of an officer to the same post. The one of the following statements which is the LEAST important advantage of such permanent assignment is that under this system,

   A. it is more likely that events which do not fit into the normal pattern of activity on the post will be noticed
   B. the officer becomes well-acquainted with many persons residing on his post
   C. there is a saving of time and effort due to the familiarity of the officer with his post-relieving point
   D. there is less joint responsibility for conditions on any given post

19. The performance of continuous routine patrol service should generally be provided by the patrol division and not by special divisions.
This statement is

A. *true;* the patrol division should not be subordinated to any other police unit
B. *false;* special divisions frequently are staffed with many of the most competent housing officers
C. *true;* officers engaged in special patrol are less likely to be alert for patrol conditions outside the field of their specialization
D. *false;* special divisions have a basic patrol responsibility equal to that of the patrol division

20. Specialization in the performance of administrative planning duties is not an example of an undesirable specialization of duty being made at the expense of the patrol force. This statement is GENERALLY

    A. *false;* specialization of any kind inevitably results in some depletion of the patrol force
    B. *true;* specialization is desirable to the extent that it efficiently performs part of the actual patrol duty
    C. *false;* this type of duty can be performed efficiently by the individual supervising officer
    D. *true;* these duties cannot be performed by officers in the course of their regular patrol

21. The one of the following which MOST indicates a definite need for the establishment of a specialized enforcement unit, in addition to the regular patrol force, is that

    A. a community group requests that extra enforcement activity be directed towards problems of public morals
    B. a substantial number of patrol personnel have been trained in specialized areas of police work
    C. business interests in the community demand police protection during transfers of cash to banks
    D. the patrol force is unable to perform the total police task in some area

22. The one of the following which indicates the BEST method by which a supervising police officer may check on the quality of patrol performance by the officers under his supervision is to

    A. ask the community residents if they are receiving satisfactory police service
    B. determine the number of arrests for serious crimes made by each officer
    C. observe the officers while they are actually performing patrol
    D. question the more experienced officers concerning the performance of other members of the force

23. The police force should de-emphasize the pursuit of criminals and stress crime prevention.
    For a supervising police officer, this should mean that his CHIEF emphasis should be on the

    A. importance of complete patrol coverage
    B. importance of physical fitness
    C. proficiency of his subordinates with firearms
    D. value of morale in police work

24. Supervising police officers should be instructed how to use manpower to prevent distribution of forces on unproductive assignments.
    This statement is

    A. *false;* only time can tell whether any assignment will be unproductive or not
    B. *true;* the supervising officer cannot perform any supervisory duty without such instructions
    C. *false;* assignments should be made solely in response to public demand for police protection
    D. *true;* the assignment of men should be aimed at securing the maximum police protection

25. An officer on patrol is approached by a resident who excitedly informs him that she has just observed a stranger trying the doors of several apartments on the second floor of the project building in which she lives. She also states that the stranger is wearing a dark hat and topcoat. The officer goes to the building and encounters a man hurriedly leaving, who is wearing a gray hat and topcoat. The officer questions him about his presence in the building. The action of the officer was

    A. *poor;* his duty is to go to the second floor as quickly as possible
    B. *good;* everyone in the vicinity of a crime who acts suspiciously should be arrested
    C. *poor;* the tenant stated that the stranger trying the doors was wearing a dark hat and topcoat
    D. *good;* the man about to leave the building may be the same one who was trying the apartment doors

KEY (CORRECT ANSWERS)

1. C   11. D
2. D   12. B
3. A   13. A
4. C   14. B
5. C   15. D

6. B   16. B
7. B   17. B
8. C   18. C
9. D   19. C
10. D   20. D

21. D
22. C
23. A
24. D
25. D

TEST 2

DIRECTIONS: Each question or incomplete statement is followed by several suggested answers or completions. Select the one that BEST answers the question or completes the statement. *PRINT THE LETTER OF THE CORRECT ANSWER IN THE SPACE AT THE RIGHT.*

1. A supervisor who is training several inexperienced subordinates on patrol in the best way to handle the various patrol situations likely to arise should respond with them to calls for their services and

    A. avoid correcting any mistakes as they are made to discuss the overall handling of the situation later
    B. correct all mistakes as they are made and also discuss the overall handling of the situation later
    C. correct all mistakes as they are made and then avoid future discussion of these mistakes
    D. correct serious mistakes as they are made and discuss the overall handling of the situation later

2. For an officer who is supervising patrol to make a notation in his memorandum book whenever he strongly reprimands a subordinate verbally is

    A. *inadvisable,* chiefly because an undue amount of supervisory time will be devoted to recording such information
    B. *advisable,* chiefly because the sergeant is developing a fund of information which will be useful in the future handling of the subordinate
    C. *inadvisable,* chiefly because the subordinate may resent such a procedure
    D. *advisable,* chiefly because all subordinates will make greater efforts to improve their job performance since they will not be sure of the nature of the notations

3. A supervisor is attempting to discuss some important and practical applications of a new law to police work with a group of his subordinates who have little knowledge of this law. He notices that the group is passive and uninterested in the discussion.
Of the following, it would be BEST for the supervisor to

    A. explain the law and its application carefully and as thoroughly as possible and ask provocative questions
    B. order the group to participate in the discussion since it is for their own good
    C. give the factual information on the law and then stay out of the discussion as much as possible
    D. postpone further discussion until some future time when the group has shown some interest in the law

4. While on patrol, a supervisor is required to issue a fairly important order to a subordinate. Due to the pressure of other duties, the supervisor issues the order very quickly and briefly while *on the run.*
An IMPORTANT weakness of the issuance of the order in this manner is that

    A. the subordinate is likely to regard the order as less important than it really is
    B. the supervisor is giving the subordinate more responsibility than is proper
    C. orders require explanation in order to convey the intended meaning
    D. the supervisor is likely to forget this order and to whom it was issued

5. In giving orders, a supervisor will give more details at certain times than at other times. The one of the following situations in which the LEAST amount of detail should be given is when the order is concerned with a procedure which

   A. has hazardous features
   B. is of a special or infrequent nature
   C. has been generally performed in a standardized manner
   D. is to be carried out by several subordinates of limited experience

6. Briefing a subordinate on the circumstances which have made an order necessary is desirable MAINLY because the

   A. subordinate thereby has greater respect for the supervisor for his demonstrated knowledge of the job
   B. supervisor is thereby making allowances for differences among subordinates in their ability to understand orders
   C. subordinate will not tend to view the order as a personal or arbitrary command
   D. supervisor will be better able to test the quality of the execution of the order by *follow-up* procedures

7. Disciplinary action will, in most instances, be initiated by the immediate superior of the person to be disciplined. This is so MAINLY because

   A. it permits the higher superiors to be able to devote most of their attention and effort to broader and more generalized problems of administration
   B. it helps to develop a forceful image of the immediate superior which will serve to prevent other overt acts of misconduct by other subordinates
   C. the immediate superior is the one most qualified to make recommendations as to the severity of punishment to be applied
   D. the immediate superior is usually in the best position to observe derelictions of duty requiring some kind of corrective action

8. Having decided to institute disciplinary action against a subordinate in his command, a supervisor speaks to the subordinate for the purpose of informing him of the action to be taken.
   At this interview, it would be LEAST advisable for the supervisor to explain to the subordinate

   A. the procedural steps which will follow the institution of disciplinary action
   B. the specific reason for the disciplinary action
   C. that the purpose of discipline is the punishment of the offender
   D. what is expected of the subordinate in the future, especially as related to the behavior which resulted in disciplinary action being taken

9. The repeated use by a superior officer of a call for volunteers to get a job done is objectionable MAINLY because

   A. it may create a feeling of animosity between the volunteers and the non-volunteers
   B. it may indicate that the superior is avoiding responsibility for making assignments which will be most productive
   C. it is an indication that the superior is not familiar with the individual capabilities of his men
   D. it is unfair to men who, for valid reasons, do not or cannot volunteer

10. Of the following statements concerning subordinates, expressions to a supervisor of their opinions and feelings concerning work situations, the one which is MOST correct is that

    A. by listening and responding to such expressions the supervisor encourages the development of complaints
    B. the lack of such expressions should indicate to the supervisor that there is a high level of job satisfaction
    C. the more the supervisor listens to and responds to such expressions, the more he demonstrates lack of supervisory ability
    D. by listening and responding to such expressions, the supervisor will enable many subordinates to understand and solve their own problems on the job

11. Usually one thinks of communication as a single step, essentially that of transmitting an idea. Actually, however, this is only part of a total process, the FIRST step of which should be

    A. the prompt dissemination of the idea to those who may be affected by it
    B. motivating those affected to take the required action
    C. clarifying the idea in one's own mind
    D. deciding to whom the idea is to be communicated

12. Research studies on patterns of informal communication have concluded that most individuals in a group tend to be passive recipients of news, while a few make it their business to spread it around in an organization.
    With this conclusion in mind, it would be MOST correct for the supervisor to attempt to identify these few individuals and

    A. give them the complete facts on important matters in advance of others
    B. inform the other subordinates of the identity of these few individuals so that their influence may be minimized
    C. keep them straight on the facts on important matters
    D. warn them to cease passing along any information to others

13. The one of the following which is the PRINCIPAL advantage of making an oral report is that it

    A. affords an immediate opportunity for two-way communication between the subordinate and superior
    B. is an easy method for the superior to use in transmitting information to others of equal rank
    C. saves the time of all concerned
    D. permits more precise pinpointing of praise or blame by means of follow-up questions by the superior

14. Supervisory training is designed to develop skills in human relationships while work-skill training attempts to alter the relationship between a person and a machine or material of some sort.
    The one of the following which MOST accurately describes an important difference between these two types of training is that

A. resistance to work-skill training is likely to be greater than resistance to supervisory training
B. skills acquired from supervisory training should be less flexible than skills acquired from work-skill training
C. skills acquired from supervisory training are usually less directly and routinely applied than skills acquired from work-skill training
D. trainees are more apt to feel more secure in attempting to utilize skills acquired through supervisory training than those acquired from work-skill training

15. The quantity and quality of work performed by one subordinate is below the level that he is capable of attaining. Because of this, the supervisor gives this subordinate the least difficult assignments only.
This action taken by the supervisor is

   A. *poor,* chiefly because the subordinate should be motivated to perform work of greater responsibility
   B. *good,* chiefly because each subordinate should be allowed to work in the manner he finds most satisfactory
   C. *poor,* chiefly because the supervisor should make his assignments such that all subordinates are given an equal amount of work and responsibility
   D. *good,* chiefly because otherwise the supervisor will have to give a greater amount of supervisory attention to this subordinate than to other subordinates

16. It has been the practice in some communities to substantially base the efficiency rating of police commanders on incidence of crime.
This practice is inadvisable MAINLY because

   A. crime figures also reflect many community factors beyond the control of the commander
   B. such figures may be incomplete and unreliable
   C. there is little or no relation between such figures and police efficiency
   D. there is a great need for improved techniques of processing and analysis of crime figures

17. Even though officers are assigned on a permanent basis to tours of duty at night, experts in plant security recommend that arrangements be made for them to make a complete tour of the premises during the daytime.
The CHIEF reason for this suggestion is to

   A. enable them to coordinate their patrol work better with that of the officers assigned to daytime duty
   B. discover those areas in which teenage groups congregate during the day and which are, therefore, most vulnerable to night-time crime
   C. allow them to become more familiar with the general layout of the premises and with specific locations that may be of importance to them in their work
   D. give them a clearer daytime view of the exact conditions they may expect to encounter during their tours of duty at night

18. It has been suggested that housing officers on duty at night record the names of all Authority employees remaining in or leaving the project considerably after their normal working hours.
The CHIEF reason for taking this precaution would be to

A. assist the housing police force in interrogating the supervisors of these employees to determine whether they have any valid reason for remaining after their working hours
B. enable the housing police force to determine more promptly whether these employees are involved in any illegal activity during their off-duty hours
C. assist the housing police force to direct its questioning to these employees if it later develops that something improper occurred during this period of time
D. enable the housing police force to scrutinize more closely the activities of these employees during their regular working hours

19. The one of the following which is a distinct advantage of an organization's special police force over the regular police force is that the special police force GENERALLY

    A. has a limited area of jurisdiction in which only certain types of crimes occur
    B. has a limited responsibility for exercising diligence in patrol
    C. is able to limit its surveillance to only those persons who are not tenants or employees
    D. knows that most persons with whom it comes in contact on post are known to it as tenants or employees of the organization

20. From a management point of view, the BEST of the following reasons why it is better for police to emphasize the prevention of theft and vandalism, rather than the detection of such crimes or the apprehension of persons involved, is that preventive measures generally

    A. expedite the more prompt reporting of acts of vandalism and thefts because any actual occurrence of such offenses would be made more obvious
    B. minimize the need for the more unpleasant and costly procedures involved in apprehending and prosecuting guilty employees
    C. result in offenders being easily caught in the act of committing the crime
    D. involve stricter screening of employees and thus prevent any would-be criminals from becoming employees

21. It is generally recommended that the security division or special force of an organization be organized and trained in the measures needed to disperse or control a milling crowd and prevent it from turning into a rioting mob CHIEFLY in order to

    A. avoid the necessity of seeking outside assistance in quelling a purely local disturbance involving the organization
    B. quickly isolate and apprehend the leaders of the mob so that the police can take proper punitive action
    C. prevent injury or death to persons and damage to organization plant and equipment
    D. prevent the mob from spreading out into territory where the special police force has no jurisdiction

22. The CHIEF reason why the issuance of identification badges should be carefully controlled and why one should never be reissued with the same serial number as one which has been previously reported lost is to

A. insure against duplications of identification and establish a clear record of who is authorized to possess a particular badge
B. minimize the possibility of their being stolen or counterfeited by unauthorized persons
C. make sure that identification badges are returned
D. prevent unauthorized persons from mutilating or altering a validly issued identification badge

23. The rotation of officers has been recommended, in terms of both time and place of operation.
The CHIEF of the following reasons for applying this recommendation to experienced officers would be to

   A. enable them to gain more experience by exposing them to the different supervisory methods of various superior officers
   B. keep them alert by making them uncertain as to the varying degrees of diligence required by the different superior officers to whom they are assigned
   C. prevent them from becoming overly friendly with the residents and shopkeepers in the neighborhood
   D. make them more aware of problems existing in the various communities

24. Supervisors often feel that police recruits today do not accept direction as willingly as in the past.
The one of the following which is the MOST likely explanation for such a reaction by some recruits is the

   A. emphasis on individuality found in the home and in the school which tends to substitute tolerance and freedom for strict discipline
   B. increasingly complex nature of society which does not permit authoritarian concepts of discipline
   C. negative reaction to authority of men who have fulfilled a required military service obligation
   D. current notion that frequent direction by superiors constitutes undemocratic supervision

25. Police officers on patrol are constantly warned to be on the alert for suspicious persons, actions, and circumstances. With this in mind, a supervisor should emphasize the need for them to

   A. be cautious and suspicious when dealing officially with any civilian, regardless of the latter's overt actions or the circumstances surrounding his dealings with the police
   B. become thoroughly familiar with the usual on their posts so as to be better able to detect the unusual
   C. take aggressive police action immediately against any unusual person or condition detected on their posts, regardless of any other circumstances
   D. keep looking for the unusual persons, actions, and circumstances on their posts and pay less attention to the usual occurrences

KEY (CORRECT ANSWERS)

1. D
2. B
3. A
4. A
5. C

6. C
7. D
8. C
9. B
10. D

11. C
12. C
13. A
14. C
15. A

16. A
17. C
18. C
19. D
20. B

21. C
22. A
23. C
24. A
25. B

TEST 3

DIRECTIONS: Each question or incomplete statement is followed by several suggested answers or completions. Select the one that BEST answers the question or completes the statement. *PRINT THE LETTER OF THE CORRECT ANSWER IN THE SPACE AT THE RIGHT.*

1. The most competent leaders seldom have to resort to a display of authority. Of the following, the MOST important quality of this type of leader is that he

    A. is able to inspire subordinates to perform satisfactorily
    B. makes sure that his men know the point beyond which punitive action will be taken
    C. secures compliance with orders by formalized disciplinary procedures
    D. secures compliance with orders by implied threats of disciplinary action

1.___

2. Demands for more police officers are frequently made by police administrators before they have first adopted methods that will assure a more effective use of the present forces.
In view of this statement, the BEST of the following guides to the most effective utilization of police personnel is the

    A. analysis of reports, complaints, and statistics to indicate needed services
    B. demands of various community groups for special kinds of police protection
    C. fullest use of new scientific equipment in records management
    D. requests of commanders of specialized units who seek to increase the effectiveness of their units by the assignment of additional men

2.___

3. An organization such as a police agency is not generally confronted by such unique problems as to make impossible the application of certain administrative principles that have been found applicable in other organizations.
Of the following, the MOST valid deduction to make from this statement is that

    A. practices of other organizations reveal that police problems are not generally susceptible to solution by standardized management techniques
    B. questions of size are relevant in evaluating the applicability of common administrative principles
    C. some management guides can serve both police and non-police administrators equally well
    D. superficial familiarity with police organizations often leads to the application of invalid administrative techniques

3.___

4. Formal police training programs should generally be conducted during the officers' off-duty time; otherwise, the public funds allotted to police services are not being properly used.
This statement is GENERALLY

    A. *false;* close supervision during the actual performance of duties provides the only practical training technique
    B. *true;* the most effective training is usually conducted in an environment completely different from the one in which job performance takes place
    C. *true;* only those training activities which relate to the performance of extremely difficult duties should be conducted during on-duty time
    D. *false;* more effective performance of duties by the trainees will compensate for any on-duty time devoted to training

4.___

5. The ultimate responsibility for police training lies with the top echelon of command, and the supervising police officer should not properly be held accountable for any part of this supervisory function.
   This statement is

   A. *true;* the supervising police officer should devote the major portion of his time to the performance of patrol
   B. *false;* the supervising police officer is in a key position to assist in training
   C. *true;* the duty of a supervising police officer to correct the improper patrol performance of subordinates cannot be classified as training
   D. *false;* the supervising police officer's primary responsibility is the training of subordinates

6. Periodic training of all police personnel, experienced officers as well as recruits, is a necessary requirement for effective police operations.
   This statement is GENERALLY

   A. *false;* methods of police operation are relatively stable and, therefore, additional training is unnecessary
   B. *true;* experienced personnel and recruits both require continued training at essentially the same level
   C. *false;* such training would undermine the morale of the experienced officers and seriously affect their job performance
   D. *true;* the original training may be forgotten or made obsolete by changing community conditions and improved methods

7. There is considerable merit to the idea that the police agency have only one telephone number listed in the telephone directory so that the general public, when seeking police assistance, will be required to contact a central complaint desk.
   The one of the following which is the MOST important advantage of this procedure is that

   A. direct public contact with the central complaint desk will insure that the most appropriate police action will be taken
   B. it makes less likely the possibility of a complaint being ignored or not investigated
   C. it makes unnecessary any future public contact with the local police unit
   D. it prevents any complaints from being registered in any local police unit

8. A system of complete decentralization of police records, with the line operating units maintaining their own records, constitutes the most advisable system.
   This statement is GENERALLY

   A. *false;* decentralization of record keeping tends to turn the line operating units into small and almost independent police organizations
   B. *true;* decentralization of record keeping fixes responsibility in a manner superior to the centralization of record keeping
   C. *false;* such complete decentralization of records would prevent any coordination of the line operating units
   D. *true;* police records should remain in the unit of their origin so that ready reference may be made to them

9. Much of the difficulty encountered in the process of administrative communication arises from a failure to realize that many words have varied, rather than a single, meaning. Accordingly, in issuing complex orders, it would be MOST important for the newly appointed supervising police officer to

   A. carefully check the meaning of difficult words in proposed orders
   B. issue written orders, rather than verbal orders, wherever possible
   C. review and discuss the orders with his subordinates
   D. revise the wording of all orders in order to clarify their meaning

10. As a supervising police officer, you have informed your subordinates that the Chief wants them to come to him directly at any suitable time to discuss problems, grievances, or suggestions for improvement of patrol performance. You have noticed, after a lapse of several months, that none of your subordinates have gone to the Chief for any of these purposes.
    The one of the following which is the LEAST likely explanation of this reluctance on the part of your subordinates is

    A. the natural reluctance of subordinates to freely express their ideas in the presence of higher authority
    B. that the subordinates may be reluctant to bypass your authority as their immediate supervisor
    C. the fear of being considered *troublemakers* by other superior officers in the department
    D. that good supervision has completely eliminated problems, grievances, and the need for suggestions

11. As a supervising police officer, you feel that a certain officer under your supervision is responsible for starting several unfounded rumors concerning police matters in the precinct.
    Of the following possible courses of action, the one which would be the MOST effective in dealing with the problem is to

    A. ignore the situation since none of the rumors contained any elements of truth
    B. provide sufficient facts about police matters in the precinct to establish a basis upon which rumors may be evaluated
    C. institute formal disciplinary action against the suspected officer
    D. speak to your subordinates, as a group, on the undesirable effects of spreading false information

12. Although the increasing complexity of police work strongly favors the specialist, experienced administrators are alert to the dangers in this tendency and strive to maintain flexible arrangements whenever specialized techniques threaten unity of action.
    Of the following, the MOST valid conclusion from this statement is that

    A. complexity of police work requires specialization to insure unity of action
    B. flexibility is needed to offset the occasional undesirable effects of specialization
    C. the role of the specialist in police work has become more important due to the influence of experienced administrators
    D. unity of action, although increased by specialization, can at the same time be inflexible because of police complexity

13. The quality of police service is more strongly influenced by the competence of the individual members of the force than by any other single factor.
The one of the following aspects of police administration which contributes LEAST to the development of such competence is the

    A. absence of morale-destroying influences
    B. promptness and certainty of disciplinary procedures
    C. existence of a suitable recruit training program
    D. survey of needed changes in organizational structure

14. Some law enforcement agencies do not wait for the legal disposition of an arrest case by the courts but close the arrest record when their custody of a prisoner ends. Such a procedure is GENERALLY considered to be

    A. *good;* strict impartiality by the police in the administration of criminal law requires that they be unaffected by either the conviction or acquittal of a prisoner
    B. *good;* the long delays frequently accompanying court procedure would unduly add to the work involved in the record keeping function
    C. *poor;* the legal disposition of a case should have some bearing on evaluating the work of the agency
    D. *poor;* court dispositions provide the only sure indication of the quality of the police investigative procedures

15. A maintenance man continually brings to the attention of a housing officer matters of a minor nature about building upkeep which are not the proper concern of the housing officer force. The housing officer has told the maintenance man that these problems are not a concern of the housing police personnel. However, the maintenance man continues to bring these matters to the attention of the housing officer. The housing officer tells his supervising officer about the situation.
Of the following, the BEST course of action for the supervising officer to take is to

    A. advise the housing officer to listen to the complaints of the maintenance man and then to ignore them
    B. ask the housing manager to take steps to change the conduct of the maintenance man
    C. have the housing officer transferred to another assignment so that he will not come in contact with the maintenance man
    D. suggest to the housing manager that the maintenance man be transferred since the latter is interfering with police duties

16. The one of the following factors which provides the BEST indication of the number of officers to be assigned to the inspection of store doors during the night hours is the

    A. average distance between the stores to be inspected
    B. number of complaints received from the owners of the stores to be inspected
    C. number of man-hours required to perform these inspections properly
    D. number of stores that are to be inspected

17. When properly performed, patrol plays a leading role in the accomplishment of the police purpose of crime prevention CHIEFLY by

    A. apprehending offenders and impressing them with the omnipotence of the police
    B. being the only form of police service that directly attempts to eliminate the opportunities for crime

C. gaining public support by the prompt investigation of offenses and recovery of stolen property
D. influencing public attitudes against crime in its routine daily associations with the public

18. The theory of police patrol which, if properly applied, should have the GREATEST deterrent effect on crime is that which favors patrolling

    A. all areas in such a manner as to make the police officers as unnoticeable as possible
    B. all areas in such a manner as to attract the maximum of attention to the police
    C. areas of high incidence of crime in an obvious manner and on a frequent and fixed schedule
    D. areas of low incidence of crime obviously and irregularly and areas of high incidence of crime on an irregular schedule and attracting a minimum of attention

19. It has been said that police patrol should aim at giving the impression of omnipresence at all times.
The one of the following which is the PRIMARY reason for this statement is that generally the

    A. planning for successful theft must be changed by the potential offender's expectation of apprehension
    B. potential thief's desire to steal is diminished by the presence of a uniformed officer
    C. potential thief's belief in the opportunity for successful theft is diminished by his expectation of apprehension
    D. potential thief's desire to steal is diminished by his expectation of apprehension

20. Whenever new tasks and duties are assigned to the police force, the question arises as to whether they should be assigned to the regular patrol force or to a specialized unit.
It would be MOST desirable in such a situation for the new tasks and duties to be so assigned as to give the

    A. regular patrol force all tasks and duties which it can perform as well as if done by specialists and which do not interfere with regular patrol duties
    B. specialized units all tasks and duties which they can perform as efficiently as the regular patrol force
    C. regular patrol force only those tasks and duties which are clearly in keeping with patrol duties and which are of a non-specialized nature
    D. specialized units all those tasks and duties which are of a specialized nature regardless of their relationship to regular patrol duties

21. An undesirable result of specialization in police work is the

    A. assignment to regular patrol officers of the primary responsibility for the enforcement of regulations in specialized areas of enforcement
    B. assignment of regular patrol officers to render many services to the specialized branches of service
    C. performance by patrol officers during the course of their regular patrol of tasks which can be performed by specialists at any other time
    D. performance by specialists of tasks that should be performed by patrol officers in the course of their regular patrol

22. There has been a marked trend during the past thirty years toward a greater public demand for extra services from the patrol force and also a trend toward increased specialization in police work.
The CHIEF drawback to both of these tendencies is the

    A. difficulty of choosing the members of the force to be assigned to both these tasks
    B. decrease in the number of members of the force available for assignment to patrol
    C. poorer technical knowledge of the patrol sergeant in his supervisory dealings with police specialists
    D. reduction in authority and prestige of the members of the force assigned to patrol duties in contrast to that of those assigned to special units

22.____

23. It is not enough for a police agency's services to be of a high quality; attention must also be given to the acceptability of these services to the general public. This statement is GENERALLY

    A. *false;* a superior quality of police service automatically wins public support
    B. *true;* the police cannot generally progress beyond the understanding and support of the public
    C. *false;* the acceptance by the public of police services determines their quality
    D. *true;* the police are generally unable to engage in any effective enforcement activity without public support

23.____

24. Final decisions regarding quality and extent of police services to be provided should rest with those politically responsible for the conduct of a city's affairs.
The PRINCIPAL reason for this point of view is that

    A. only those officials responsible for the overall conduct of city affairs have the authority to make such decisions
    B. city and state legislation determine the limits of the activities of the police
    C. these officials have the advantage of readily available technical advice and information from police officials
    D. the level of governmental services is, in the final analysis, dependent solely upon budgetary considerations

24.____

25. Of the following, the LEAST likely way in which a records system may serve a supervising police officer is in

    A. developing a sympathetic and cooperative public attitude toward the police
    B. improving the quality of supervision by permitting a check on the accomplishment of subordinates
    C. permitting a precise prediction of the exact crime incidence in specific categories for the following year
    D. helping to take the guesswork out of the distribution of the force

25.____

KEY (CORRECT ANSWERS)

1. A
2. A
3. C
4. D
5. B

6. D
7. B
8. A
9. C
10. D

11. B
12. B
13. D
14. C
15. B

16. C
17. B
18. B
19. C
20. A

21. D
22. B
23. B
24. A
25. A

PHILOSOPHY, PRINCIPLES, PRACTICES, AND TECHNICS OF SUPERVISION, ADMINISTRATION, MANAGEMENT, AND ORGANIZATION

TABLE OF CONTENTS

	Page
MEANING OF SUPERVISION	1
THE OLD AND THE NEW SUPERVISION	1
THE EIGHT (8) BASIC PRINCIPLES OF THE NEW SUPERVISION	1
I. Principle of Responsibility	1
II. Principle of Authority	2
III. Principle of Self-Growth	2
IV. Principle of Individual Worth	2
V. Principle of Creative Leadership	2
VI. Principle of Success and Failure	2
VII. Principle of Science	3
VIII. Principle of Cooperation	3
WHAT IS ADMINISTRATION?	3
I. Practices Commonly Classed as "Supervisory"	3
II. Practices Commonly Classed as "Administrative"	3
III. Practices Commonly Classed as Both "Supervisory" and "Administrative"	4
RESPONSIBILITIES OF THE SUPERVISOR	4
COMPETENCIES OF THE SUPERVISOR	4
THE PROFESSIONAL SUPERVISOR-EMPLOYEE RELATIONSHIP	4
MINI-TEXT IN SUPERVISION, ADMINISTRATION, MANAGEMENT, AND ORGANIZATION	5
I. Brief Highlights	5
A. Levels of Management	6
B. What the Supervisor Must Learn	6
C. A Definition of Supervision	6
D. Elements of the Team Concept	6
E. Principles of Organization	6
F. The Four Important Parts of Every Job	7
G. Principles of Delegation	7
H. Principles of Effective Communications	7
I. Principles of Work Improvement	7
J. Areas of Job Improvement	7
K. Seven Key Points in Making Improvements	8

	L.	Corrective Techniques for Job Improvement	8
	M.	A Planning Checklist	8
	N.	Five Characteristics of Good Directions	9
	O.	Types of Directions	9
	P.	Controls	9
	Q.	Orienting the New Employee	9
	R.	Checklist for Orienting New Employees	9
	S.	Principles of Learning	10
	T.	Causes of Poor Performance	10
	U.	Four Major Steps in On-the-Job Instructions	10
	V.	Employees Want Five Things	10
	W.	Some Don'ts in Regard to Praise	11
	X.	How to Gain Your Workers' Confidence	11
	Y.	Sources of Employee Problems	11
	Z.	The Supervisor's Key to Discipline	11
	AA.	Five Important Processes of Management	12
	BB.	When the Supervisor Fails to Plan	12
	CC.	Fourteen General Principles of Management	12
	DD.	Change	12
II.	Brief Topical Summaries		13
	A.	Who/What is the Supervisor?	13
	B.	The Sociology of Work	13
	C.	Principles and Practices of Supervision	14
	D.	Dynamic Leadership	14
	E.	Processes for Solving Problems	15
	F.	Training for Results	15
	G.	Health, Safety, and Accident Prevention	16
	H.	Equal Employment Opportunity	16
	I.	Improving Communications	16
	J.	Self-Development	17
	K.	Teaching and Training	17
		1. The Teaching Process	17
		a. Preparation	17
		b. Presentation	18
		c. Summary	18
		d. Application	18
		e. Evaluation	18
		2. Teaching Methods	18
		a. Lecture	18
		b. Discussion	18
		c. Demonstration	19
		d. Performance	19
		e. Which Method to Use	19

PHILOSOPHY, PRINCIPLES, PRACTICES, AND TECHNICS
OF
SUPERVISION, ADMINISTRATION, MANAGEMENT, AND ORGANIZATION

MEANING OF SUPERVISION

The extension of the democratic philosophy has been accompanied by an extension in the scope of supervision. Modern leaders and supervisors no longer think of supervision in the narrow sense of being confined chiefly to visiting employees, supplying materials, or rating the staff. They regard supervision as being intimately related to all the concerned agencies of society, they speak of the supervisor's function in terms of "growth," rather than the "improvement" of employees.

This modern concept of supervision may be defined as follows: Supervision is leadership and the development of leadership within groups which are cooperatively engaged in inspection, research, training, guidance, and evaluation.

THE OLD AND THE NEW SUPERVISION

TRADITIONAL
1. Inspection
2. Focused on the employee
3. Visitation
4. Random and haphazard
5. Imposed and authoritarian
6. One person usually

MODERN
1. Study and analysis
2. Focused on aims, materials, methods, supervisors, employees, environment
3. Demonstrations, intervisitation, workshops, directed reading, bulletins, etc.
4. Definitely organized and planned (scientific)
5. Cooperative and democratic
6. Many persons involved (creative)

THE EIGHT (8) BASIC PRINCIPLES OF THE NEW SUPERVISION

I. Principle of Responsibility
   Authority to act and responsibility for acting must be joined.
   A. If you give responsibility, give authority.
   B. Define employee duties clearly.
   C. Protect employees from criticism by others.
   D. Recognize the rights as well as obligations of employees.
   E. Achieve the aims of a democratic society insofar as it is possible within the area of your work.
   F. Establish a situation favorable to training and learning.
   G. Accept ultimate responsibility for everything done in your section, unit, office, division, department.
   H. Good administration and good supervision are inseparable.

II. Principle of Authority
The success of the supervisor is measured by the extent to which the power of authority is not used.
   A. Exercise simplicity and informality in supervision
   B. Use the simplest machinery of supervision
   C. If it is good for the organization as a whole, it is probably justified.
   D. Seldom be arbitrary or authoritative.
   E. Do not base your work on the power of position or of personality.
   F. Permit and encourage the free expression of opinions.

III. Principle of Self-Growth
The success of the supervisor is measured by the extent to which, and the speed with which, he is no longer needed.
   A. Base criticism on principles, not on specifics.
   B. Point out higher activities to employees.
   C. Train for self-thinking by employees to meet new situations.
   D. Stimulate initiative, self-reliance, and individual responsibility
   E. Concentrate on stimulating the growth of employees rather than on removing defects.

IV. Principle of Individual Worth
Respect for the individual is a paramount consideration in supervision.
   A. Be human and sympathetic in dealing with employees.
   B. Don't nag about things to be done.
   C. Recognize the individual differences among employees and seek opportunities to permit best expression of each personality.

V. Principle of Creative Leadership
The best supervision is that which is not apparent to the employee.
   A. Stimulate, don't drive employees to creative action.
   B. Emphasize doing good things.
   C. Encourage employees to do what they do best.
   D. Do not be too greatly concerned with details of subject or method.
   E. Do not be concerned exclusively with immediate problems and activities.
   F. Reveal higher activities and make them both desired and maximally possible.
   G. Determine procedures in the light of each situation but see that these are derived from a sound basic philosophy.
   H. Aid, inspire, and lead so as to liberate the creative spirit latent in all good employees.

VI. Principle of Success and Failure
There are no unsuccessful employees, only unsuccessful supervisors who have failed to give proper leadership.
   A. Adapt suggestions to the capacities, attitudes, and prejudices of employees.
   B. Be gradual, be progressive, be persistent.
   C. Help the employee find the general principle; have the employee apply his own problem to the general principle.
   D. Give adequate appreciation for good work and honest effort.
   E. Anticipate employee difficulties and help to prevent them.
   F. Encourage employees to do the desirable things they will do anyway.
   G. Judge your supervision by the results it secures.

VII. Principle of Science
Successful supervision is scientific, objective, and experimental. It is based on facts, not on prejudices.
   A. Be cumulative in results.
   B. Never divorce your suggestions from the goals of training.
   C. Don't be impatient of results.
   D. Keep all matters on a professional, not a personal, level.
   E. Do not be concerned exclusively with immediate problems and activities.
   F. Use objective means of determining achievement and rating where possible.

VIII. Principle of Cooperation
Supervision is a cooperative enterprise between supervisor and employee.
   A. Begin with conditions as they are.
   B. Ask opinions of all involved when formulating policies.
   C. Organization is as good as its weakest link.
   D. Let employees help to determine policies and department programs.
   E. Be approachable and accessible—physically and mentally.
   F. Develop pleasant social relationships.

WHAT IS ADMINISTRATION

Administration is concerned with providing the environment, the material facilities, and the operational procedures that will promote the maximum growth and development of supervisors and employees. (Organization is an aspect and a concomitant of administration.)

There is no sharp line of demarcation between supervision and administration; these functions are intimately interrelated and, often, overlapping. They are complementary activities.

I. Practices Commonly Classed as "Supervisory"
   A. Conducting employees' conferences
   B. Visiting sections, units, offices, divisions, departments
   C. Arranging for demonstrations
   D. Examining plans
   E. Suggesting professional reading
   F. Interpreting bulletins
   G. Recommending in-service training courses
   H. Encouraging experimentation
   I. Appraising employee morale
   J. Providing for intervisitation

II. Practices Commonly Classified as "Administrative"
   A. Management of the office
   B. Arrangement of schedules for extra duties
   C. Assignment of rooms or areas
   D. Distribution of supplies
   E. Keeping records and reports
   F. Care of audio-visual materials
   G. Keeping inventory records
   H. Checking record cards and books

      I.   Programming special activities
      J.   Checking on the attendance and punctuality of employees

III.   Practices Commonly Classified as Both "Supervisory" and "Administrative"
      A.   Program construction
      B.   Testing or evaluating outcomes
      C.   Personnel accounting
      D.   Ordering instructional materials

RESPONSIBILITIES OF THE SUPERVISOR

A person employed in a supervisory capacity must constantly be able to improve his own efficiency and ability. He represent the employer to the employees and only continuous self-examination can make him a capable supervisor.

Leadership and training are the supervisor's responsibility. An efficient working unit is one in which the employees work with the supervisor. It is his job to bring out the best in his employees. He must always be relaxed, courteous, and calm in his association with his employees. Their feelings are important, and a harsh attitude does not develop the most efficient employees.

COMPETENCES OF THE SUPERVISOR

I.   Complete knowledge of the duties and responsibilities of his position.
II.   To be able to organize a job, plan ahead, and carry through.
III.   To have self-confidence and initiative.
IV.   To be able to handle the unexpected situation and make quick decisions.
V.   To be able to properly train subordinates in the positions they are best suited for.
VI.   To be able to keep good human relations among his subordinates.
VII. To be able to keep good human relations between his subordinates and himself and to earn their respect and trust.

THE PROFESSIONAL SUPERVISOR-EMPLOYEE RELATIONSHIP

There are two kinds of efficiency: one kind is only apparent and is produced in organizations through the exercise of mere discipline; this is but a simulation of the second, or true, efficiency which springs from spontaneous cooperation. If you are a manager, no matter how great or small your responsibility, it is your job, in the final analysis, to create and develop this involuntary cooperation among the people whom you supervise. For, no matter how powerful a combination of money, machines, and materials a company may have, this is a dead and sterile thing without a team of willing, thinking, and articulate people to guide it.

The following 21 points are presented as indicative of the exemplary basic relationship that should exist between supervisor and employee:

1. Each person wants to be liked and respected by his fellow employee and wants to be treated with consideration and respect by his superior.
2. The most competent employee will make an error. However, in a unit where good relations exist between the supervisor and his employees, tenseness and fear do not exist. Thus, errors are not hidden or covered up, and the efficiency of a unit is not impaired.

3. Subordinates resent rules, regulations, or orders that are unreasonable or unexplained.
4. Subordinates are quick to resent unfairness, harshness, injustices, and favoritism.
5. An employee will accept responsibility if he knows that he will be complimented for a job well done, and not too harshly chastised for failure; that his supervisor will check the cause of the failure, and, if it was the supervisor's fault, he will assume the blame therefore. If it was the employee's fault, his supervisor will explain the correct method or means of handling the responsibility.
6. An employee wants to receive credit for a suggestion he has made, that is used. If a suggestion cannot be used, the employee is entitled to an explanation. The supervisor should not say "no" and close the subject.
7. Fear and worry slow up a worker's ability. Poor working environment can impair his physical and mental health. A good supervisor avoids forceful methods, threats, and arguments to get a job done.
8. A forceful supervisor is able to train his employees individually and as a team, and is able to motivate them in the proper channels.
9. A mature supervisor is able to properly evaluate his subordinates and to keep them happy and satisfied.
10. A sensitive supervisor will never patronize his subordinates.
11. A worthy supervisor will respect his employees' confidences.
12. Definite and clear-cut responsibilities should be assigned to each executive.
13. Responsibility should always be coupled with corresponding authority.
14. No change should be made in the scope or responsibilities of a position without a definite understanding to that effect on the part of all persons concerned.
15. No executive or employee, occupying a single position in the organization, should be subject to definite orders from more than one source.
16. Orders should never be given to subordinates over the head of a responsible executive. Rather than do this, the officer in question should be supplanted.
17. Criticisms of subordinates should, whoever possible, be made privately, and in no case should a subordinate be criticized in the presence of executives or employees of equal or lower rank.
18. No dispute or difference between executives or employees as to authority or responsibilities should be considered too trivial for prompt and careful adjudication.
19. Promotions, wage changes, and disciplinary action should always be approved by the executive immediately superior to the one directly responsible.
20. No executive or employee should ever be required, or expected, to be at the same time an assistant to, and critic of, another.
21. Any executive whose work is subject to regular inspection should, wherever practicable, be given the assistance and facilities necessary to enable him to maintain an independent check of the quality of his work.

MINI-TEXT IN SUPERVISION, ADMINISTRATION, MANAGEMENT, AND ORGANIZATION

I. Brief Highlights

Listed concisely and sequentially are major headings and important data in the field for quick recall and review.

A. Levels of Management
Any organization of some size has several levels of management. In terms of a ladder, the levels are:

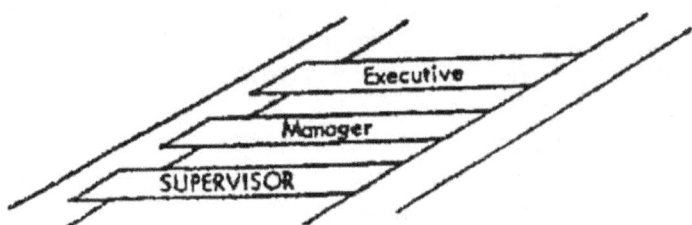

The first level is very important because it is the beginning point of management leadership.

B. What the Supervisor Must Learn
A supervisor must learn to:
1. Deal with people and their differences
2. Get the job done through people
3. Recognize the problems when they exist
4. Overcome obstacles to good performance
5. Evaluate the performance of people
6. Check his own performance in terms of accomplishment

C. A Definition of Supervisor
The term supervisor means any individual having authority, in the interests of the employer, to hire, transfer, suspend, lay-off, recall, promote, discharge, assign, reward, or discipline other employees or responsibility to direct them, or to adjust their grievances, or effectively to recommend such action, if, in connection with the foregoing, exercise of such authority is not of a merely routine or clerical nature but requires the use of independent judgment.

D. Elements of the Team Concept
What is involved in teamwork? The component parts are:
1. Members
2. A leader
3. Goals
4. Plans
5. Cooperation
6. Spirit

E. Principles of Organization
1. A team member must know what his job is.
2. Be sure that the nature and scope of a job are understood.
3. Authority and responsibility should be carefully spelled out.
4. A supervisor should be permitted to make the maximum number of decisions affecting his employees.
5. Employees should report to only one supervisor.
6. A supervisor should direct only as many employees as he can handle effectively.
7. An organization plan should be flexible.

8. Inspection and performance of work should be separate.
9. Organizational problems should receive immediate attention.
10. Assign work in line with ability and experience.

F. The Four Important Parts of Every Job
1. Inherent in every job is the *accountability* for results.
2. A second set of factors in every job is *responsibilities*.
3. Along with duties and responsibilities one must have the *authority* to act within certain limits without obtaining permission to proceed.
4. No job exists in a vacuum. The supervisor is surrounded by key *relationships*.

G. Principles of Delegation
Where work is delegated for the first time, the supervisor should think in terms of these questions:
1. Who is best qualified to do this?
2. Can an employee improve his abilities by doing this?
3. How long should an employee spend on this?
4. Are there any special problems for which he will need guidance?
5. How broad a delegation can I make?

H. Principles of Effective Communications
1. Determine the media.
2. To whom directed?
3. Identification and source authority.
4. Is communication understood?

I. Principles of Work Improvement
1. Most people usually do only the work which is assigned to them.
2. Workers are likely to fit assigned work into the time available to perform it.
3. A good workload usually stimulates output.
4. People usually do their best work when they know that results will be reviewed or inspected.
5. Employees usually feel that someone else is responsible for conditions of work, workplace layout, job methods, type of tools/equipment, and other such factors.
6. Employees are usually defensive about their job security.
7. Employees have natural resistance to change.
8. Employees can support or destroy a supervisor.
9. A supervisor usually earns the respect of his people through his personal example of diligence and efficiency.

J. Areas of Job Improvement
The areas of job improvement are quite numerous, but the most common ones which a supervisor can identify and utilize are:
1. Departmental layout
2. Flow of work
3. Workplace layout
4. Utilization of manpower
5. Work methods
6. Materials handling

7. Utilization
8. Motion economy

K. Seven Key Points in Making Improvements
1. Select the job to be improved
2. Study how it is being done now
3. Question the present method
4. Determine actions to be taken
5. Chart proposed method
6. Get approval and apply
7. Solicit worker participation

l. Corrective Techniques of Job Improvement
Specific Problems
1. Size of workload
2. Inability to meet schedules
3. Strain and fatigue
4. Improper use of men and skills
5. Waste, poor quality, unsafe conditions
6. Bottleneck conditions that hinder output
7. Poor utilization of equipment and machine
8. Efficiency and productivity of labor

General Improvement
1. Departmental layout
2. Flow of work
3. Work plan layout
4. Utilization of manpower
5. Work methods
6. Materials handling
7. Utilization of equipment
8. Motion economy

Corrective Techniques
1. Study with scale model
2. Flow chart study
3. Motion analysis
4. Comparison of units produced to standard allowance
5. Methods analysis
6. Flow chart and equipment study
7. Down time vs. running time
8. Motion analysis

M. A Planning Checklist
1. Objectives
2. Controls
3. Delegations
4. Communications
5. Resources
6. Manpower

7. Equipment
8. Supplies and materials
9. Utilization of time
10. Safety
11. Money
12. Work
13. Timing of improvements

N. Five Characteristics of Good Directions
In order to get results, directions must be:
1. Possible of accomplishment
2. Agreeable with worker interests
3. Related to mission
4. Planned and complete
5. Unmistakably clear

O. Types of Directions
1. Demands or direct orders
2. Requests
3. Suggestion or implication
4. volunteering

P. Controls
A typical listing of the overall areas in which the supervisor should establish controls might be:
1. Manpower
2. Materials
3. Quality of work
4. Quantity of work
5. Time
6. Space
7. Money
8. Methods

Q. Orienting the New Employee
1. Prepare for him
2. Welcome the new employee
3. Orientation for the job
4. Follow-up

R. Checklist for Orienting New Employees   Yes   No
1. Do you appreciate the feelings of new employees
   when they first report for work?   ___   ___
2. Are you aware of the fact that the new employee must
   make a big adjustment to his job?   ___   ___
3. Have you given him good reasons for liking the job and
   the organization?   ___   ___
4. Have you prepared for his first day on the job?   ___   ___
5. Did you welcome him cordially and make him feel needed?   ___   ___

		Yes	No
6.	Did you establish rapport with him so that he feels free to talk and discuss matters with you?	___	___
7.	Did you explain his job to him and his relationship to you?	___	___
8.	Does he know that his work will be evaluated periodically on a basis that is fair and objective?	___	___
9.	Did you introduce him to his fellow workers in such a way that they are likely to accept him?	___	___
10.	Does he know what employee benefits he will receive?	___	___
11.	Does he understand the importance of being on the job and what to do if he must leave his duty station?	___	___
12.	Has he been impressed with the importance of accident prevention and safe practice?	___	___
13.	Does he generally know his way around the department?	___	___
14.	Is he under the guidance of a sponsor who will teach the right way of doing things?	___	___
15.	Do you plan to follow-up so that he will continue to adjust successfully to his job?	___	___

S. Principles of Learning
  1. Motivation
  2. Demonstration or explanation
  3. Practice

T. Causes of Poor Performance
  1. Improper training for job
  2. Wrong tools
  3. Inadequate directions
  4. Lack of supervisory follow-up
  5. Poor communications
  6. Lack of standards of performance
  7. Wrong work habits
  8. Low morale
  9. Other

U. Four Major Steps in On-The-Job Instruction
  1. Prepare the worker
  2. Present the operation
  3. Tryout performance
  4. Follow-up

V. Employees Want Five Things
  1. Security
  2. Opportunity
  3. Recognition
  4. Inclusion
  5. Expression

W. Some Don'ts in Regard to Praise
   1. Don't praise a person for something he hasn't done.
   2. Don't praise a person unless you can be sincere.
   3. Don't be sparing in praise just because your superior withholds it from you.
   4. Don't let too much time elapse between good performance and recognition of it

X. How to Gain Your Workers' Confidence
   Methods of developing confidence include such things as:
   1. Knowing the interests, habits, hobbies of employees
   2. Admitting your own inadequacies
   3. Sharing and telling of confidence in others
   4. Supporting people when they are in trouble
   5. Delegating matters that can be well handled
   6. Being frank and straightforward about problems and working conditions
   7. Encouraging others to bring their problems to you
   8. Taking action on problems which impede worker progress

Y. Sources of Employee Problems
   On-the-job causes might be such things as:
   1. A feeling that favoritism is exercised in assignments
   2. Assignment of overtime
   3. An undue amount of supervision
   4. Changing methods or systems
   5. Stealing of ideas or trade secrets
   6. Lack of interest in job
   7. Threat of reduction in force
   8. Ignorance or lack of communications
   9. Poor equipment
   10. Lack of knowing how supervisor feels toward employee
   11. Shift assignments

   Off-the-job problems might have to do with:
   1. Health
   2. Finances
   3. Housing
   4. Family

Z. The Supervisor's Key to Discipline
   There are several key points about discipline which the supervisor should keep in mind:
   1. Job discipline is one of the disciplines of life and is directed by the supervisor.
   2. It is more important to correct an employee fault than to fix blame for it.
   3. Employee performance is affected by problems both on the job and off.
   4. Sudden or abrupt changes in behavior can be indications of important employee problems.
   5. Problems should be dealt with as soon as possible after they are identified.
   6. The attitude of the supervisor may have more to do with solving problems than the techniques of problem solving.
   7. Correction of employee behavior should be resorted to only after the supervisor is sure that training or counseling will not be helpful.

8. Be sure to document your disciplinary actions.
9. Make sure that you are disciplining on the basis of facts rather than personal feelings.
10. Take each disciplinary step in order, being careful not to make snap judgments, or decisions based on impatience.

AA. Five Important Processes of Management
1. Planning
2. Organizing
3. Scheduling
4. Controlling
5. Motivating

BB. When the Supervisor Fails to Plan
1. Supervisor creates impression of not knowing his job
2. May lead to excessive overtime
3. Job runs itself—supervisor lacks control
4. Deadlines and appointments missed
5. Parts of the work go undone
6. Work interrupted by emergencies
7. Sets a bad example
8. Uneven workload creates peaks and valleys
9. Too much time on minor details at expense of more important tasks

CC. Fourteen General Principles of Management
1. Division of work
2. Authority and responsibility
3. Discipline
4. Unity of command
5. Unity of direction
6. Subordination of individual interest to general interest
7. Remuneration of personnel
8. Centralization
9. Scalar chain
10. Order
11. Equity
12. Stability of tenure of personnel
13. Initiative
14. Esprit de corps

DD. Change

Bringing about change is perhaps attempted more often, and yet less well understood, than anything else the supervisor does. How do people generally react to change? (People tend to resist change that is imposed upon them by other individuals or circumstances.

Change is characteristic of every situation. It is a part of every real endeavor where the efforts of people are concerned.

1. Why do people resist change?
   People may resist change because of:
   a. Fear of the unknown
   b. Implied criticism
   c. Unpleasant experiences in the past
   d. Fear of loss of status
   e. Threat to the ego
   f. Fear of loss of economic stability

2. How can we best overcome the resistance to change?
   In initiating change, take these steps:
   a. Get ready to sell
   b. Identify sources of help
   c. Anticipate objections
   d. Sell benefits
   e. Listen in depth
   f. Follow up

II. Brief Topical Summaries

   A. Who/What is the Supervisor?
      1. The supervisor is often called the "highest level employee and the lowest level manager."
      2. A supervisor is a member of both management and the work group. He acts as a bridge between the two.
      3. Most problems in supervision are in the area of human relations, or people problems.
      4. Employees expect: Respect, opportunity to learn and to advance, and a sense of belonging, and so forth.
      5. Supervisors are responsible for directing people and organizing work. Planning is of paramount importance.
      6. A position description is a set of duties and responsibilities inherent to a given position.
      7. It is important to keep the position description up-to-date and to provide each employee with his own copy.

   B. The Sociology of Work
      1. People are alike in many ways; however, each individual is unique.
      2. The supervisor is challenged in getting to know employee differences. Acquiring skills in evaluating individuals is an asset.
      3. Maintaining meaningful working relationships in the organization is of great importance.
      4. The supervisor has an obligation to help individuals to develop to their fullest potential.
      5. Job rotation on a planned basis helps to build versatility and to maintain interest and enthusiasm in work groups.
      6. Cross training (job rotation) provides backup skills.

7. The supervisor can help reduce tension by maintaining a sense of humor, providing guidance to employees, and by making reasonable and timely decisions. Employees respond favorably to working under reasonably predictable circumstances.
8. Change is characteristic of all managerial behavior. The supervisor must adjust to changes in procedures, new methods, technological changes, and to a number of new and sometimes challenging situations.
9. To overcome the natural tendency for people to resist change, the supervisor should become more skillful in initiating change.

C. Principles and Practices of Supervision
1. Employees should be required to answer to only one superior.
2. A supervisor can effectively direct only a limited number of employees, depending upon the complexity, variety, and proximity of the jobs involved.
3. The organizational chart presents the organization in graphic form. It reflects lines of authority and responsibility as well as interrelationships of units within the organization.
4. Distribution of work can be improved through an analysis using the "Work Distribution Chart."
5. The "Work Distribution Chart" reflects the division of work within a unit in understandable form.
6. When related tasks are given to an employee, he has a better chance of increasing his skills through training.
7. The individual who is given the responsibility for tasks must also be given the appropriate authority to insure adequate results.
8. The supervisor should delegate repetitive, routine work. Preparation of recurring reports, maintaining leave and attendance records are some examples.
9. Good discipline is essential to good task performance. Discipline is reflected in the actions of employees on the job in the absence of supervision.
10. Disciplinary action may have to be taken when the positive aspects of discipline have failed. Reprimand, warning, and suspension are examples of disciplinary action.
11. If a situation calls for a reprimand, be sure it is deserved and remember it is to be done in private.

D. Dynamic Leadership
1. A style is a personal method or manner of exerting influence.
2. Authoritarian leaders often see themselves as the source of power and authority.
3. The democratic leader often perceives the group as the source of authority and power.
4. Supervisors tend to do better when using the pattern of leadership that is most natural for them.
5. Social scientists suggest that the effective supervisor use the leadership style that best fits the problem or circumstances involved.
6. All four styles—telling, selling, consulting, joining—have their place. Using one does not preclude using the other at another time.

7. The theory X point of view assumes that the average person dislikes work, will avoid it whenever possible, and must be coerced to achieve organizational objectives.
8. The theory Y point of view assumes that the average person considers work to be a natural as play, and, when the individual is committed, he requires little supervision or direction to accomplish desired objectives.
9. The leader's basic assumptions concerning human behavior and human nature affect his actions, decisions, and other managerial practices.
10. Dissatisfaction among employees is often present, but difficult to isolate. The supervisor should seek to weaken dissatisfaction by keeping promises, being sincere and considerate, keeping employees informed, and so forth.
11. Constructive suggestions should be encouraged during the natural progress of the work.

E. Processes for Solving Problems
1. People find their daily tasks more meaningful and satisfying when they can improve them.
2. The causes of problems, or the key factors, are often hidden in the background. Ability to solve problems often involves the ability to isolate them from their backgrounds. There is some substance to the cliché that some persons "can't see the forest for the trees."
3. New procedures are often developed from old ones. Problems should be broken down into manageable parts. New ideas can be adapted from old one.
4. People think differently in problem-solving situations. Using a logical, patterned approach is often useful. One approach found to be useful includes these steps:
    a. Define the problem
    b. Establish objectives
    c. Get the facts
    d. Weigh and decide
    e. Take action
    f. Evaluate action

F. Training for Results
1. Participants respond best when they feel training is important to them.
2. The supervisor has responsibility for the training and development of those who report to him.
3. When training is delegated to others, great care must be exercised to insure the trainer has knowledge, aptitude, and interest for his work as a trainer.
4. Training (learning) of some type goes on continually. The most successful supervisor makes certain the learning contributes in a productive manner to operational goals.
5. New employees are particularly susceptible to training. Older employees facing new job situations require specific training, as well as having need for development and growth opportunities.
6. Training needs require continuous monitoring.
7. The training officer of an agency is a professional with a responsibility to assist supervisors in solving training problems.

8. Many of the self-development steps important to the supervisor's own growth are equally important to the development of peers and subordinates. Knowledge of these is important when the supervisor consults with others on development and growth opportunities.

G. Health, Safety, and Accident Prevention
1. Management-minded supervisors take appropriate measures to assist employees in maintaining health and in assuring safe practices in the work environment.
2. Effective safety training and practices help to avoid injury and accidents.
3. Safety should be a management goal. All infractions of safety which are observed should be corrected without exception.
4. Employees' safety attitude, training and instruction, provision of safe tools and equipment, supervision, and leadership are considered highly important factors which contribute to safety and which can be influenced directly by supervisors.
5. When accidents do occur, they should be investigated promptly for very important reasons, including the fact that information which is gained can be used to prevent accidents in the future.

H. Equal Employment Opportunity
1. The supervisor should endeavor to treat all employees fairly, without regard to religion, race, sex, or national origin.
2. Groups tend to reflect the attitude of the leader. Prejudice can be detected even in very subtle form. Supervisors must strive to create a feeling of mutual respect and confidence in every employee.
3. Complete utilization of all human resources is a national goal. Equitable consideration should be accorded women in the work force, minority-group members, the physically and mentally handicapped, and the older employee. The important question is: "Who can do the job?"
4. Training opportunities, recognition for performance, overtime assignments, promotional opportunities, and all other personnel actions are to be handled on an equitable basis.

I. Improving Communications
1. Communications is achieving understanding between the sender and the receiver of a message. It also means sharing information—the creation of understanding.
2. Communication is basic to all human activity. Words are means of conveying meanings; however, real meanings are in people.
3. There are very practical differences in the effectiveness of one-way, impersonal, and two-way communications. Words spoken face-to-face are better understood. Telephone conversations are effective, but lack the rapport of person-to-person exchanges. The whole person communicates.
4. Cooperation and communication in an organization go hand in hand. When there is a mutual respect between people, spelling out rules and procedures for communicating is unnecessary.
5. There are several barriers to effective communications. These include failure to listen with respect and understanding, lack of skill in feedback, and misinterpreting the meanings of words used by the speaker. It is also common

practice to listen to what we want to hear, and tune out things we do not want to hear.
6. Communication is management's chief problem. The supervisor should accept the challenge to communicate more effectively and to improve interagency and intra-agency communications.
7. The supervisor may often plan for and conduct meetings. The planning phase is critical and may determine the success or the failure of a meeting.
8. Speaking before groups usually requires extra effort. Stage fright may never disappear completely, but it can be controlled.

J. Self-Development
1. Every employee is responsible for his own self-development.
2. Toastmaster and toastmistress clubs offer opportunities to improve skills in oral communications.
3. Planning for one's own self-development is of vital importance. Supervisors know their own strengths and limitations better than anyone else.
4. Many opportunities are open to aid the supervisor in his developmental efforts, including job assignments; training opportunities, both governmental and non-governmental—to include universities and professional conferences and seminars.
5. Programmed instruction offers a means of studying at one's own rate.
6. Where difficulties may arise from a supervisor's being away from his work for training, he may participate in televised home study or correspondence courses to meet his self-development needs.

K. Teaching and Training
1. The Teaching Process
Teaching is encouraging and guiding the learning activities of students toward established goals. In most cases this process consists of five steps: preparation, presentation, summarization, evaluation, and application.

   a. Preparation
   Preparation is two-fold in nature; that of the supervisor and the employee. Preparation by the supervisor is absolutely essential to success. He must know what, when, where, how, and whom he will teach. Some of the factors that should be considered are:
   1) The objectives
   2) The materials needed
   3) The methods to be used
   4) Employee participation
   5) Employee interest
   6) Training aids
   7) Evaluation
   8) Summarization

   Employee preparation consists in preparing the employee to receive the material. Probably the most important single factor in the preparation of the employee is arousing and maintaining his interest. He must know the objectives of the training, why he is there, how the material can be used, and its importance to him.

b. Presentation
   In presentation, have a carefully designed plan and follow it. The plan should be accurate and complete, yet flexible enough to meet situations as they arise. The method of presentation will be determined by the particular situation and objectives.

c. Summary
   A summary should be made at the end of every training unit and program. In addition, there may be internal summaries depending on the nature of the material being taught. The important thing is that the trainee must always be able to understand how each part of the new material relates to the whole.

d. Application
   The supervisor must arrange work so the employee will be given a chance to apply new knowledge or skills while the material is still clear in his mind and interest is high. The trainee does not really know whether he has learned the material until he has been given a chance to apply it. If the material is not applied, it loses most of its value.

e. Evaluation
   The purpose of all training is to promote learning. To determine whether the training has been a success or failure, the supervisor must evaluate this learning.
   In the broadest sense, evaluation includes all the devices, methods, skills, and techniques used by the supervisor to keep himself and the employees informed as to their progress toward the objectives they are pursuing. The extent to which the employee has mastered the knowledge, skills, and abilities, or changed his attitudes, as determined by the program objectives, is the extent to which instruction has succeeded or failed.
   Evaluation should not be confined to the end of the lesson, day, or program but should be used continuously. We shall note later the way this relates to the rest of the teaching process.

2. Teaching Methods
   A teaching method is a pattern of identifiable student and instructor activity used in presenting training material.
   All supervisors are faced with the problem of deciding which method should be used at a given time.

   a. Lecture
      The lecture is direct oral presentation of material by the supervisor. The present trend is to place less emphasis on the trainer's activity and more on that of the trainee.

   b. Discussion
      Teaching by discussion or conference involves using questions and other techniques to arouse interest and focus attention upon certain areas, and by doing so creating a learning situation. This can be one of the most

valuable methods because it gives the employees an opportunity to express their ideas and pool their knowledge.

    c. Demonstration

    The demonstration is used to teach how something works or how to do something. It can be used to show a principle or what the results of a series of actions will be. A well-staged demonstration is particularly effective because it shows proper methods of performance in a realistic manner.

    d. Performance

    Performance is one of the most fundamental of all learning techniques or teaching methods. The trainee may be able to tell how a specific operation should be performed but he cannot be sure he knows how to perform the operation until he has done so.
    As with all methods, there are certain advantages and disadvantages to each method.

    e. Which Method to Use

    Moreover, there are other methods and techniques of teaching. It is difficult to use any method without other methods entering into it. In any learning situation, a combination of methods is usually more effective than any one method alone.

Finally, evaluation must be integrated into the other aspects of the teaching-learning process.

It must be used in the motivation of the trainees; it must be used to assist in developing understanding during the training; and it must be related to employee application of the results of training.

This is distinctly the role of the supervisor.

POLICE SCIENCE NOTES
DETENTION PROCEDURES

Introduction

Generally detention is thought of as confinement of a prisoner in a jail facility from his formal booking to his formal release. This includes a period of time when he is merely held for bail or court appearance, when he is held after trial for formal sentencing, and when he is actually serving time in a jail or prison. Actually his arrest restricts or removes his freedom and places him under official restraint; thus, it is at this point that his actual detention begins.

Responsibility for the prisoner before booking may be solely that of the arresting officer or it may be given over to jail personnel assigned to transport him to the detention facility. We are concerned, therefore, as a practical matter with the entire time the prisoner is in official custody beginning with his arrest and ending with his release from custody.

Security is the essence of detention and implies assurance against escape or rescue of the prisoner. It also implies a full measure of personal safety for the officers, the prisoner himself, other inmates and visitors and other citizens.

Although it has been implied, and is true in fact, that our concern is with persons arrested for the commission of crimes, our responsibility is a broader one. The more broad responsibility will be increasingly important in time of natural disaster or civil defense emergency. The latter includes the "holding" for safekeeping of the mentally and physically incompetent, children without parents or who are lost or abandoned, persons who are threatened by mobs or individuals, and those who must be held as material witnesses. While legal and procedural provisions must be made to handle each of the above, this is a local matter not detailed here.

Transportation

Usually an arresting officer makes a search of his prisoner at the time of arrest for dangerous weapons, means of self-destruction, and less frequently, for evidence of a crime. Officers should be trained and required to make this search. Nonetheless, since it is often made under unusual conditions of stress, transporting and booking officers should also conduct searches with final responsibility lying with the booking officer. Adequate search is a protection to police and jailers, to the prisoner and other inmates, and to visitors and other citizens.

The search, however, only removes one kind of danger; the security measure of adequate restraint must be provided to avoid loss of the prisoner by his own actions or those of others. The restraint is also provided, of course, as another means of preventing injury to the prisoner and to others.

Transportation should be considered as any means used to get the prisoner from one point to another which is usually considered to be from the location of arrest to the place of detention. Transportation, however, is also involved in taking the prisoner to court, in moving him from one place of detention to another, and in taking him to the site of work details or assignments. For our purposes we must assume that transportation may mean moving the prisoner on foot, in a special or regular police automobile, in a special prisoner vehicle (paddywagon or prisoner van) or by other means including aircraft or boats.

The same general precautions apply to all means of transport because the need for security and restraint exists in all. Transport by walking should only be considered in the absence of a proper vehicle, for very short distances, or when physical circumstances may require it, as in moving the prisoner from a detention facility to a court. The number of officers required varies according to apparent need but also according to prescribed regulations. Only one officer is required in the transport of noncriminal nonviolent persons in protective custody and these include children, the aged, minor offenders, and others. Two officers should be used normally for a person under criminal arrest if there is even a nominal possibility of escape or rescue. Three or more officers should be used in serious criminal cases, cases involving a violent prisoner, or where there is likely to be a serious attempt to escape, rescue, or attack the prisoner.

Two officers should almost always be used in prisoner transport by vehicle except in minor cases when the prisoner is placed in a separate, secure and specially designed section of the vehicle screened off from the driver. When a vehicle is used all doors should be locked and inside handles removed from the prisoner section, as in the rear of an automobile.

Minimal restraint is required when the prisoner is in a secure and separate section of the vehicle unless conflict among prisoners may develop. Reasonable restraint should be used otherwise and will usually involve the use of handcuffs. Whenever handcuffs and other restraining devices are required public display of their use should be avoided.

Special precautions should be used at the place of detention because this is the most likely point of escape or rescue. It is important that detention officers assist transporting officers in placing prisoners in the detention facility. Although the prisoner has been under restraint since his arrest, detention in a formal sense begins when he is placed in the detention facility. Properly booking and admitting the prisoner is of utmost importance and carefully prescribed admittance procedures should be established and followed. The latter, of course, must conform to State and local legal requirements. A prisoner's property, and evidence also, must be properly identified, receipted, and secured. Identification of property should be witnessed under most circumstances and especially when the prisoner is unable to sign for it. Securing property implies controlling it so that it may be returned intact on the prisoner's release.

Fingerprinting and photographing of each prisoner should be required in all criminal cases and in emergency conditions where accurate identification is important as when the prisoner is suffering from amnesia. Exceptions to this practice may be established, i.e., if the prisoner had been previously arrested and his identification established prior to the present arrest.

A final detailed and complete search must be made. The search should be for evidence if this is appropriate under the circumstances; however, the principal purpose at this point is probably to remove offensive weapons and means of self-destruction. Before a prisoner is placed in a cell it should be carefully searched also.

Capabilities for medical examination of incoming prisoners, especially those who are sick or injured, should be provided. This is not only humane but may prevent serious problems later including criticism for failure to provide proper care. Under some circumstances a detailed medical examination for all prisoners may be practicable. In this case, by formal regulation, prisoners falling in certain categories must be examined. Categories should include any person over 60 years of age as this age group will usually contain a much higher percentage of persons requiring care than would those who are younger; any person with a history of illness or disability known to the officers by prior acquaintance with the person or through medical records he carries on his person; any person who is apparently, although not necessarily obviously, ill or injured; any prisoner who complains of illness or injury; and any person who is unconscious or comatose.

It is standard practice in detention facilities to provide for separation of prisoners by age and sex. Quite obviously juveniles and adults should not be quartered together, nor should men be placed with women. Those who have communicable diseases or who may have been exposed to them should be placed in quarantine sections. Those who are perverts or who exhibit tendencies to perversion should be separated from others, particularly children. Those who are mentally deranged, or who apparently become so, must also be isolated. This may be an especially important consideration under emer-gency conditions. Less serious offenders should be separated from the more serious offenders to avoid recruiting prisoners to the ranks of major criminals. The use of psychiatrists and medical personnel is recommended to assist in determining necessary separation in the case of perversion and mental derangement.

Providing adequate security is essential. All offensive weapons and means of self-destruction must be physically protected and adequately guarded. None should be within reach of any prisoner. Guards should not carry firearms while in any prisoner section. Full control of all means of entrance and exit must be provided. No guard should have on his person a set of keys which would allow escape from or admittance to the full facility or a series of its sections. All tools require close control because they may be used as weapons, escape devices, or provide the means to make such items. Prisoners being returned to cells from corridors, shops, and dining rooms should be searched.

Medical supplies must be carefully controlled. Their possession by prisoners provide means of self-destruction and barter. Under some circumstances prisoners would maliciously destroy essential medical provisions.

On a frequent, intermittent basis, quarters and inmates must be inspected and prisoners counted.

To avoid emotional problems, provide exercise, and for other reasons prisoners who warrant the trust can be given some freedom in the facility and be put to minor but productive tasks. Classification of prisoners as "trusties" or available for light work must be carefully done to avoid escapes and other problems.

All security measures must be established on a basis that allows prompt implementation of plans for evacuation of prisoners in the event of fire or facility destruction by other means. Planning must also provide full means of protection against the consequences of riot and mob attempts at rescue or attack. This may require provisions to quickly and inconspicuously move key prisoners to other detention.

Detention When Jails Unavailable

Most shelters and relocation facilities are not designed for detention purposes. This will require imaginative improvisation of both quarters and procedures. Two things must be provided in spite of adverse circumstances: (1) Basic security for prisoners, officers, and other occupants; and (2) separation of various categories of prisoners.

Large rooms, of course, can be used for group detention if adequate security is provided and if the need for separation is minimal or absent. Such use of space, however, may require the use of additional guards constantly on the alert to avoid altercations or plotting for escape.

In shelters the problems of security and separation may require unusual use of restraining devices and materials. Individual prisoners can be handcuffed to pipes, doorknobs, stanchions, or window bars. If this is done, adequate free space around the prisoner should be provided to avoid improper and dangerous contact with other prisoners or occupants of the shelter. Two prisoners can be secured with a single set of handcuffs merely by passing the cuffs behind a pipe set close to a wall or the floor, or behind a bar in a barred window or door.

Ropes, belts, and similar material may be used in lieu of handcuffs, but require unusual care to avoid injury or escapes. Although it may be necessary to occasionally check handcuffs to see that they are not too tight for the comfort or safety of the prisoner, frequent inspection of rope and other nonmetallic material is essential. These may quickly become either too tight and thus cause injury, or too loose and thus permit escape. Restraints of material must also be checked if they become wet, or dry out after being wet.

Sedatives may be used under unusual circumstances by a doctor or by a nurse under his direction. Sedatives have a particular value when handling a violent person and may be used both as a restraint and treatment in many cases.

Expensive, but necessary on occasion, will be the use of guards or officers on the basis of one guard to a prisoner. This should be avoided if possible because of the excessive drain it puts on available personnel.

Conclusion

It should be said once again that security is the essence of detention. The safety of officers, prisoners, and others is dependent on strict adherence to carefully prepared procedures.

CLASSIFICATION OF JAIL PRISONERS

TABLE OF CONTENTS

Preface

The Jailer's Needs to Know 1

The Development and Testing of
a Classification Tool 5

    Design of an experimental procedure 5

    Preliminary tests 7

        Prisoner inventory form 9

        Major test findings 17

    Future possibilities 19

Appendix A 23

    Description of test jails and summary of
        of test experiences

Appendix B 27

    Summary report.

CLASSIFICATION OF JAIL PRISONERS

THE JAILER'S NEEDS TO KNOW

The days have gone forever when jails, other than those in large metropolitan areas, dealt almost exclusively with local citizens. Not only were the reputations and backgrounds of these people generally known, but commitment to jail was a conspicuous event. From his own knowledge and information readily available to him, the jailer could quickly size up the situation and determine how best to handle each prisoner. In these days of rapid community growth and mobility, when it is commonplace for people to relocate frequently and travel from one end of the country to the other in a few hours, increasing numbers of jail prisoners are commited as total strangers. Moreover, these people may have no ties whatever to the community in which the jail is located. The proper handling of prisoners who are strangers is an entirely different problem than dealing with people who are well known.

Within the limits of the law and the framework of judicial and public expectations, the chief jailer and his staff have wide latitude for making institutional policy decisions, establishing or changing operating procedures and introducing new methods, programs and services. While the exercise of this responsibility is in the interest of increasing the efficiency and effectiveness of basic jail functions, the inescapable fact is that jail personnel deal with people. For this reason, the manner in which policies, rules and procedures are applied have great importance. In part, this becomes a matter of sensitizing personnel to prisoners' needs, problems and feelings. In part, also, it is a matter of having information about individual prisoners with which to distinguish among them and to make decision choices based on these distinctions.

Just a brief look at a few ordinary jail activities will indicate how acute the need for information about prisoners can be. Take housing, for example. Any policy of housing jail prisoners will have to be determined to some extent by the kind and location of available accommodations. Yet, when choices are possible, common sense will dictate that: juvenile and female prisoners are held in seperate quarters; weak and submissive prisoners are not placed in dormitories or group cells with aggressive predatory types; prisoners with incapacitating physical handicaps are assigned to quarters on the main floor; young impressionable prisoners are separated from those who are sophisticated and calloused. Further reflection will suggest other distinctions.

2

One of the surest ways of inviting a law-suit, official or public censure and adverse prisoner reaction is to ignore or be unaware of a prisoner's need for emergency medical care. Will commitment policies permit the receiving officer to refuse acceptance of a person in need of immediate medical attention? If so, how does he discover that a problem exists and in what ways does he exercise this discretion? With whom and in what ways can prisoners register complaints of being ill? What is done about such complaints? What other kinds of emergency needs might arise which, if ignored, might cause great personal or family hardship or extreme and unnecessary inconvenience?

What is the work assignment policy at the jail? What should it be? How are trusties selected? Work release candidates? Many factors besides security have to be considered in making work assignment decisions. Is the prisoner physically able to the work required? A person with a heart condition, for example, or one subject to seizures should not be assigned to work in high places or at tasks requiring extreme physical exertion. Does the prisoner have the intelligence and emotional stability to follow instructions? Does he have the skills or experience that may be required? Will he take care of tools and equipment? Can he work cooperatively with others?

Adequate feeding can present problems. There may be dietary considerations, as for those who are under special medical care or those who live under strict religious observances. Food handlers should meet at least minimum public health standards of being free from infectious disease and neat in personal cleanliness. If there is a central dining room, it may be necessary to feed certain prisoners separately from certain others, such as a material witness who is to testify against a prisoner awaiting trial. When meals are served in housing units, there is a need to assure that the food is properly conveyed and that rations are distributed equitably. In this connection, it must be remembered that in group cells or dormitories weak inmates can be victimized by aggressive prisoners who will get more than their share.

Whatever correctional programs and services may be available obviously are intended for those prisoners who need them and who are eligible to participate in them. Increasing attention is being given such non-traditional pretrial programs as early diversion, pretrial liberty and emergency services to defendants and such post-conviction procedures as extending the limits of confinement. These suggest a number of possible new roles for jails for which new capabilities and more information about prisoners will be needed.

So the jailer has various needs for various kinds of information about prisoners; and these can be defined in fairly specific terms. One kind of information is that which has *predictive value*. Information of this kind is essential to good decision-making. To illustrate: it must be decided whether to place a prisoner under maximum or minimum supervision. The prisoner's stability is an important factor in such a decision. Residence is one indicator of stability, but how long he has been a resident of the community probably is more relevant than other kinds of information about residence. Thus, in this illustration, length of residence has predictive value in determining a person's stability, whereas the address or amount of rent does not.

Another kind of information is that which can be used for *identification purposes*. Essential distinctions are made among prisoners constantly. Is he in jail awaiting trial or serving a sentence? It makes a difference. It also matters whether he will be in jail a few days or several months. Identifying information is indispensible to good decision-making. It would make little sense, for example, to enroll in Alcoholics Anonymous a prisoner who did not at least have a serious drinking problem.

A third kind of information is that which is needed for *management evaluations*. Budget requests are sought and defended in such terms as daily per capita costs for care, custody and various kinds of programs and services. Changes in policy and other management adjustments are made in part on evaluations of day-to-day operations and activities. Planning for future requirements cannot proceed very far without factual accounts of the present and careful analyses of trends. These are but a few examples of many needs for information about prisoners, their circumstances, their management and control.

5

THE DEVELOPMENT AND TESTING OF A CLASSIFICATION TOOL

The focus of concern in this project is the jailer's decision-making responsibility and whether certain kinds of information about prisoners can be obtained and used in ways which will contribute to more prompt and reliable decisions. The jailer makes many decisions of many kinds. This project is limited primarily to determinations of prisoner custody (supervision requirements) and housing assignments. These are important basic decisions that are made tens of thousands of times every day in jails throughout the United States.

This is not a new concern. For a long time jailers have rightly complained of the extreme difficulties imposed upon them in exercising their responsibilities for the safekeeping of all kinds of prisoners who come and go daily. Underlying the burden is the absence of essential information with which to make important decisions based on factual experience and differences in prisoners. Past attempts have been made to adapt to the jail setting diagnostic and case management techniques of major prisons and reformatories. These efforts have been quite unproductive for reasons which are increasingly apparent. Informational needs have not been pin-pointed. Although both prisons and jails are lock-ups, the operation of a local jail is very much unlike that of a prison for sentenced felons. Most jails have neither the staff specialists nor the time to apply diagnostic procedures that are suitable for prisons.

Development of this experimental classification tool has been predictated on certain beliefs or assumptions. (1) It is possible to pin-point the jailers information needs and to distinguish various kinds of information in accordance with the uses for it. (2) From an array of information it is possible to select specific items which will have identification and predictive value for decision-making. (3) The kinds of information needed for basic decisions related to the management and control of jail prisoners can be obtained promptly and easily. (4) Information uses can be simplified and standardized.

DESIGN OF AN EXPERIMENTAL PROCEDURE

From years of experience in classifying sentenced prisoners and from published designs of bail reform procedures, items of information

6

were listed which were thought to have a significant bearing on decisions as to prisoner supervision and housing assignments. More specifically, the object was to find what were thought to be the best indicators of emotional stability and mature behavior habits. The list was revised many times to insure that it included only the kinds of information that could be obtained during a brief interview, subject to quick and simple verification as might be necessary. The list was reduced to what was thought to be only key items and it was arranged so that it could be recorded by simply checking "yes" or "no" responses to direct questions.

The next task was to isolate the stability indicators and assign reasonable numerical weights to them since it could be expected that some items would be better predictors than others. It was also thought that some variables would be predictors only when measured in combination with other variables. Classification experience also suggested that not every important information item lends itself to variable weighting. Some items produce simple "either"-"or" decisions. It was known only that, by whatever means, the predictive values of the information at hand would have to be substantially greater than chance or the information would be useless as a decision-making aid.

With these considerations in mind, the information list was amended further and converted into an inventory of basic prisoner data which contained a mix of both predictive variables and items of identification that presumably would be helpful in decision-making, plus a few other items that might be useful for other purposes. Two overlay sheets were designed: one intended as an aid in determining degree of supervision required; the other as an aid to making housing assignments. Both were adapted to a prisoner inventory form with window cut-outs matched to the possible responses to certain information questions. The supervision overlay was geared to three grades of custody (maximum, medium and minimum supervision) in contrast to the usual two (trusties and all others) and included both "either"-"or" and weighted variable items of information. The housing overlay was limited to "either"-"or" items of information with a coded explanation of how these should be considered in making housing assignments.

The prisoner inventory and the two overlays were subjected to two pretests. The first was against the case records of 50 randomly selected Federal prisoners. This group was not like a random group of jail prisoners in that they were all adult males serving sentences, but they had been classified as to custody and housing. Inventory sheets were completed from information contained in the case records. Both overlay sheets were applied. The housing overlay showed nothing significant but the custody overlay produced a spread of maximum, medium and minimum custody decision recommendations that conformed roughly with decisions that had already been made.

Adjustments were made in some of the inventory items and in the scoring weights of the custody overlay. These manipulations produced greater conformity with the 50 case records of decisions already made. These revisions were further pretested with nearby jail prisoners A set of 109 additional inventories were completed from actual interviews. The revised custody overlay produced tabulated results that showed a nearly normal distribution of maximum, medium and minimum custody candidates. Unfortunately, there was no way of comparing these findings with actual custody decisions since neither of the cooperating jails had such a classification system. Likewise, because of the nature of both facilities, there was no way of utilizing the housing assignment overlay.

PRELIMINARY TESTS

With this encouragement, it was decided that the materials should be put to experimental use. The items of information for decision-making were rearranged again to further simplify their recording and use. A few new items were added, not for decision-making but to demonstrate the convenience and usefulness of a single record of basic information that could serve many administrative and management purposes. It was also thought that the numerically weighted values of certain information items used for custody decisions could also be used to predict certain kinds of actual behavior. In other words, it was assumed that the higher the numerical score the more likely the prisoner would be to accept the circumstances of his imprisonment and to relate satisfactorily to fellow prisoners and staff members. Accordingly, a questionnaire was added to the back of the prisoner inventory to test this assumption.

Following is the experimental Prisoner Inventory as it was prepared for use during a predetermined 60 day test period at selected jails. Both overlays were readied by final editing to insure that self-contained instructions were as complete and clear as possible. To these was added a set of general instructions for the actual use tests.

Prisoner Inventory Test

INSTRUCTIONS FOR PRISONER INVENTORY

It is intended that the Prisoner Inventory be completed for each prisoner admitted to jail, on the basis of a brief interview and such additional verifications as may be necessary. This may be done as part of the booking process. If not done then, the Inventory should be completed as soon after booking as possible. NOTE: The Prisoner Inventory is designed to be used only for healthy male prisoners. Females and prisoners who obviously are in need of immediate medical care should be considered special cases.

The upper part of the Prisoner Inventory consists of information items that have a bearing on decisions as to housing and supervision required. Overlay sheets, which carry their own instructions, are provided to assist in making these two decisions. The information contained in this portion of the Inventory, along with that appearing on the lower part, may have other possible uses as well. Check the YES or NO column for each category of items. Most check marks will appear in the YES column, but check only the one that is appropriate. Example, in the category of "AGE", the prisoner is either legally a juvenile, under 21, between 21 and 25, between 26 and 35 or over 35. Check one.

As a guide to deciding the degree of custody or amount of supervision required for the prisoner, *carefully* place the Supervision overlay sheet on top of the completed Prisoner Inventory so that the proper items show through the windows. Look first for W items that show through, then add the numerical values of all the other items that show. Enter W or the total score on the top of the Inventory sheet. Consult the instructions on the overlay sheet as a guide to custody decision. There is reason to believe that this indication is reliable, *but it is not a substitute for common sense.*

For housing decisions follow the same procedure of matching the overlay sheet to the Inventory form. The numbers at the windows, however, are not to be added. They are code numbers that are keyed to specific instructions on the bottom of the overlay sheet. Note that these are not substitutes for common sense.

10

To assist in the experimental use of these forms, enter the custody classification and housing assignment at the upper left hand corner of the Prisoner Inventory form. Whenever either of these classifications may be changed, enter the date and the change on the top of the form, from left to right, so that the last entry on the right will be the current one.

There is a question as to whether the decision-maker should be the same person who completed the Prisoner Inventory. For experimental purposes this does not matter. If the same employee performs both functions he may develop certain biases that will cause him to complete the Inventory to coincide with what he thinks the outcome should be. It is possible, too, that in some jails decisions of this kind are made only by supervisory personnel. On the other hand, a rating instrument of any kind can never be all-inclusive or perfect. This one is not a substitute either for common sense or for knowledge, experience and skills in dealing with people. From this point of view, it is possible that the person completing the Inventory can make better decisions because his personal contact with the prisoner is better than relying entirely on a piece of paper that somebody else provided.

Again, because of great differences in the nature of jail operations, it may not be necessary to complete the Prisoner Inventory form on all persons booked. For example, the value of completed forms for offenders who will be held in jail for only a few hours or a day or two may be questioned.

On the back of the Prisoner Inventory form is a questionnaire relative to prisoner characteristics and behavior that were observed. This should be completed as part of the experiment by the jail supervisor or other staff member who is in a posistion to know. The evaluation should be made on the day of the prisoner's release from jail or at the end of the 60-day experiment, whichever comes first. Simply place a check mark in the appropriate column as to each item, record any additional comments; enter date, signature and title.

All Prisoner Inventory forms must be picked up by the Jail Inspector at the conclusion of the 60-day trial period and mailed promptly to the Bureau. Review and analysis of the data will be primarily for the purpose of determining the reliability of the forms as a decision-making guide. In addition, it is hoped that the forms will be an aid in predicting the behavior of certain catagories of prisoners.

DEGREE OF SUPERVISION REQUIRED*   **PRISONER INVENTORY**

	RATING	YES	NO		RATING	YES	NO		RATING	YES	NO
COMMITMENT STATUS								**MENTAL CONDITION OR ATTITUDE**			
								Appears or acts —			
On writ	W							questionable	W		
Other	W			**RESIDENCE**				abnormal	W		
				Duration— ** (see footnote)							
				under 6 mos.	1-0						
Possible detainers	W			6 mos. to 1 yr.	2-1						
				over 1 yr.	3-2						
				Duration in community —							
				under 6 mos.	1-0						
				6 mos. to 1 yr.	2-1						
Prior commitment	3			over 1 yr.	3-2						
AGE				Rents by —							
Juvenile	W										
				month	2						
				Leasing or pur.	3						
21-25	1			Lives with family	3						
26-35	2			**RECENT WORK HISTORY**							
Over 35	3										
				Employed or in school —							
				full time	3						
				part time	2						
MARITAL STATUS											
Married	3			under 6 mos.	1						
Family support —				6 mos. to 1 yr.	2						
total	3			over 1 yr.	3						
major	2										
partial	1										

* to be used for healthy male prisoners only—females, and prisoners in need of medical care, are to be considered special cases.

** if residence is in local cummunity, use left hand rating figures; if not, use right hand rating figures.

NOTES

Purpose: Only those items of the Prisoner Inventory thought to have a direct bearing on custody decisions are used.

Rating legend: 3 denotes a good indicator of stability.
                2 denotes a fair indicator of stability.
                1 denotes a minimum indicator of stability.
                W (Warning) is an indicator of probable instability.
                (Any W item checked means that in the absence of any compeling reason to the contrary, the prisoner should not be placed in reduced custody and may require maximum supervision at all times.)

Scoring: W: If a check mark appears for any item rated W, the prisoner should be classified maximum custody until further investigation or a change of circumstances suggests otherwise.
        10 or less : a good candidate for maximum custody.
        11 - 15   : a questionable candidate for medium custody.
        16 - 20   : a good candidate for medium custody.
        21 - 25   : a questionable candidate for minimum custody.
        26 - 30   : a good candidate for minimum custody.

PRISONER INVENTORY

NAME: _____ NUMBER: _____ DATE: _____ TIME: _____

	YES	NO		YES	NO		YES	NO
COMMITMENT STATUS			ESTIMATED STAY			MENTAL CONDITION		
Awaiting trial			One day or less			OR ATTITUDE		
Awaiting sentence			2 days to 1 wk.			Appears or acts —	////	////
Awaiting appeal			Over 1 wk. to 1 mo.			normal		
Direct sentence or fine			Over 1 mo. to 6 mos.			questionable		
Parole violation			Over 6 mos. to 1 yr.			abnormal		
On writ			Over 1 yr.			describe:	////	////
Other			RESIDENCE				////	////
specify:	////	////	Address:	////	////		////	////
	////	////		////	////		////	////
	////	////	Duration —				////	////
	////	////	under 6 mos.				////	////
Possible detainers			6 mos. to 1 yr.			PHYSICAL CONDITION		
explain:	////	////	over 1 yr.					
	////	////	Duration in community —	////	////	General appearance —	////	////
	////	////	under 6 mos.			good		
	////	////	6 mos. to 1 yr.			questionable		
	////	////	over 1 yr.			poor		
Prior commitment			Rents by —	////	////	Present complaint		
AGE			day or week			explain:	////	////
Juvenile			month				////	////
Under 21			Leasing or purchasing				////	////
21-25			Lives with family				////	////
26-35			RECENT WORK HISTORY				////	////
Over 35			Employer's name	////	////	Taking medication		
SEX			and address:	////	////	description:	////	////
Male				////	////		////	////
Female				////	////		////	////
CHARGE OR OFFENSE				////	////		////	////
Against person			Employed or in school —				////	////
Sex			full time			Doctor's care		
Property			part time			physician's name:	////	////
Public order			odd jobs				////	////
Other			unemployed				////	////
MARITAL STATUS			under 6 mos.				////	////
Married			6 mos. to 1 yr.				////	////
Family support —	////	////	over 1 yr.				////	////
total			WORK SKILLS (describe)			Appearance or	////	////
major				////	////	history of —	////	////
partial				////	////	alcohol		
none				////	////	drugs		

Describe prisoner's responsibilities, if any:

Persons interested in this prisoner:

Name	Address	Tel.	Relation
_____	_____	_____	_____
_____	_____	_____	_____
_____	_____	_____	_____

Immediate problems: (list in order of importance)   (Action indicated)

Other observations or comments:

14

Prisoner Characteristics and Behavior	True	More True Than False	More False Than True	Un-true	Don't Know
General Adjustment					
1. Accepted circumstances without complaints.					
2. Behavior was satisfactory and dependable.					
3. Participated in available activities regularly.					
4. Positive outlook toward release.					
5. Escaped or attempted escape.		/////////////	/////////////		/////////
Relationships with Personnel					
1. Cooperative and respectful.					
2. Accepted instructions and constructive criticism.					
3. Sought no personal favors; did not fraternize.					
4. Enjoyed the confidence and respect of personnel.					
Relationships with Prisoners					
1. Sought few associates and chose them carefully.					
2. Respectful and considerate.					
3. Self-assured; maintained own identity.					
4. Enjoyed the confidence and respect of others.					

Comments:

Date:	Signature:	Title:

15

HOUSING* **PRISONER INVENTORY**

	CODE NO.	YES	NO		CODE NO.	YES	NO
COMMITMENT STATUS				**MENTAL CONDITION OR ATTITUDE**			
Awaiting trial	1			Appears or acts —			
Awaiting sentence	1			questionable	9		
				abnormal	9		
Other	2						
				PHYSICAL CONDITION			
				General appearance —			
Prior commitment	3			questionable	9		
AGE				poor	9		
Juvenile	4						
Under 21	5						
SEX							
Female	6			Doctor's care	9		
CHARGE OR OFFENSE							
Against person	7						
Sex	8						
				Appearance or history of —			
				alcohol	9		
				drugs	9		

*to be used for all commitments

Code No	Action
1	Should be kept apart from sentenced prisoners if possible.
2	Should be kept apart from sentenced prisoners if possible and if material witness, awaiting sanity hearing, etc., may require separate quarters.
3	The degree of supervision required and the conduct record of a prior commitment are good indicators of what can be expected on this commitment.
4	Must be kept entirely separate from all adults.
5	If weak submissive type, may need protection from sophisticated, aggressive types.
6	Must be kept entirely separate from all males.
7	Others may need protection from aggressive, predatory types.
8	Child molesters and rapists may need protection from others. Aggressive homosexuals may need to be segregated, passive homosexuals may need protection.
9	Obtain medical advice for housing requirements.

For an adequate test it was hoped that five or six jails could be selected that would represent geographical spread, different size and various kinds of operations. It was also hoped that local jail officials could be found who would be willing and able to make operational changes during the 60-day test period in order that decisions called for by the classification forms could actually be applied. Six such jails were identified and the Federal Jail Inspectors responsible for them were brought together for briefings on the test and discussions of the kinds of operational changes that might be considered. They were also informed how to help jail personnel prepare for the test experience. The kinds of assistance that might be needed to complete the experiment were anticipated. It was determined that the test period should run from May 1 to June 30, 1970. As soon as the test ended the Inspectors involved were to collect all of the completed forms and send them to the private consulting agency in New York City with whom a contract was made for processing and analyzing the test data. (See Appendix B for the summary report).

Major test findings: A single general conclusion about the experiment, such as that it succeeded or failed, would have little meaning. The fact is that in both operational and analytical terms the test experience was highly encouraging in a number of particulars and just as disappointing in others. The experiment also produced some outcomes that were unforeseen.

Findings related to basic assumptions. Assumption (1): It is possible to pin-point the jailers information needs and to distinguish various kinds of information in accordance with the uses for it. The test confirmed this. All information items used in the test were specific and they were of three distinct types, all of which were applied in one way or another. Assumption (2): From an array of information it is possible to select specific items which will have identification and predictive value for decision-making. The test confirmed this. See discussion of findings related to experimental assumptions, below, and Appendix B. Assumption (3): The kinds of information needed for basic decisions can be obtained promptly and easily. The test confirmed this. Interviews with new prisoners were conducted at the time of booking or soon thereafter. Interviews were completed in ten minutes or less each by line officers who were given minimum instructions in how to conduct such interviews. Decisions as to custody and housing assignments were made instantly. Assumption (4): Information uses can be simplified and standardized. The test confirmed this. See the custody and housing overlays both of which were used simultaneously in six different jails for a period of 60 days.

Findings related to experimental assumptions. Assumption (a): It is possible to classify jail prisoners into three grades of custody, instead of the usual two. The test confimed this. Of 1,735 prisoners processed in six jails over a 60-day period 743 were classified maximum custody, 886 medium custody and 106 minimum custody. Assumption (b): An instrument can be designed which will reliably identify which prisoners should be classified maximum, medium and minimum custody. The test provided statistical encouragement that this is possible. See Appendix B. There was about a .70 level of correlation between recommended custody and actual custody decisions in all test jails. Assumption (c): An instrument can be designed which will help to avoid improper and unwise housing assignments. The test provided neither positive nor negative clues as to this. Whether because of lack of understanding or reluctance to modify operational customs for a limited test period, there was little indication that available housing accommodations were differentiated or stratified to enable a test of this assumption. Assumption (d): The scoring values used in making custody decisions can also be used to predict prisoner behavior. The test provided neither positive nor negative clues as to this. No answers were recorded on this part of the Prisoner Inventory forms in over three-fourths of them. With many entries incomplete on the remaining one-forth, meaningful data analysis was impossible.

While these results are directly related to the primary purposes of the test, the experiment produced a number of other significant findings:

The Prisoner Inventory itself can be a useful identifier of prisoner types. Examples: Officials at one jail expressed surprise at finding so high a proportion of drug users. At another jail staff expressed surprise at the number of young prisoners awaiting trial on serious charges. At a third jail the Prisoner Inventory documented the burdensome process of repeated bookings of habitual drunks.

The Prisoner Inventory can provide information that is useful in identifying correctional needs of prisoners. The jail with the high proportion of drug users planned to seek the assistance of the county medical association in treating this problem. The same jail began to think about ways of increasing prisoners' educational achievement.

In the four test jails where breakdowns of one kind or another did not force abandonment of the experiment, jail officials were unanimous in their observation that the project contributed to a marked improvement in prisoner attitudes and staff morale. The possibility of this kind of benefit had not been foreseen in the experimental design and in the absence of scientific measures of what actually happened one can only speculate about it. Perhaps the prisoners who were interviewed reacted in positive ways to the attention they received (and possibly to the implicit expectation that the interviews were conducted for some beneficial purpose). It is possible that personnel found reassurance in a better understanding of prisoners as people with the new information produced. It could be that the face-to-face relationship which an interview requires has its own training value for staff. This is to say that as staff begins to look upon prisoners in new and different ways, this triggers new thoughts and ideas about prisoners and about the job of managing them in jail.

The test produced another important finding: this or any other approach to the classification of jail prisoners will fail without (a) real commitment to it by administrators and supervisors; (b) adequate staff training and operational preparation and (c) supervision to insure consistency in application. These lessons can be clearly seen in Appendix A which briefly describes each of the test jails and summarizes each of the test experiences. Despite the best of pretest intentions to minimize breakdowns and misunderstandings, the facts are that two jails abandoned the project after the first week or two, none completed all of the Prisoner Inventory forms and none fully applied the kinds of decisions that the project was supposed to test. This is not stated as an indictment at all and any blame for this disappointing performance must be shared by the project directors and the Jail Inspectors involved. This finding is invaluable as an aid to any further experimentation.

FUTURE POSSIBILITIES

Although the experiment was incomplete in a number of respects it has demonstrated some of its potentials of one approach to the classification of jail prisoners. Preliminary experience with this approach suggests that it can be useful to jail managers in a number of ways and that it can be applied with relative safety.

That the basic Prisoner Inventory and the overlays need further refinement is beyond question. While, as a whole, the Prisoner Inventory form produced very few "no answers" during the test some items were responded to more completely than others. Further adjustments are needed to reduce "no answers" to absolute minimums. Through application in other jail settings and further analysis it should be possible to increase the sensitivity and reliability of the system as a decision-making aid. The underlying concept, and the forms used can be developed to meet other jail management needs. For example, information can be gathered and recorded to create an essential prisoner information system. Information can be used to identify and assess the nature of prisoners' correctional needs. Further experimentation may enable the development of classification materials as diagnostic and predictive instruments for the use of correctional program managers, judges and other concerned officials both within and outside the criminal justice system.

An effective prisoner classification system can have even more immediate operational benefits. (1) Improved security and control of prisoners will be assured through identifying and providing necessary surveillance for those who need closest supervision. Direct benefits should be realized in fewer escapes, assaults, destruction of property and similar behavior which is disruptive and threatening to good order and safety. (2) It should be possible for administrators and supervisors to use available personnel more efficiently. When prisoner housing assignments, work assigments and other activities are stratified and regulated according to custody classifications, supervision and controls are applied where needed and only to the extent circumstances require. (3) The combination of (1) and (2) should result in greater flexibility in jail operations. For example, minimum custody prisoners can be permitted more activity than others. Minimum custody housing units can be of less secure construction, more remotely located and checked less frequently than others. Personnel deployment can be concentrated or diluted in accordance with custody groups of prisoners, as well as the supervision requirements of various activities and the time of day. (4) When privileges and opportunities to participate in various activities are geared to custody classifications there will be built-in incentive for most prisoners to aspire to the most favorable grades of custody. This implies that prisoners can and will be reclassified upward or downward as their attitudes, behavior and circumstances warrant. (5) An effective system of prisoner classification will provide a data base for periodic reexamination of policy, evaluations of operating efficiency and future planning. This is to say that factual information about prisoner characteristics, their needs for control and services and the manner of their adaptation to confinement can be translated into requirements of correctional program planning and architectural design of new facilities.

Hopefully, this project has suggested a degree of confidence is warranted that a system for classifying jail prisoners can be engineered and applied. There can be no question that the pay-offs of such a system will be worth the effort and expense. May the project have provided the inspiration for further explorations.

Appendix A

JAIL A is a small, rural type jail in the Southwest built in 1919 with a total capacity of 74. Many of the prisoners are local Indians serving short sentences on drunkenness charges. Housing is of inside cell type with a day room. All maintenance work is performed by 8 trusties. Activities are limited to religious services conducted by lay preachers, day room recreation, use of donated reading materials and personal radios.

A few of the Prisoner Inventory forms were completed but no attempt was made to use the information for decision-making and the statisticians were unable to process the data. The Jail Sergeant felt that the forms did help discover a possible T.B. case and identify a number of prisoners who were supposed to be on some type of medication. For the most part, he felt, the Inventory was of no value. In his words, "It sure don't work on Indians."

JAIL B is a fairly new metropolitan jail in the Southeast with a rated capacity of 955. Two other separate units are operated conjointly with it; a new lock-up for traffic offenders and a minimum security stockade, primarily for sentenced prisoners. At the main jail there are several types of single and group cell housing. All work except food service is performed by stockade trusties. Other activities include worship services and religious education classes, individual and group counseling, central radio, TV and dayroom recreation.

This jail was, by far, the largest contributor to the test sample. Nearly 1,200 prisoners were processed during the two-month period. Unfortunately, entries were not made on the back of the Prisoner Inventory form. Thus it was not possible to analyze the relationship between supervision scores and subsequently observed behavior and characteristics. During the test period all newly-commited prisoners were kept in holding cells until they were classified. The test material was used in limited ways for housing assignments, selection of trusties and seperation of medical cases needing special attention. Jail officials expressed surprise at finding so high a proportion of young offenders and unmarried drug users. It was thought that more minimum custody candidates should have been identified by the classification material and staff began to see the need for additional information on the Prisoner Inventory form, such as drug use and educational achievement.

Staff consensus was that test materials were highly useful. It was observed that prisoners were more at ease and more cooperative than formerly. This was attributed to the personal attention given during classification interviews. Staff planned to seek County Medical Association help for the drug users and educational and guidance opportunities for the younger offenders. Officials planned to continue the project after the test period ended and to use the experience as a basis for developing their own classification system.

JAIL C is another new city jail and is located on the Gulf Coast. It has a normal capcity of 487 and operates as a detention center primarily for adult males awaiting trial and sentenced prisoners on appeal. All booking occurs at a separate 166-man unit downtown. The main jail has a unit of maximum security single cells, a minimum custody wing and units of 4-man group cells. Unit day rooms are provided. Sentenced prisoners work on the farm and perform maintenance chores. Other activities include chapel services for minimum custody prisoners, dayroom recreation and donated reading material.

Staff used the classification material to a limited extent in making both housing and work assignments. Staff expressed surprise at the number of young prisoners awaiting trial on serious charges. They felt that the Prisoner Inventory form enabled the identification of medical problems that otherwise might have been missed. The form was used to check identity of visitors. The "who-to-notify" item was used several times. Staff experimented in using the classification material to identify additional prisoners who would be allowed to attend Chapel services. This ended when a "grand fight" resulted from unknown enemies getting together. Despite this, it was felt that the classification interviews enabled staff to know the prisoners better and that this tended to ease prisoner stress. It was also felt that Inventory information would be useful in planning a new jail by enabling design to meet the needs of more specific prisoner types.

JAIL D too, is a new jail located in a North Central city. With a normal capacity of 256, housing accomodations consist of 12-bed dormitories and inside single cells. An attempt is made to employ all sentenced prisoners. In addition to performing maintenance chores around the jail, trusties perform such work in town as doing the janitor work at the court house. Other activities include remedial education, group therapy, Alcoholics Anonymous, psychological testing, vocational training in auto mechanics and welding and reading materials furnished by the State Library.

Classification interviews were conducted by two identification officers immediately after booking. The information was used in making work assignments for sentenced prisoners, but many prisoners were well known to staff and this knowledge tended to override decisions indicated by the classification rating sheet. Housing unit officers completed the back of the Prisoner Inventory form as required. Staff discovered that a large proportion of prisoners booked were actually held only a few hours or a day or two. The Inventory forms also documented the burdensome process of repeated bookings of habitual drunks. The Sheriff intended to use these facts to support an attempt to find ways of circumventing customary jail routines for these offenders. The Sheriff also thought that morale of both prisoners and staff improved during the test period. This was attributed to positive prisoner reaction to the attention given them and a corresponding tendency of staff to relax. Staff thought that the classification project would be even more valuable in a large metropolitan jail where most of the prisoners are unknown.

JAIL E is located in a South Central city. With a normal capacity of 364, this jail was built in 1925 but it was renovated and remodeled twice in the 1960's. Housing consists of single cells with front day rooms. This unit operates in conjunction with another 150-man holding facility for lesser offenders and the County Penal Farm. The Farm is intended for all sentenced prisoners as well as persons who will await trial for any length of time. As a result, activities at the main jail are rather limited. Only a few prisoners are assigned to maintenance chores. There is day room recreation, central radio, worship services and reading material furnished by local church and civic groups.

At the outset of the test period, arrangements had been made for one staff member to do all the classification interviewing but he became ill and the interviewing was relegated to housing unit officers on each of 3 floors whose work shifts changed every 4 weeks. This unfortunate circumstance interfered with proper completion of the Prisoner Inventory forms and with experimental decision-making. Despite this, there was staff consensus that the experimental rating sheets tended to confirm "seat of the pants" impressions of prisoners. Staff expressed surprise at the large number of persons who were released on bond after booking and expressed the general view that classification interviews tended to relieve prisoner anxiety. On the basis of this fragmentary experience the Sheriff intends to improve the prisoner records system to reflect more information about each prisoner and to develop their own classification program.

JAIL F is a city jail on the Mexican border. It has a normal capacity of 448. Housing consists of both inside single and group cells, in addition to which there are dormitories for trusties. Sentenced misdemeanants perform necessary maintenance chores around the jail and they are housed separately. At the time of the test there were few other activities but plans had been completed for a demonstration grant to finance a group of correctional programs clustered around vocational training and work release.

Rather elaborate plans were made for the experimental classification project to insure that both housing and work assignments were based on the test materials. Tentative arrangements were also made for follow-up counseling and referral of prisoner problems to local agencies. All new prisoners were to be kept in holding cells until they were classified. Interviewing was to be done by booking officers under the supervision of a counselor who was to have functioned in effect as project director. Everything went as planned for the first two weeks but then the counselor left, several English-speaking jailers went on vacation and there was not sufficient help left to conduct interviews and do the paper work. A week after the experiment was prematurely terminated one prisoner murdered another. There was some speculation that this might have been avoided had the original classification plan been in effect. By the end of the test period some stratification of housing was left but there was no formal means of classifying prisoners.

Appendix B

PRISONER INVENTORY STUDY

October, 1970

OBJECTIVES

The purpose of the present study was to evaluate the effectiveness of two scoring systems currently being developed to help estimate required supervision for prisoners and housing requirements. The two scoring systems were:

1) the Estimated Supervision Score based on answers to the Prisoner Inventory — a series of questions about the prisoners commitment status, background and appearance.

2) the Prisoners Characteristics Score, based on answers to questions about prisoners adjustment and relationships to personnel and other prisoners.

Each of these two estimated scores were constructed based on responses from a sample of jails, and *validated* against an *actual* supervision code assigned by wardens using normal procedures.

In addition, the present study offered an opportunity to evaluate other aspects of the effectiveness of the scoring systems such as *ease of response, sensitivity* of the scores and of the items making up the scores, and *reliability* of the scores across the various jails.

METHOD

1. Sample

   The sample size was 1,846. The surveys were taken in five jails: Dade County, East Baton Rouge County, Ingham County, El Paso County, and Shelby County.

2. Data Problems

   The following is a discussion of the problems which were incurred in the initial retrieval of the data from the forms.

   a. Dade County did not fill in the backs of the questionnaires.

   b. Dade County sent carbon copies which were not properly aligned.

   c. Instructions for filling out both the Estimated Supervision Code and the Housing Code were not followed at all.

   d. Housing Classification (single, group, dorm) was not coded.

e. Multiple responses were listed, in which case the first response was recorded.

f. The Charge or Offense category was often qualified and/or answered as "other". Possibly this category should be expanded.

3. <u>Definitions of Calculations</u>

   a. Estimated Supervision Code was calculated according to specification.

   b. Housing Code was calculated according to specification. If the person fell into two or more codes, each was counted.

   c. The average scores for General Adjustment, Relations and Personnel, Relations with Prisoners and Prisoner Characteristics, were determined in the following manner:

      1) Drop all "Don't know" answers.
      2) Assign the following values:
         a) true = 1
         b) more false than true = 2
         c) more true than false = 3
         d) false = 4
      3) Sum all values for each category.
      4) Multiply the above sum by 10.
      5) Divide the result in 4) by the number of "1-4" answers in each category.

   The Prisoner Characteristics Average Score includes all categories.

CONCLUSION

1. IS THE ESTIMATED SUPERVISION SCORE BASED ON THE PRISONER INVENTORY AN EFFECTIVE SYSTEM FOR ESTIMATING DEGREE OF SUPERVISION REQUIRED?

   Yes. The ESS was based on questions which elicited high levels of response from wardens. It appears to be a *sensitive* and *reliable* tool, most importantly, a *valid* means of estimating the actual supervision code for prisoners.

a. Response rates for ESS questions

As a whole, the ESS questions resulted in very few "no answers" indicating that the Prisoner Inventory questions are practical and easy to obtain answers for.

Some items, however, were less completely responded to than others, indicating possibilities for further refinement of questions to minimize "no answers" which adversely affects the ESS. (See Tables 29-50 for items in the Prisoner Inventory where "no answers" exceed 3% — e.g. family support, length of employment, etc.)

b. Sensitivity and Reliability of the ESS

The ESS appears to be a potentially sensitive tool. Scores from the sample for this study were distributed fairly equally across the whole scale, indicating a broad range of classifications which the ESS is capable of measuring. This dispersion of scores occurred in each of the five participating jails. (Table 1)

The ESS also appears to be a reliable tool: scores developed for each of the participating jails indicated a reasonably consistent dispersion of scores across all five jails. The ESS did as well as the Actual Supervision Codes on dispersion of the scores and consistency across jails. (Table 1, 2 through 7)

c. Validity of the ESS Relative to Actual Supervision Code.

The ESS appears to be a reasonably good estimate of the actual supervision code assigned by wardens under current practices. The ESS correlates well with both the "first" supervision code and the "last" supervision code — at about .70 level of correlation.

This holds true for the total sample of all jails and also for each of the individual jails as well. (Tables 81 to 86, 96 to 105).

2. DOES THE PRISONERS CHARACTERISTICS SCORE REPRESENT AN EFFECTIVE SYSTEM FOR ESTIMATING DEGREE OF SUPERVISION REQUIRED?

No. The questions on which this score was based were poorly responded to, both in number of responses and quality of response. Given the relatively poor raw data for this score, it is not surprising that the PCS did not prove to be a good predictor of the Actual Supervision Code. Nonetheless, there are some indications that the concept of the PCS as an estimating tool could work if improvements are made in the data obtained.

a. Response rates for the PCS questions

The bulk of the sample for this study, the 1176 residents (out of 1846) from Dade County, as well as about 300 respondents from the other cities, did not answer any of the questions on the Prisoners Characteristics and Behavior. Of those who *did* answer this section of the questionaire, many did not respond to all of the questions. (Tables 51-63)

b. Sensitivity and reliability of the PCS

In addition to the low response rates, the quality of responses to the PCS questions was very poor — many respondents checked the same answer for all items, not discriminating in their responses. As a result, the Prisoners Characteristics Score is not a potentially sensitive score. Most of the respondents fell into the most favorable category, indicating that the respondent gave a "True" answer to all 10 questions, excepting only the attempted "Escape" question.

Prisoner Characteristic Score	%
10 (Good)	54
11 to 19	35
20 + (Bad)	11
(See Tables 101 to 108)	100

There is also little consistency in the pattern of responses across the various jails — in one jail, as many as 85% are in the 10 score category, whereas in another jail, only 2% fell in the 10 score group, an indication of both a lack of reliability as well as a lack of sensitvity in the estimated score.
(Tables 109 — 140)

c. Validity of the PCS vs. Actual Supervision Code

As might be expected, given the poor data in the PCS, it does not correlate well with the actual supervision code (correlation of .23). Neither the total PCS, nor the components of the PCS — the average score on General Adjustment, or the average score on Relationships with Personnel, or the average score on Relationships with Prisoners — is a good estimate of the Actual Supervision Code. However, there is still an indication of a *slight* relationship even with the current PCS, when analyzed on a gross basis, suggesting that a PCS could work if the input data were better.

	Estimated PCS					
Actual First Supervision Code	Minimum (10 score)		Medium (11-19)		Maximum (20+)	
	#	%	#	%	#	%
Minimum	9	8	2	3	2	9
Medium	63	57	19	31	6	29
Maximum	38	35	40	66	13	62
	110	100	61	100	21	100

(See Tables 102, 104, 106, 108)

3. BASED ON THE PRESENT STUDY, WHAT ARE SOME WAYS IN WHICH THE TWO ESTIMATING TOOLS — THE ESS AND PCS — MIGHT BE IMPROVED?

The experience with the present study suggests that improvements could be made in the following aspects of these tools:

- improving response rates
- improving sensitivity of the scores by improving discrimination in responses to specific items.
- improving ease of handling data for analysis

a. Response rates — ESS and PCS

The ESS is reasonably effective as it now stands, and the only obvious area for improvement is to decrease no-answers by clarifying or amplifying some of the questions in the Prisoner Inventory.

The bigger problems lie with PCS. Presumably, response rates could be improved with clearer instructions to the respondents and stressing the importance of the questions on the back of the questionnaire.

34

    b. <u>Increasing sensitivity of PCS</u>

In addition, however, changes should be made in the questions. The balanced 4 point scale currently used (True, More true than false, More false than true, False) for responses to the questions, resulted in answers clustering in either the first or second box; hardly anyone responded in the two "false" boxes. Thus, it would seem desirable to use either an unbalanced 4 point scale, (e.g. Completely true, Usually true, Sometimes true. Not true; where three boxes are positive, and only one is negative) or better yet, a 6 point or 10 point unbalanced scale. (e.g. Completely true, Very true, Quite true, Somewhat true, Not true, Not very true, Not at all true is a 6 point unbalanced scale — 4 positives and 2 negatives.)

    c. <u>Ease of handling data — ESS and PCS</u>

Finally, greater ease in tabulating and handling the data could be accomplished by pre-coding the questionnaire for both ESS and PCS and by altering the layout somewhat. This might also serve a double purpose in making the questionnaire easier to answer for the respondents, thus increasing response rates as well.

4. <u>Process</u>

After the forms had been filled in, they were sent by each jail to the private consulting agency. Each form was then stamped with an identification number to identify the form and jail. The forms were then hand coded so that they could be keypunched. After the keypunching, they were edited to correct possible coding and keypunch errors. For this process the Data Check Express software package was used. Tabulation specifications were changed somewhat in view of the data. After seeing the results of the first set of tables, a second set was run to explore certain areas of the Supervision Codes.

GLOSSARY OF LEGAL TERMS

TABLE OF CONTENTS

	Page
Action ... Affiant	1
Affidavit ... At Bar	2
At Issue ... Burden of Proof	3
Business ... Commute	4
Complainant ... Conviction	5
Cooperative ... Demur (v.)	6
Demurrage ... Endorsement	7
Enjoin ... Facsimile	8
Factor ... Guilty	9
Habeas Corpus ... Incumbrance	10
Indemnify ... Laches	11
Landlord and Tenant ... Malice	12
Mandamus ... Obiter Dictum	13
Object (v.) ... Perjury	14
Perpetuity ... Proclamation	15
Proffered Evidence ... Referee	16
Referendum ... Stare Decisis	17
State ... Term	18
Testamentary ... Warrant (Warranty) (v.)	19
Warrant (n.) ... Zoning	20

GLOSSARY OF LEGAL TERMS

A

ACTION - "Action" includes a civil action and a criminal action.
A FORTIORI - A term meaning you can reason one thing from the existence of certain facts.
A POSTERIORI - From what goes after; from effect to cause.
A PRIORI - From what goes before; from cause to effect.
AB INITIO - From the beginning.
ABATE - To diminish or put an end to.
ABET - To encourage the commission of a crime.
ABEYANCE - Suspension, temporary suppression.
ABIDE - To accept the consequences of.
ABJURE - To renounce; give up.
ABRIDGE - To reduce; contract; diminish.
ABROGATE - To annul, repeal, or destroy.
ABSCOND - To hide or absent oneself to avoid legal action.
ABSTRACT - A summary.
ABUT - To border on, to touch.
ACCESS - Approach; in real property law it means the right of the owner of property to the use of the highway or road next to his land, without obstruction by intervening property owners.
ACCESSORY - In criminal law, it means the person who contributes or aids in the commission of a crime.
ACCOMMODATED PARTY - One to whom credit is extended on the strength of another person signing a commercial paper.
ACCOMMODATION PAPER - A commercial paper to which the accommodating party has put his name.
ACCOMPLICE - In criminal law, it means a person who together with the principal offender commits a crime.
ACCORD - An agreement to accept something different or less than that to which one is entitled, which extinguishes the entire obligation.
ACCOUNT - A statement of mutual demands in the nature of debt and credit between parties.
ACCRETION - The act of adding to a thing; in real property law, it means gradual accumulation of land by natural causes.
ACCRUE - To grow to; to be added to.
ACKNOWLEDGMENT - The act of going before an official authorized to take acknowledgments, and acknowledging an act as one's own.
ACQUIESCENCE - A silent appearance of consent.
ACQUIT - To legally determine the innocence of one charged with a crime.
AD INFINITUM - Indefinitely.
AD LITEM - For the suit.
AD VALOREM - According to value.
ADJECTIVE LAW - Rules of procedure.
ADJUDICATION - The judgment given in a case.
ADMIRALTY - Court having jurisdiction over maritime cases.
ADULT - Sixteen years old or over (in criminal law).
ADVANCE - In commercial law, it means to pay money or render other value before it is due.
ADVERSE - Opposed; contrary.
ADVOCATE - (v.) To speak in favor of;
    (n.) One who assists, defends, or pleads for another.
AFFIANT - A person who makes and signs an affidavit.

AFFIDAVIT - A written and sworn to declaration of facts, voluntarily made.
AFFINITY- The relationship between persons through marriage with the kindred of each other; distinguished from consanguinity, which is the relationship by blood.
AFFIRM - To ratify; also when an appellate court affirms a judgment, decree, or order, it means that it is valid and right and must stand as rendered in the lower court.
AFOREMENTIONED; AFORESAID - Before or already said.
AGENT - One who represents and acts for another.
AID AND COMFORT - To help; encourage.
ALIAS - A name not one's true name.
ALIBI - A claim of not being present at a certain place at a certain time.
ALLEGE - To assert.
ALLOTMENT - A share or portion.
AMBIGUITY - Uncertainty; capable of being understood in more than one way.
AMENDMENT - Any language made or proposed as a change in some principal writing.
AMICUS CURIAE - A friend of the court; one who has an interest in a case, although not a party in the case, who volunteers advice upon matters of law to the judge. For example, a brief amicus curiae.
AMORTIZATION - To provide for a gradual extinction of (a future obligation) in advance of maturity, especially, by periodical contributions to a sinking fund which will be adequate to discharge a debt or make a replacement when it becomes necessary.
ANCILLARY - Aiding, auxiliary.
ANNOTATION - A note added by way of comment or explanation.
ANSWER - A written statement made by a defendant setting forth the grounds of his defense.
ANTE - Before.
ANTE MORTEM - Before death.
APPEAL - The removal of a case from a lower court to one of superior jurisdiction for the purpose of obtaining a review.
APPEARANCE - Coming into court as a party to a suit.
APPELLANT - The party who takes an appeal from one court or jurisdiction to another (appellate) court for review.
APPELLEE - The party against whom an appeal is taken.
APPROPRIATE - To make a thing one's own.
APPROPRIATION - Prescribing the destination of a thing; the act of the legislature designating a particular fund, to be applied to some object of government expenditure.
APPURTENANT - Belonging to; accessory or incident to.
ARBITER - One who decides a dispute; a referee.
ARBITRARY - Unreasoned; not governed by any fixed rules or standard.
ARGUENDO - By way of argument.
ARRAIGN - To call the prisoner before the court to answer to a charge.
ASSENT - A declaration of willingness to do something in compliance with a request.
ASSERT - Declare.
ASSESS - To fix the rate or amount.
ASSIGN - To transfer; to appoint; to select for a particular purpose.
ASSIGNEE - One who receives an assignment.
ASSIGNOR - One who makes an assignment.
AT BAR - Before the court.

AT ISSUE - When parties in an action come to a point where one asserts something and the other denies it.
ATTACH - Seize property by court order and sometimes arrest a person.
ATTEST - To witness a will, etc.; act of attestation.
AVERMENT - A positive statement of facts.

B

BAIL - To obtain the release of a person from legal custody by giving security and promising that he shall appear in court; to deliver (goods, etc.) in trust to a person for a special purpose.
BAILEE - One to whom personal property is delivered under a contract of bailment.
BAILMENT - Delivery of personal property to another to be held for a certain purpose and to be returned when the purpose is accomplished.
BAILOR - The party who delivers goods to another, under a contract of bailment.
BANC (OR BANK) - Bench; the place where a court sits permanently or regularly; also the assembly of all the judges of a court.
BANKRUPT - An insolvent person, technically, one declared to be bankrupt after a bankruptcy proceeding.
BAR - The legal profession.
BARRATRY - Exciting groundless judicial proceedings.
BARTER - A contract by which parties exchange goods for other goods.
BATTERY - Illegal interfering with another's person.
BEARER - In commercial law, it means the person in possession of a commercial paper which is payable to the bearer.
BENCH - The court itself or the judge.
BENEFICIARY - A person benefiting under a will, trust, or agreement.
BEST EVIDENCE RULE, THE - Except as otherwise provided by statute, no evidence other than the writing itself is admissible to prove the content of a writing. This section shall be known and may be cited as the best evidence rule.
BEQUEST - A gift of personal property under a will.
BILL - A formal written statement of complaint to a court of justice; also, a draft of an act of the legislature before it becomes a law; also, accounts for goods sold, services rendered, or work done.
BONA FIDE - In or with good faith; honestly.
BOND - An instrument by which the maker promises to pay a sum of money to another, usually providing that upon performances of a certain condition the obligation shall be void.
BOYCOTT - A plan to prevent the carrying on of a business by wrongful means.
BREACH - The breaking or violating of a law, or the failure to carry out a duty.
BRIEF - A written document, prepared by a lawyer to serve as the basis of an argument upon a case in court, usually an appellate court.
BURDEN OF PRODUCING EVIDENCE - The obligation of a party to introduce evidence sufficient to avoid a ruling against him on the issue.
BURDEN OF PROOF - The obligation of a party to establish by evidence a requisite degree of belief concerning a fact in the mind of the trier of fact or the court. The burden of proof may require a party to raise a reasonable doubt concerning the existence of nonexistence of a fact or that he establish the existence or nonexistence of a fact by a preponderance of the evidence, by clear and convincing proof, or by proof beyond a reasonable doubt.

Except as otherwise provided by law, the burden of proof requires proof by a preponderance of the evidence.

BUSINESS, A - Shall include every kind of business, profession, occupation, calling or operation of institutions, whether carried on for profit or not.

BY-LAWS - Regulations, ordinances, or rules enacted by a corporation, association, etc., for its own government.

C

CANON - A doctrine; also, a law or rule, of a church or association in particular.

CAPIAS - An order to arrest.

CAPTION - In a pleading, deposition or other paper connected with a case in court, it is the heading or introductory clause which shows the names of the parties, name of the court, number of the case on the docket or calendar, etc.

CARRIER - A person or corporation undertaking to transport persons or property.

CASE - A general term for an action, cause, suit, or controversy before a judicial body.

CAUSE - A suit, litigation or action before a court.

CAVEAT EMPTOR - Let the buyer beware. This term expresses the rule that the purchaser of an article must examine, judge, and test it for himself, being bound to discover any obvious defects or imperfections.

CERTIFICATE - A written representation that some legal formality has been complied with.

CERTIORARI - To be informed of; the name of a writ issued by a superior court directing the lower court to send up to the former the record and proceedings of a case.

CHANGE OF VENUE - To remove place of trial from one place to another.

CHARGE - An obligation or duty; a formal complaint; an instruction of the court to the jury upon a case.

CHARTER - (n.) The authority by virtue of which an organized body acts;
(v.) in mercantile law, it means to hire or lease a vehicle or vessel for transportation.

CHATTEL - An article of personal property.

CHATTEL MORTGAGE - A mortgage on personal property.

CIRCUIT - A division of the country, for the administration of justice; a geographical area served by a court.

CITATION - The act of the court by which a person is summoned or cited; also, a reference to legal authority.

CIVIL (ACTIONS) - It indicates the private rights and remedies of individuals in contrast to the word "criminal" (actions) which relates to prosecution for violation of laws.

CLAIM (n.) - Any demand held or asserted as of right.

CODICIL - An addition to a will.

CODIFY - To arrange the laws of a country into a code.

COGNIZANCE - Notice or knowledge.

COLLATERAL - By the side; accompanying; an article or thing given to secure performance of a promise.

COMITY - Courtesy; the practice by which one court follows the decision of another court on the same question.

COMMIT - To perform, as an act; to perpetrate, as a crime; to send a person to prison.

COMMON LAW - As distinguished from law created by the enactment of the legislature (called statutory law), it relates to those principles and rules of action which derive their authority solely from usages and customs of immemorial antiquity, particularly with reference to the ancient unwritten law of England. The written pronouncements of the common law are found in court decisions.

COMMUTE - Change punishment to one less severe.

COMPLAINANT - One who applies to the court for legal redress.
COMPLAINT - The pleading of a plaintiff in a civil action; or a charge that a person has committed a specified offense.
COMPROMISE - An arrangement for settling a dispute by agreement.
CONCUR - To agree, consent.
CONCURRENT - Running together, at the same time.
CONDEMNATION - Taking private property for public use on payment therefor.
CONDITION - Mode or state of being; a qualification or restriction.
CONDUCT - Active and passive behavior; both verbal and nonverbal.
CONFESSION - Voluntary statement of guilt of crime.
CONFIDENTIAL COMMUNICATION BETWEEN CLIENT AND LAWYER - Information transmitted between a client and his lawyer in the course of that relationship and in confidence by a means which, so far as the client is aware, discloses the information to no third persons other than those who are present to further the interest of the client in the consultation or those to whom disclosure is reasonably necessary for the transmission of the information or the accomplishment of the purpose for which the lawyer is consulted, and includes a legal opinion formed and the advice given by the lawyer in the course of that relationship.
CONFRONTATION - Witness testifying in presence of defendant.
CONSANGUINITY - Blood relationship.
CONSIGN - To give in charge; commit; entrust; to send or transmit goods to a merchant, factor, or agent for sale.
CONSIGNEE - One to whom a consignment is made.
CONSIGNOR - One who sends or makes a consignment.
CONSPIRACY - In criminal law, it means an agreement between two or more persons to commit an unlawful act.
CONSPIRATORS - Persons involved in a conspiracy.
CONSTITUTION - The fundamental law of a nation or state.
CONSTRUCTION OF GENDERS - The masculine gender includes the feminine and neuter.
CONSTRUCTION OF SINGULAR AND PLURAL - The singular number includes the plural; and the plural, the singular.
CONSTRUCTION OF TENSES - The present tense includes the past and future tenses; and the future, the present.
CONSTRUCTIVE - An act or condition assumed from other parts or conditions.
CONSTRUE - To ascertain the meaning of language.
CONSUMMATE - To complete.
CONTIGUOUS - Adjoining; touching; bounded by.
CONTINGENT - Possible, but not assured; dependent upon some condition.
CONTINUANCE - The adjournment or postponement of an action pending in a court.
CONTRA - Against, opposed to; contrary.
CONTRACT - An agreement between two or more persons to do or not to do a particular thing.
CONTROVERT - To dispute, deny.
CONVERSION - Dealing with the personal property of another as if it were one's own, without right.
CONVEYANCE - An instrument transferring title to land.
CONVICTION - Generally, the result of a criminal trial which ends in a judgment or sentence that the defendant is guilty as charged.

COOPERATIVE - A cooperative is a voluntary organization of persons with a common interest, formed and operated along democratic lines for the purpose of supplying services at cost to its members and other patrons, who contribute both capital and business.
CORPUS DELICTI - The body of a crime; the crime itself.
CORROBORATE - To strengthen; to add weight by additional evidence.
COUNTERCLAIM - A claim presented by a defendant in opposition to or deduction from the claim of the plaintiff.
COUNTY - Political subdivision of a state.
COVENANT - Agreement.
CREDIBLE - Worthy of belief.
CREDITOR - A person to whom a debt is owing by another person, called the "debtor."
CRIMINAL ACTION - Includes criminal proceedings.
CRIMINAL INFORMATION - Same as complaint.
CRITERION (sing.)
CRITERIA (plural) - A means or tests for judging; a standard or standards.
CROSS-EXAMINATION - Examination of a witness by a party other than the direct examiner upon a matter that is within the scope of the direct examination of the witness.
CULPABLE - Blamable.
CY-PRES - As near as (possible). The rule of *cy-pres* is a rule for the construction of instruments in equity by which the intention of the party is carried out *as near as may be*, when it would be impossible or illegal to give it literal effect.

D

DAMAGES - A monetary compensation, which may be recovered in the courts by any person who has suffered loss, or injury, whether to his person, property or rights through the unlawful act or omission or negligence of another.
DECLARANT - A person who makes a statement.
DE FACTO - In fact; actually but without legal authority.
DE JURE - Of right; legitimate; lawful.
DE MINIMIS - Very small or trifling.
DE NOVO - Anew; afresh; a second time.
DEBT - A specified sum of money owing to one person from another, including not only the obligation of the debtor to pay, but the right of the creditor to receive and enforce payment.
DECEDENT - A dead person.
DECISION - A judgment or decree pronounced by a court in determination of a case.
DECREE - An order of the court, determining the rights of all parties to a suit.
DEED - A writing containing a contract sealed and delivered; particularly to convey real property.
DEFALCATION - Misappropriation of funds.
DEFAMATION - Injuring one's reputation by false statements.
DEFAULT - The failure to fulfill a duty, observe a promise, discharge an obligation, or perform an agreement.
DEFENDANT - The person defending or denying; the party against whom relief or recovery is sought in an action or suit.
DEFRAUD - To practice fraud; to cheat or trick.
DELEGATE (v.)- To entrust to the care or management of another.
DELICTUS - A crime.
DEMUR (v.) - To dispute the sufficiency in law of the pleading of the other side.

DEMURRAGE - In maritime law, it means, the sum fixed or allowed as remuneration to the owners of a ship for the detention of their vessel beyond the number of days allowed for loading and unloading or for sailing; also used in railroad terminology.
DENIAL - A form of pleading; refusing to admit the truth of a statement, charge, etc.
DEPONENT - One who gives testimony under oath reduced to writing.
DEPOSITION - Testimony given under oath outside of court for use in court or for the purpose of obtaining information in preparation for trial of a case.
DETERIORATION - A degeneration such as from decay, corrosion or disintegration.
DETRIMENT - Any loss or harm to person or property.
DEVIATION - A turning aside.
DEVISE - A gift of real property by the last will and testament of the donor.
DICTUM (sing.)
DICTA (plural) - Any statements made by the court in an opinion concerning some rule of law not necessarily involved nor essential to the determination of the case.
DIRECT EVIDENCE - Evidence that directly proves a fact, without an inference or presumption, and which in itself if true, conclusively establishes that fact.
DIRECT EXAMINATION - The first examination of a witness upon a matter that is not within the scope of a previous examination of the witness.
DISAFFIRM - To repudiate.
DISMISS - In an action or suit, it means to dispose of the case without any further consideration or hearing.
DISSENT - To denote disagreement of one or more judges of a court with the decision passed by the majority upon a case before them.
DOCKET (n.) - A formal record, entered in brief, of the proceedings in a court.
DOCTRINE - A rule, principle, theory of law.
DOMICILE - That place where a man has his true, fixed and permanent home to which whenever he is absent he has the intention of returning.
DRAFT (n.) - A commercial paper ordering payment of money drawn by one person on another.
DRAWEE - The person who is requested to pay the money.
DRAWER - The person who draws the commercial paper and addresses it to the drawee.
DUPLICATE - A counterpart produced by the same impression as the original enlargements and miniatures, or by mechanical or electronic re-recording, or by chemical reproduction, or by other equivalent technique which accurately reproduces the original.
DURESS - Use of force to compel performance or non-performance of an act.

E

EASEMENT - A liberty, privilege, or advantage without profit, in the lands of another.
EGRESS - Act or right of going out or leaving; emergence.
EIUSDEM GENERIS - Of the same kind, class or nature. A rule used in the construction of language in a legal document.
EMBEZZLEMENT - To steal; to appropriate fraudulently to one's own use property entrusted to one's care.
EMBRACERY - Unlawful attempt to influence jurors, etc., but not by offering value.
EMINENT DOMAIN - The right of a state to take private property for public use.
ENACT - To make into a law.
ENDORSEMENT - Act of writing one's name on the back of a note, bill or similar written instrument.

ENJOIN - To require a person, by writ of injunction from a court of equity, to perform or to abstain or desist from some act.
ENTIRETY - The whole; that which the law considers as one whole, and not capable of being divided into parts.
ENTRAPMENT - Inducing one to commit a crime so as to arrest him.
ENUMERATED - Mentioned specifically; designated.
ENURE - To operate or take effect.
EQUITY - In its broadest sense, this term denotes the spirit and the habit of fairness, justness, and right dealing which regulate the conduct of men.
ERROR - A mistake of law, or the false or irregular application of law as will nullify the judicial proceedings.
ESCROW - A deed, bond or other written engagement, delivered to a third person, to be delivered by him only upon the performance or fulfillment of some condition.
ESTATE - The interest which any one has in lands, or in any other subject of property.
ESTOP - To stop, bar, or impede.
ESTOPPEL - A rule of law which prevents a man from alleging or denying a fact, because of his own previous act.
ET AL. (alii) - And others.
ET SEQ. (sequential) - And the following.
ET UX. (uxor) - And wife.
EVIDENCE - Testimony, writings, material objects, or other things presented to the senses that are offered to prove the existence or non-existence of a fact.
   Means from which inferences may be drawn as a basis of proof in duly constituted judicial or fact finding tribunals, and includes testimony in the form of opinion and hearsay.
EX CONTRACTU
EX DELICTO - In law, rights and causes of action are divided into two classes, those arising *ex contractu* (from a contract) and those arising *ex delicto* (from a delict or tort).
EX OFFICIO - From office; by virtue of the office.
EX PARTE - On one side only; by or for one.
EX POST FACTO - After the fact.
EX POST FACTO LAW - A law passed after an act was done which retroactively makes such act a crime.
EX REL. (relations) - Upon relation or information.
EXCEPTION - An objection upon a matter of law to a decision made, either before or after judgment by a court.
EXECUTOR (male)
EXECUTRIX (female) - A person who has been appointed by will to execute the will.
EXECUTORY - That which is yet to be executed or performed.
EXEMPT - To release from some liability to which others are subject.
EXONERATION - The removal of a burden, charge or duty.
EXTRADITION - Surrender of a fugitive from one nation to another.

F

F.A.S.- "Free alongside ship"; delivery at dock for ship named.
F.O.B.- "Free on board"; seller will deliver to car, truck, vessel, or other conveyance by which goods are to be transported, without expense or risk of loss to the buyer or consignee.
FABRICATE - To construct; to invent a false story.
FACSIMILE - An exact or accurate copy of an original instrument.

FACTOR - A commercial agent.
FEASANCE - The doing of an act.
FELONIOUS - Criminal, malicious.
FELONY - Generally, a criminal offense that may be punished by death or imprisonment for more than one year as differentiated from a misdemeanor.
FEME SOLE - A single woman.
FIDUCIARY - A person who is invested with rights and powers to be exercised for the benefit of another person.
FIERI FACIAS - A writ of execution commanding the sheriff to levy and collect the amount of a judgment from the goods and chattels of the judgment debtor.
FINDING OF FACT - Determination from proof or judicial notice of the existence of a fact. A ruling implies a supporting finding of fact; no separate or formal finding is required unless required by a statute of this state.
FISCAL - Relating to accounts or the management of revenue.
FORECLOSURE (sale) - A sale of mortgaged property to obtain satisfaction of the mortgage out of the sale proceeds.
FORFEITURE - A penalty, a fine.
FORGERY - Fabricating or producing falsely, counterfeited.
FORTUITOUS - Accidental.
FORUM - A court of justice; a place of jurisdiction.
FRAUD - Deception; trickery.
FREEHOLDER - One who owns real property.
FUNGIBLE - Of such kind or nature that one specimen or part may be used in the place of another.

G

GARNISHEE - Person garnished.
GARNISHMENT - A legal process to reach the money or effects of a defendant, in the possession or control of a third person.
GRAND JURY - Not less than 16, not more than 23 citizens of a county sworn to inquire into crimes committed or triable in the county.
GRANT - To agree to; convey, especially real property.
GRANTEE - The person to whom a grant is made.
GRANTOR - The person by whom a grant is made.
GRATUITOUS - Given without a return, compensation or consideration.
GRAVAMEN - The grievance complained of or the substantial cause of a criminal action.
GUARANTY (n.) - A promise to answer for the payment of some debt, or the performance of some duty, in case of the failure of another person, who, in the first instance, is liable for such payment or performance.
GUARDIAN - The person, committee, or other representative authorized by law to protect the person or estate or both of an incompetent (or of a *sui juris* person having a guardian) and to act for him in matters affecting his person or property or both. An incompetent is a person under disability imposed by law.
GUILTY - Establishment of the fact that one has committed a breach of conduct; especially, a violation of law.

H

HABEAS CORPUS - You have the body; the name given to a variety of writs, having for their object to bring a party before a court or judge for decision as to whether such person is being lawfully held prisoner.
HABENDUM - In conveyancing; it is the clause in a deed conveying land which defines the extent of ownership to be held by the grantee.
HEARING - A proceeding whereby the arguments of the interested parties are heared.
HEARSAY - A type of testimony given by a witness who relates, not what he knows personally, but what others have told hi, or what he has heard said by others.
HEARSAY RULE, THE - (a) "Hearsay evidence" is evidence of a statement that was made other than by a witness while testifying at the hearing and that is offered to prove the truth of the matter stated; (b) Except as provided by law, hearsay evidence is inadmissible; (c) This section shall be known and may be cited as the hearsay rule.
HEIR - Generally, one who inherits property, real or personal.
HOLDER OF THE PRIVILEGE - (a) The client when he has no guardian or conservator; (b) A guardian or conservator of the client when the client has a guardian or conservator; (c) The personal representative of the client if the client is dead; (d) A successor, assign, trustee in dissolution, or any similar representative of a firm, association, organization, partnership, business trust, corporation, or public entity that is no longer in existence.
HUNG JURY - One so divided that they can't agree on a verdict.
HUSBAND-WIFE PRIVILEGE - An accused in a criminal proceeding has a privilege to prevent his spouse from testifying against him.
HYPOTHECATE - To pledge a thing without delivering it to the pledgee.
HYPOTHESIS - A supposition, assumption, or toehry.

I

I.E. (id est) - That is.
IB., OR IBID.(ibidem) - In the same place; used to refer to a legal reference previously cited to avoid repeating the entire citation.
ILLICIT - Prohibited; unlawful.
ILLUSORY - Deceiving by false appearance.
IMMUNITY - Exemption.
IMPEACH - To accuse, to dispute.
IMPEDIMENTS - Disabilities, or hindrances.
IMPLEAD - To sue or prosecute by due course of law.
IMPUTED - Attributed or charged to.
IN LOCO PARENTIS - In place of parent, a guardian.
IN TOTO - In the whole; completely.
INCHOATE - Imperfect; unfinished.
INCOMMUNICADO - Denial of the right of a prisoner to communicate with friends or relatives.
INCOMPETENT - One who is incapable of caring for his own affairs because he is mentally deficient or undeveloped.
INCRIMINATION - A matter will incriminate a person if it constitutes, or forms an essential part of, or, taken in connection with other matters disclosed, is a basis for a reasonable inference of such a violation of the laws of this State as to subject him to liability to punishment therefor, unless he has become for any reason permanently immune from punishment for such violation.
INCUMBRANCE - Generally a claim, lien, charge or liability attached to and binding real property.

INDEMNIFY - To secure against loss or damage; also, to make reimbursement to one for a loss already incurred by him.
INDEMNITY - An agreement to reimburse another person in case of an anticipated loss falling upon him.
INDICIA - Signs; indications.
INDICTMENT - An accusation in writing found and presented by a grand jury charging that a person has committed a crime.
INDORSE - To write a name on the back of a legal paper or document, generally, a negotiable instrument
INDUCEMENT - Cause or reason why a thing is done or that which incites the person to do the act or commit a crime; the motive for the criminal act.
INFANT - In civil cases one under 21 years of age.
INFORMATION - A formal accusation of crime made by a prosecuting attorney.
INFRA - Below, under; this word occurring by itself in a publication refers the reader to a future part of the publication.
INGRESS - The act of going into.
INJUNCTION - A writ or order by the court requiring a person, generally, to do or to refrain from doing an act.
INSOLVENT - The condition of a person who is unable to pay his debts.
INSTRUCTION - A direction given by the judge to the jury concerning the law of the case.
INTERIM - In the meantime; time intervening.
INTERLOCUTORY - Temporary, not final; something intervening between the commencement and the end of a suit which decides some point or matter, but is not a final decision of the whole controversy.
INTERROGATORIES - A series of formal written questions used in the examination of a party or a witness usually prior to a trial.
INTESTATE - A person who dies without a will.
INURE - To result, to take effect.
IPSO FACTO - By the fact iself; by the mere fact.
ISSUE (n.) The disputed point or question in a case,

J

JEOPARDY - Danger, hazard, peril.
JOINDER - Joining; uniting with another person in some legal steps or proceeding.
JOINT - United; combined.
JUDGE - Member or members or representative or representatives of a court conducting a trial or hearing at which evidence is introduced.
JUDGMENT - The official decision of a court of justice.
JUDICIAL OR JUDICIARY - Relating to or connected with the administration of justice.
JURAT - The clause written at the foot of an affidavit, stating when, where and before whom such affidavit was sworn.
JURISDICTION - The authority to hear and determine controversies between parties.
JURISPRUDENCE - The philosophy of law.
JURY - A body of persons legally selected to inquire into any matter of fact, and to render their verdict according to the evidence.

L

LACHES - The failure to diligently assert a right, which results in a refusal to allow relief.

LANDLORD AND TENANT - A phrase used to denote the legal relation existing between the owner and occupant of real estate.

LARCENY - Stealing personal property belonging to another.

LATENT - Hidden; that which does not appear on the face of a thing.

LAW - Includes constitutional, statutory, and decisional law.

LAWYER-CLIENT PRIVILEGE - (1) A "client" is a person, public officer, or corporation, association, or other organization or entity, either public or private, who is rendered professional legal services by a lawyer, or who consults a lawyer with a view to obtaining professional legal services from him; (2) A "lawyer" is a person authorized, or reasonably believed by the client to be authorized, to practice law in any state or nation; (3) A "representative of the lawyer" is one employed to assist the lawyer in the rendition of professional legal services; (4) A communication is "confidential" if not intended to be disclosed to third persons other than those to whom disclosure is in furtherance of the rendition of professional legal services to the client or those reasonably necessary for the transmission of the communication.

General rule of privilege - A client has a privilege to refuse to disclose and to prevent any other person from disclosing confidential communications made for the purpose of facilitating the rendition of professional legal services to the client, (1) between himself or his representative and his lawyer or his lawyer's representative, or (2) between his lawyer and the lawyer's representative, or (3) by him or his lawyer to a lawyer representing another in a matter of common interest, or (4) between representatives of the client or between the client and a representative of the client, or (5) between lawyers representing the client.

LEADING QUESTION - Question that suggests to the witness the answer that the examining party desires.

LEASE - A contract by which one conveys real estate for a limited time usually for a specified rent; personal property also may be leased.

LEGISLATION - The act of enacting laws.

LEGITIMATE - Lawful.

LESSEE - One to whom a lease is given.

LESSOR - One who grants a lease

LEVY - A collecting or exacting by authority.

LIABLE - Responsible; bound or obligated in law or equity.

LIBEL (v.) - To defame or injure a person's reputation by a published writing.

(n.) - The initial pleading on the part of the plaintiff in an admiralty proceeding.

LIEN - A hold or claim which one person has upon the property of another as a security for some debt or charge.

LIQUIDATED - Fixed; settled.

LIS PENDENS - A pending civil or criminal action.

LITERAL - According to the language.

LITIGANT - A party to a lawsuit.

LITATION - A judicial controversy.

LOCUS - A place.

LOCUS DELICTI - Place of the crime.

LOCUS POENITENTIAE - The abandoning or giving up of one's intention to commit some crime before it is fully completed or abandoning a conspiracy before its purpose is accomplished.

M

MALFEASANCE - To do a wrongful act.

MALICE - The doing of a wrongful act Intentionally without just cause or excuse.

MANDAMUS - The name of a writ issued by a court to enforce the performance of some public duty.
MANDATORY (adj.) Containing a command.
MARITIME - Pertaining to the sea or to commerce thereon.
MARSHALING - Arranging or disposing of in order.
MAXIM - An established principle or proposition.
MINISTERIAL - That which involves obedience to instruction, but demands no special discretion, judgment or skill.
MISAPPROPRIATE - Dealing fraudulently with property entrusted to one.
MISDEMEANOR - A crime less than a felony and punishable by a fine or imprisonment for less than one year.
MISFEASANCE - Improper performance of a lawful act.
MISREPRESENTATION - An untrue representation of facts.
MITIGATE - To make or become less severe, harsh.
MITTIMUS - A warrant of commitment to prison.
MOOT (adj.) Unsettled, undecided, not necessary to be decided.
MORTGAGE - A conveyance of property upon condition, as security for the payment of a debt or the performance of a duty, and to become void upon payment or performance according to the stipulated terms.
MORTGAGEE - A person to whom property is mortgaged.
MORTGAGOR - One who gives a mortgage.
MOTION - In legal proceedings, a "motion" is an application, either written or oral, addressed to the court by a party to an action or a suit requesting the ruling of the court on a matter of law.
MUTUALITY - Reciprocation.

N

NEGLIGENCE - The failure to exercise that degree of care which an ordinarily prudent person would exercise under like circumstances.
NEGOTIABLE (instrument) - Any instrument obligating the payment of money which is transferable from one person to another by endorsement and delivery or by delivery only.
NEGOTIATE - To transact business; to transfer a negotiable instrument; to seek agreement for the amicable disposition of a controversy or case.
NOLLE PROSEQUI - A formal entry upon the record, by the plaintiff in a civil suit or the prosecuting officer in a criminal action, by which he declares that he "will no further prosecute" the case.
NOLO CONTENDERE - The name of a plea in a criminal action, having the same effect as a plea of guilty; but not constituting a direct admission of guilt.
NOMINAL - Not real or substantial.
NOMINAL DAMAGES - Award of a trifling sum where no substantial injury is proved to have been sustained.
NONFEASANCE - Neglect of duty.
NOVATION - The substitution of a new debt or obligation for an existing one.
NUNC PRO TUNC - A phrase applied to acts allowed to be done after the time when they should be done, with a retroactive effect.("Now for then.")

O

OATH - Oath includes affirmation or declaration under penalty of perjury.
OBITER DICTUM - Opinion expressed by a court on a matter not essentially involved in a case and hence not a decision; also called dicta, if plural.

OBJECT (v.) - To oppose as improper or illegal and referring the question of its propriety or legality to the court.
OBLIGATION - A legal duty, by which a person is bound to do or not to do a certain thing.
OBLIGEE - The person to whom an obligation is owed.
OBLIGOR - The person who is to perform the obligation.
OFFER (v.) - To present for acceptance or rejection.
(n.) - A proposal to do a thing, usually a proposal to make a contract.
OFFICIAL INFORMATION - Information within the custody or control of a department or agency of the government the disclosure of which is shown to be contrary to the public interest.
OFFSET - A deduction.
ONUS PROBANDI - Burden of proof.
OPINION - The statement by a judge of the decision reached in a case, giving the law as applied to the case and giving reasons for the judgment; also a belief or view.
OPTION - The exercise of the power of choice; also a privilege existing in one person, for which he has paid money, which gives him the right to buy or sell real or personal property at a given price within a specified time.
ORDER - A rule or regulation; every direction of a court or judge made or entered in writing but not including a judgment.
ORDINANCE - Generally, a rule established by authority; also commonly used to designate the legislative acts of a municipal corporation.
ORIGINAL - Writing or recording itself or any counterpart intended to have the same effect by a person executing or issuing it. An "original" of a photograph includes the negative or any print therefrom. If data are stored in a computer or similar device, any printout or other output readable by sight, shown to reflect the data accurately, is an "original."
OVERT - Open, manifest.

P

PANEL - A group of jurors selected to serve during a term of the court.
PARENS PATRIAE - Sovereign power of a state to protect or be a guardian over children and incompetents.
PAROL - Oral or verbal.
PAROLE - To release one in prison before the expiration of his sentence, conditionally.
PARITY - Equality in purchasing power between the farmer and other segments of the economy.
PARTITION - A legal division of real or personal property between one or more owners.
PARTNERSHIP - An association of two or more persons to carry on as co-owners a business for profit.
PATENT (adj.) - Evident.
(n.) - A grant of some privilege, property, or authority, made by the government or sovereign of a country to one or more individuals.
PECULATION - Stealing.
PECUNIARY - Monetary.
PENULTIMATE - Next to the last.
PER CURIAM - A phrase used in the report of a decision to distinguish an opinion of the whole court from an opinion written by any one judge.
PER SE - In itself; taken alone.
PERCEIVE - To acquire knowledge through one's senses.
PEREMPTORY - Imperative; absolute.
PERJURY - To lie or state falsely under oath.

PERPETUITY - Perpetual existence; also the quality or condition of an estate limited so that it will not take effect or vest within the period fixed by law.
PERSON - Includes a natural person, firm, association, organization, partnership, business trust, corporation, or public entity.
PERSONAL PROPERTY - Includes money, goods, chattels, things in action, and evidences of debt.
PERSONALTY - Short term for personal property.
PETITION - An application in writing for an order of the court, stating the circumstances upon which it is founded and requesting any order or other relief from a court.
PLAINTIFF - A person who brings a court action.
PLEA - A pleading in a suit or action.
PLEADINGS - Formal allegations made by the parties of their respective claims and defenses, for the judgment of the court.
PLEDGE - A deposit of personal property as a security for the performance of an act.
PLEDGEE - The party to whom goods are delivered in pledge.
PLEDGOR - The party delivering goods in pledge.
PLENARY - Full; complete.
POLICE POWER - Inherent power of the state or its political subdivisions to enact laws within constitutional limits to promote the general welfare of society or the community.
POLLING THE JURY - Call the names of persons on a jury and requiring each juror to declare what his verdict is before it is legally recorded.
POST MORTEM - After death.
POWER OF ATTORNEY - A writing authorizing one to act for another.
PRECEPT - An order, warrant, or writ issued to an officer or body of officers, commanding him or them to do some act within the scope of his or their powers.
PRELIMINARY FACT - Fact upon the existence or nonexistence of which depends the admissibility or inadmissibility of evidence. The phrase "the admissibility or inadmissibility of evidence" includes the qualification or disqualification of a person to be a witness and the existence or non-existence of a privilege.
PREPONDERANCE - Outweighing.
PRESENTMENT - A report by a grand jury on something they have investigated on their own knowledge.
PRESUMPTION - An assumption of fact resulting from a rule of law which requires such fact to be assumed from another fact or group of facts found or otherwise established in the action.
PRIMA FACUE - At first sight.
PRIMA FACIE CASE - A case where the evidence is very patent against the defendant.
PRINCIPAL - The source of authority or rights; a person primarily liable as differentiated from "principle" as a primary or basic doctrine.
PRO AND CON - For and against.
PRO RATA - Proportionally.
PROBATE - Relating to proof, especially to the proof of wills.
PROBATIVE - Tending to prove.
PROCEDURE - In law, this term generally denotes rules which are established by the Federal, State, or local Governments regarding the types of pleading and courtroom practice which must be followed by the parties involved in a criminal or civil case.
PROCLAMATION - A public notice by an official of some order, intended action, or state of facts.

PROFFERED EVIDENCE - The admissibility or inadmissibility of which is dependent upon the existence or nonexistence of a preliminary fact.
PROMISSORY (NOTE) - A promise in writing to pay a specified sum at an expressed time, or on demand, or at sight, to a named person, or to his order, or bearer.
PROOF - The establishment by evidence of a requisite degree of belief concerning a fact in the mind of the trier of fact or the court.
PROPERTY - Includes both real and personal property.
PROPRIETARY (adj.) - Relating or pertaining to ownership; usually a single owner.
PROSECUTE - To carry on an action or other judicial proceeding; to proceed against a person criminally.
PROVISO - A limitation or condition in a legal instrument.
PROXIMATE - Immediate; nearest
PUBLIC EMPLOYEE - An officer, agent, or employee of a public entity.
PUBLIC ENTITY - Includes a national, state, county, city and county, city, district, public authority, public agency, or any other political subdivision or public corporation, whether foreign or domestic.
PUBLIC OFFICIAL - Includes an official of a political dubdivision of such state or territory and of a municipality.
PUNITIVE - Relating to punishment.

Q

QUASH - To make void.
QUASI - As if; as it were.
QUID PRO QUO - Something for something; the giving of one valuable thing for another.
QUITCLAIM (v.) - To release or relinquish claim or title to, especially in deeds to realty.
QUO WARRANTO - A legal procedure to test an official's right to a public office or the right to hold a franchise, or to hold an office in a domestic corporation.

R

RATIFY - To approve and sanction.
REAL PROPERTY - Includes lands, tenements, and hereditaments.
REALTY - A brief term for real property.
REBUT - To contradict; to refute, especially by evidence and arguments.
RECEIVER - A person who is appointed by the court to receive, and hold in trust property in litigation.
RECIDIVIST - Habitual criminal.
RECIPROCAL - Mutual.
RECOUPMENT - To keep back or get something which is due; also, it is the right of a defendant to have a deduction from the amount of the plaintiff's damages because the plaintiff has not fulfilled his part of the same contract.
RECROSS EXAMINATION - Examination of a witness by a cross-examiner subsequent to a redirect examination of the witness.
REDEEM - To release an estate or article from mortgage or pledge by paying the debt for which it stood as security.
REDIRECT EXAMINATION - Examination of a witness by the direct examiner subsequent to the cross-examination of the witness.
REFEREE - A person to whom a cause pending in a court is referred by the court, to take testimony, hear the parties, and report thereon to the court.

REFERENDUM - A method of submitting an important legislative or administrative matter to a direct vote of the people.

RELEVANT EVIDENCE - Evidence including evidence relevant to the credulity of a witness or hearsay declarant, having any tendency in reason to prove or disprove any disputed fact that is of consequence to the determination of the action.

REMAND - To send a case back to the lower court from which it came, for further proceedings.

REPLEVIN - An action to recover goods or chattels wrongfully taken or detained.

REPLY (REPLICATION) - Generally, a reply is what the plaintiff or other person who has instituted proceedings says in answer to the defendant's case.

RE JUDICATA - A thing judicially acted upon or decided.

RES ADJUDICATA - Doctrine that an issue or dispute litigated and determined in a case between the opposing parties is deemed permanently decided between these parties.

RESCIND (RECISSION) - To avoid or cancel a contract.

RESPONDENT - A defendant in a proceeding in chancery or admiralty; also, the person who contends against the appeal in a case.

RESTITUTION - In equity, it is the restoration of both parties to their original condition (when practicable), upon the rescission of a contract for fraud or similar cause.

RETROACTIVE (RETROSPECTIVE) - Looking back; effective as of a prior time.

REVERSED - A term used by appellate courts to indicate that the decision of the lower court in the case before it has been set aside.

REVOKE - To recall or cancel.

RIPARIAN (RIGHTS) - The rights of a person owning land containing or bordering on a water course or other body of water, such as lakes and rivers.

S

SALE - A contract whereby the ownership of property is transferred from one person to another for a sum of money or for any consideration.

SANCTION - A penalty or punishment provided as a means of enforcing obedience to a law; also, an authorization.

SATISFACTION - The discharge of an obligation by paying a party what is due to him; or what is awarded to him by the judgment of a court or otherwise.

SCIENTER - Knowingly; also, it is used in pleading to denote the defendant's guilty knowledge.

SCINTILLA - A spark; also the least particle.

SECRET OF STATE - Governmental secret relating to the national defense or the international relations of the United States.

SECURITY - Indemnification; the term is applied to an obligation, such as a mortgage or deed of trust, given by a debtor to insure the payment or performance of his debt, by furnishing the creditor with a resource to be used in case of the debtor's failure to fulfill the principal obligation.

SENTENCE - The judgment formally pronounced by the court or judge upon the defendant after his conviction in a criminal prosecution.

SET-OFF - A claim or demand which one party in an action credits against the claim of the opposing party.

SHALL and MAY - "Shall" is mandatory and "may" is permissive.

SITUS - Location.

SOVEREIGN - A person, body or state in which independent and supreme authority is vested.

STARE DECISIS - To follow decided cases.

STATE - "State" means this State, unless applied to the different parts of the United States. In the latter case, it includes any state, district, commonwealth, territory or insular possession of the United States, including the District of Columbia.

STATEMENT - (a) Oral or written verbal expression or (b) nonverbal conduct of a person intended by him as a substitute for oral or written verbal expression.

STATUTE - An act of the legislature. Includes a treaty.

STATUTE OF LIMITATION - A statute limiting the time to bring an action after the right of action has arisen.

STAY - To hold in abeyance an order of a court.

STIPULATION - Any agreement made by opposing attorneys regulating any matter incidental to the proceedings or trial.

SUBORDINATION (AGREEMENT) - An agreement making one's rights inferior to or of a lower rank than another's.

SUBORNATION - The crime of procuring a person to lie or to make false statements to a court.

SUBPOENA - A writ or order directed to a person, and requiring his attendance at a particular time and place to testify as a witness.

SUBPOENA DUCES TECUM - A subpoena used, not only for the purpose of compelling witnesses to attend in court, but also requiring them to bring with them books or documents which may be in their possession, and which may tend to elucidate the subject matter of the trial.

SUBROGATION - The substituting of one for another as a creditor, the new creditor succeeding to the former's rights.

SUBSIDY - A government grant to assist a private enterprise deemed advantageous to the public.

SUI GENERIS - Of the same kind.

SUIT - Any civil proceeding by a person or persons against another or others in a court of justice by which the plaintiff pursues the remedies afforded him by law.

SUMMONS - A notice to a defendant that an action against him has been commenced and requiring him to appear in court and answer the complaint.

SUPRA - Above; this word occurring by itself in a book refers the reader to a previous part of the book.

SURETY - A person who binds himself for the payment of a sum of money, or for the performance of something else, for another.

SURPLUSAGE - Extraneous or unnecessary matter.

SURVIVORSHIP - A term used when a person becomes entitled to property by reason of his having survived another person who had an interest in the property.

SUSPEND SENTENCE - Hold back a sentence pending good behavior of prisoner.

SYLLABUS - A note prefixed to a report, especially a case, giving a brief statement of the court's ruling on different issues of the case.

T

TALESMAN - Person summoned to fill a panel of jurors.

TENANT - One who holds or possesses lands by any kind of right or title; also, one who has the temporary use and occupation of real property owned by another person (landlord), the duration and terms of his tenancy being usually fixed by an instrument called "a lease."

TENDER - An offer of money; an expression of willingness to perform a contract according to its terms.

TERM - When used with reference to a court, it signifies the period of time during which the court holds a session, usually of several weeks or months duration.

TESTAMENTARY - Pertaining to a will or the administration of a will.
TESTATOR (male)
TESTATRIX (female) - One who makes or has made a testament or will.
TESTIFY (TESTIMONY) - To give evidence under oath as a witness.
TO WIT - That is to say; namely.
TORT - Wrong; injury to the person.
TRANSITORY - Passing from place to place.
TRESPASS - Entry into another's ground, illegally.
TRIAL - The examination of a cause, civil or criminal, before a judge who has jurisdiction over it, according to the laws of the land.
TRIER OF FACT - Includes (a) the jury and (b) the court when the court is trying an issue of fact other than one relating to the admissibility of evidence.
TRUST - A right of property, real or personal, held by one party for the benefit of another.
TRUSTEE - One who lawfully holds property in custody for the benefit of another.

U

UNAVAILABLE AS A WITNESS - The declarant is (1) Exempted or precluded on the ground of privilege from testifying concerning the matter to which his statement is relevant; (2) Disqualified from testifying to the matter; (3) Dead or unable to attend or to testify at the hearing because of then existing physical or mental illness or infirmity; (4) Absent from the hearing and the court is unable to compel his attendance by its process; or (5) Absent from the hearing and the proponent of his statement has exercised reasonable diligence but has been unable to procure his attendance by the court's process.
ULTRA VIRES - Acts beyond the scope and power of a corporation, association, etc.
UNILATERAL - One-sided; obligation upon, or act of one party.
USURY - Unlawful interest on a loan.

V

VACATE - To set aside; to move out.
VARIANCE - A discrepancy or disagreement between two instruments or two aspects of the same case, which by law should be consistent.
VENDEE - A purchaser or buyer.
VENDOR - The person who transfers property by sale, particularly real estate; the term "seller" is used more commonly for one who sells personal property.
VENIREMEN - Persons ordered to appear to serve on a jury or composing a panel of jurors.
VENUE - The place at which an action is tried, generally based on locality or judicial district in which an injury occurred or a material fact happened.
VERDICT - The formal decision or finding of a jury.
VERIFY - To confirm or substantiate by oath.
VEST - To accrue to.
VOID - Having no legal force or binding effect.
VOIR DIRE - Preliminary examination of a witness or a juror to test competence, interest, prejudice, etc.

W

WAIVE - To give up a right.
WAIVER - The intentional or voluntary relinquishment of a known right.
WARRANT (WARRANTY) (v.) - To promise that a certain fact or state of facts, in relation to the subject matter, is, or shall be, as it is represented to be.

WARRANT (n.) - A writ issued by a judge, or other competent authority, addressed to a sheriff, or other officer, requiring him to arrest the person therein named, and bring him before the judge or court to answer or be examined regarding the offense with which he is charged.

WRIT - An order or process issued in the name of the sovereign or in the name of a court or judicial officer, commanding the performance or nonperformance of some act.

WRITING - Handwriting, typewriting, printing, photostating, photographing and every other means of recording upon any tangible thing any form of communication or representation, including letters, words, pictures, sounds, or symbols, or combinations thereof.

WRITINGS AND RECORDINGS - Consists of letters, words, or numbers, or their equivalent, set down by handwriting, typewriting, printing, photostating, photographing, magnetic impulse, mechanical or electronic recording, or other form of data compilation.

Y

YEA AND NAY - Yes and no.

YELLOW DOG CONTRACT - A contract by which employer requires employee to sign an instrument promising as condition that he will not join a union during its continuance, and will be discharged if he does join.

Z

ZONING - The division of a city by legislative regulation into districts and the prescription and application in each district of regulations having to do with structural and architectural designs of buildings and of regulations prescribing use to which buildings within designated districts may be put.